HISTORY

OF

CASS COUNTY,

FROM 1825 TO 1875.

BY HOWARD S. ROGERS.

CASSOPOLIS, MICH.
W. H. MANSFIELD, VIGILANT BOOK AND JOB PRINT.
1875:

PREFACE.

In offering this little volume to the pioneers of Cass County and their descendants, the author is spared many fears as to its reception, by the knowledge that it will be read for the facts and incidents it contains, rather than for criticism of the style of their presentation.

It is not all he wished to make it, but is as complete and accurate as he could make it in the time alloted, and will at least serve as a starting point for future historians.

The work was undertaken last season upon the urgent and repeated requests of many old settlers and those who were interested in establishing the Cass County Pioneer Association and Museum, and his exclusive time and attention has been given to its preparation since that time.

All the early settlers and publications that could be reached, have been consulted, and the aggregate of their recollections and information is before you in a condensed form and with some attempt at chronological connection.

His earnest thanks are due and tendered to the gentlemen of the local press, the County and Township officers and many other friends too numerous to specify, to whom he is under great obligation for advice, information and substantial aid.

He is not a professional writer or speculative book-maker, and has constructed this work rather as a conservatory of facts and incidents that are in peril of being lost upon the death of the actors therein, than as a bid for literary fame by

THE AUTHOR.

MICHIGAN.

Michigan derives its name from the two words in the Chippewa language, *Mitchaw* and *Sagiegan*, meaning great, and lake. These words were applied by the members of that tribe to lakes Michigan and Huron, which at the time of the first explorations were supposed to be one. The land which these lakes so nearly surrounded, was called *Mich-sawgyegan*, meaning a lake country, hence the name, Michigan.

Of the earlist explorations by the French, little is definitely known, as the records are very limited and vague.

In 1610 a partial exploration was made, but no record of its details or extent have been preserved.

In 1632 Father Sagard visited the country along the shores of Lake Huron, and in 1634 a party of Indians, belonging to the Huron tribe, visited Quebec, and on their return were accompanied by the Jesuits, Breboeuf and Daniel, who located upon the shore of Lake Huron, and instructed the natives in religious matters.

In 1641, a number of French Jesuits came up the St. Lawrence river in bark canoes, thence up the Ottawa, crossing over to Lake Nipising, thence down the French river to Georgian Bay, and passing the islands of Lake Huron, reached the Falls of St. Mary, where they established a mission.

Rene Mesnard made an exploration of the country around Green Bay and Lake Superior in 1660, reaching in October of that year a bay on the south shore of Lake Superior, which he named St. Theressa. After remaining there about eight months, he was lost in the forest. His cloak and breviary were afterwards found among the Sioux Indians, by whom he was probably murdered.

In.1666, a mission was established at the Falls of St. Mary, now called Sault Ste. Maria, by Father Allouez, and in 1668 he was joined by Fathers Dablan and Marquette. During the next three years they made an exploration of the country along the shores of Lake Michigan, making the entire circuit of that lake.

In 1671, Marquette built a Fort and Chapel at Mackinaw, (formerly spelled Michilmackinac) and from this time Michigan properly dates her settlement, although for many years the only white inhabitants, resided in solitary Forts at wide spread distances from each other, at points where the Indians were in the habit of resorting from the fatigues of the chase, and which afforded the most ready communication by canoes, with the inland streams of the country, and served as shipping points to the headquarters of the fur trade, at Quebec and Montreal.

From the peculiar location of Mackinaw, situated on the natural highway, between the St. Lawrence and the Mississippi, its importance has ever been highly estimated. Its founder, Peere Marquette, induced a party of Huron Indians to make a settlement there in the year of its location, intending it as a nucleus for a future colony. It soon became an important rendezvous for the traders, merchants, soldiers, *couriers de bois*, missionaries, and Indians of the Northwest.

As early as 1688, the Ottawas and Hurons had villages in the vicinity of the chapel and fort, and the former had commenced to build a fortification on rising ground near by.

Near the village of the Hurons, the Jusuits had a college adjoining the chapel, enclosed with pickets, in which they exercised their influence for the conversion of the Indians. Their efforts for that object were, however, in the main unsuccessful, according to their own acknowledgments; and to be permitted to administer the sacrament to their dying children and aged Indians, was the utmost limit to which they could bring the minds of the savages.

The English and French being rivals in the fur trade, it became an important object with the former nation to secure a monopoly of the traffic in this important article of commerce. A trading expedition of the English, with the aid of the Otagamies or Fox Indians, who then inhabited the banks of the

Detroit river, arrived at Mackinaw in 1686. This tribe was unfriendly to the French, and the English as a matter of policy strengthened their relationship by presents and promises to them. At this time no permanent settlement had been made at Detroit, the French having a safer and more direct route from Montreal to the upper lakes through the Ottawa and Grand rivers. The present location of Detroit had long been looked upon as a valuable point for a settlement and a base for the fur trades, as it commanded a broad tract of country across the peninsula and was the key to the upper lakes.

While the English were looking with eager eyes to the acquisition of this point, they were anticipätd by the French, who called a grand council at Montreal for the purpose of negotiating a treaty to that effect. This council was one of great pomp and ceremony, and was composed of the principal chiefs of the different tribes from the St. Lawrence to the Mississippi, the Governor General of Canada and the most prominent men of the country. It is said to have been one of the most imposing assemblies that was ever collected together in the wilderness.

At this meeting the rights of the two claimants were fully discussed. The Iroquois claimed that the country belonged to them, and as they had forbidden the English to make a settlement there, they wished the French also to respect their rights. To this the Governor General of Canada replied that the country neither belonged to the English nor the Indians, but to the King of France, and that already there was an expedition on the way to establish a colony on the banks of the Detroit. In accordance with this determination a settlement was made on the present site of Detroit in July, 1701, by Antoine de la Motte Cadillac, acting under a commission from Louis XIV, upon a grant of fifteen acres square. He was accompanied by a Jesuit missionary and all the necessary means to establish a colony.

Before that period Detroit had not been unknown. As early as 1620 it was the resort of French missionaries, and when first visited by the French the present site was occupied by an Indian village called Teuchsa Gronde.

Cadillac erected a fort surrounded with pickets, enclosing a few houses occupied by the French traders and soldiers attached to the post. The establishment was a rude, frail affair, equipped with small cannon, which were better adapted to overawe the Indians than for effective defense.

While the French were extending their settlements along the frontier of Michigan, they were surrounded and assisted by the powerful Ottawa, Huron, Potawotamie and Menominee tribes of Indians; while the Foxes of Iroquois descent adhered to the English, and soon made their power felt against the French settlements. These Indian confederations have always been of a capricious character, the savages having an eye to the main chance—that of helping themselves—rather using the whites to farther their own designs than for any real benefit they gave them as allies.

Three years after the founding of Detroit, the

Indians were invited to Albany by the English, with a view of negotiating with them for the country. A number of Ottawa chiefs visited the place, and came back with altered feelings. During this visit they were persuaded by the English who still wished to obtain possession of the post, that the French settlements on the lakes were intending to wrest the country from their hands, and acting upon this conviction, they set fire to the town. The fire was discovered before any serious damage was done, and extinguished.

About the same time, another party of Ottawas returning from a successful expedition against the Iroquois, flushed with victory, paraded themselves in front of the fort and endeavored to induce the other Indians to join in its demolition. M. deTonti, then the French commandant, dispatched an officer for the purpose of dispersing this hostile band, in which he succeeded, putting them to flight. In the hurry of their departure they abandoned the Iroquois prisoners whom they had captured; these were sent back by the French to their tribe.

From this time until 1712, the infant settlements of Michigan, rested in comparative quietude. The Iroquois occasionally sent out marauding parties against the French and Indians, and several of the Jesuits had been murdered with the most wanton cruelty by these bands of savages. In May, 1712, the Ottogamies, then comparatively an obscure tribe, but who it appears were in secret alliance with the Iroquois, perfected a plan to demolish the town of Detroit. They were doubtless induced to do this by the Five Nations, backed by the English, who wished to destroy the post and erect one of their own on its ruins.

Accordingly on the 13th of May, the siege was commenced, but the plans which had been carefully and secretly made, were divulged by a convert to the Catholic faith before they were fully matured; and the commandant of the fort dispatched couriers to the wilderness to notify the friendly Indians, who were absent on a hunting expedition, but readily came to the summons painted and equipped for war. After a siege of nineteen days, the aggressive party were so badly beaten as to retreat some distance from the fort, closely followed by the French and friendly Indians, and after another four days fighting and killing about a thousand of their warriors they were fully conquered; the women and children, whose lives were spared, were divided as slaves among the victorious party.

The most prominent individuals at the trading post besides the commandants, were the French merchants who generally had their houses near the forts. The old French merchant was the head man of his settlement. Careful, frugal, without much enterprise, judgment, or rigid virtue. He was employed in procuring skins from the Indians and traders in exchange for manufactured goods. The policy of these traders was to exercise their influence with paternal mildness, so as to prevent rebellion, to keep on good terms with the Indians in order to secure their trade; and they frequently fostered a large number of half breed children, who were the offspring of their licentiousness. The *Couriers des Bois*, or rangers of the woods, were either French or half breeds; a hardy race, accustomed to labor and privation, and conversant with the character and habits of the Indians, from whom they procured their cargoes of furs. They were equally skilled in propelling a canoe, fishing, hunting, and trapping. If of mixed blood, they generally spoke both the languages of their parents, and knew just enough of their religions to be regardless of both. Employed by the aristocratic French companies as *voyageurs* or guides, their forms were developed to the fullest vigor by propelling the canoe through the lakes and streams, and by carrying heavy packs of goods across the portages of the interior, by straps suspended from their foreheads or shoulders. These *voyageurs* knew every rock, island, bay and shoal of the western waters.

The ordinary dress of the white portion of the French traders, was a cloth passed about the middle, a loose shirt, a blanket coat, (called a molton), and a red worsted cap. The half-breeds were demi-savage in their dress as well as in their character and appearance. They sometimes wore a surtout of coarse blue cloth reaching down to the knees, elk-skin trowsers, the seams adorned with fringes, a scarlet woolen sash tied around the waist, in which they carried a broad knife, used in dissecting the carcasses of animals taken in the chase, buckskin moccasins, and a cap made of the same material with the surtout. Affable, gay, and licentious, these men were employed by the French merchants, as guides, canoe men, steersmen, or rangers, to go in their canoes, into the remotest wilderness, to barter their European goods for peltries, depositing them at the several French depots on the lakes, whence they were transported to Quebec and Montreal.

In 1751, the fort at Detroit as well as those on the upper lakes, was in a weak condition. About thirty farms, owned by the French, were scattered along the banks of the river, and the colony contained a population of about five hundred souls beside the Indians of the three villages, who could command four hundred warriors. Detroit at this time was the most important depot of the French on the northwestern lakes. Its progress under the French was very slow, from the fact that it was controlled by exclusive companies, whose only purpose was to enrich themselves; preferring to keep the people in ignorance that they might have the better control of their labor rather than to let them become free-holders in the soil. At the same time keeping the true state of affairs from the French crown, that they might further their own selfish purposes.

The fur trade of the great lake region afforded them the largest opportunities for gain. Large canoes, laden with packs of European merchandise, were sent periodically through these lakes for the purpose of trading for peltries with the Indians, and these made their principal depots at Detroit and Mackinaw. In order to protect the interests of traders, licenses were granted by the French King, and unlicensed persons were prohibited from dealing with the Indians, in their own country under the penalty of death. The ordinary price of these licenses was six hundred crowns each, and they were mostly purchased of the Governor General by the merchants, and by them sold to the traders and *Coureurs des Bois*. The privilege granted in a single license was the loading of two large canoes, each of which was manned by six men, and freighted with merchandise valued at a thousand crowns. This was furnished to the traders at an advance of about fifteen per cent. above the price it would bring in cash at the colonies.

The actual profit on these voyages was about one hundred per cent., most of which accrued to the merchant, while the trader endured all the fatigue. On the return of the expedition, the merchant took from the gross proceeds six hundred crowns for his license, one thousand crowns for the prime cost of his goods, and from the remainder forty per cent. as bottomry, while the balance was divided equally between the six *Courieurs des Bois*, whose share for all the trials and privations undergone while on thc voyage, often proved a mere pittance.

At the capitulation of Quebec, September 18th, 1760, Detroit, Mackinaw and all the present territory of Michigan was ceded by the French to the English.

Before the conquest of the country, Michigan preserved no distinct and independent character and was far removed from the seat of war. The eastern line of the State was a ranging ground for Jesuit Missionaries and traders in their religious and mercantile operations through the wilderness. The few deasantry scattered around the military posts, cultivating their small patches of ground in quietude and happiness. The interior had been but little explored save by the wood ranger or Jesuit, who traveled through the Indian trails, which wound along pleasant landscapes, here stretching on a sunny hillside, and there overshadowed by silent primeval forests. Drafts indeed had been made by the French government to forward their campaigns, and a number of soldiers, drawn from the lake country, were present at Braddock's defeat. Hostile bands of warriors were also sent on in emergencies, from the lake shores, to devastate the English settlements, but peace in the main as yet, smiled on its dominions.

Immediately after the capitulation at Quebec, a detachment of troops under Major Rogers, was sent to take possession of Michigan. When nearing the Detroit river, they were met by the celebrated Indian Chief, Pontiac, who was for the first time then brought to the public notice, but afterwards became celebrated for his bravery, far-seeing, deep planned, and well executed expeditions. He was the chief of the Algonquin Confederacy; the autocrat of the savages along the lakes, distinguished for his noble form, commanding address and proud demeanor. He seems to have allied to himself the respect and confidence of all the Indians in this region, and was a marked example of the grandeur which is sometimes found among the savages of the American forest, with as it afterwards proved, a vein of treachery running through his organization. He was the avowed friend of the French and enemy of the English, and combined all those traits of character which distinguish men among civilized states, whether in the forum or in the field. He was grasping in his projects, his courage was unconquerable. His pride was the pride of the proudest chief of the proudest nation on earth. As an orator, he was more remarkable for pointedness and vigor, than for burning eloquence. He had watched with jealousy the progress of the English arms, and had imbibed a hatred for the English, which had been handed down in his race. He had seen them pushing their conquests through the country, destroying his people, driving the game from the hunting grounds, which had been bequeathed them from their forefathers, and crimsoning the land with the blood of his companions and friends—the French. About eight miles above Detroit, on an island, he made his summer residence, and in winter had his lodging place at an Ottawa village opposite, on the Canada shore. When he was informed of the advance of Major Rogers, who commanded the first English detachment that ever advanced into his quarters, he was aroused like a lion in his den.

On the 7th of November, when Rogers arrived at the mouth of the Chogage river, he was met by a party of Ottawa messengers who requested him to halt his forces until Pontiac came up, which was done. Pontiac's first salutation was to ask "how he dared to enter his country without his permission." He was informed by Rogers that there was no design against the Indians, but their object was to remove the French, who had been an obstacle in the way of peace between the English and Indians.

With this information friendly messages were exchanged, also several belts of wampum.

On the next morning Pontiac appeared at the English camp and informed Rogers that he had made peace with the English, and, as a pledge, both smoked the calumet.

Pontiac immediately sent messengers ahead instructing the Indians to let the English pass, and accompanied Rogers to the Detroit river, furnishing him with venison, turkeys, and parched corn, and in return received wampum and ammunition.

On the arrival of the English in the vicinity of Detroit, a dispatch was sent to the French commandant, and after some parley the post was turned over to the English, the citizens taking the oath of allegiance to that government and the French soldiers being sent to Philadelphia.

Major Rogers having made a treaty with the Indians of the country, advanced toward Lake Huron, leaving Captain Cempbell in command at Detroit.

It was his intention to take possession of Mackinaw also, but the ice prevented him from going by water, and not being prepared with snow shoes to cross the country, he returned to Detriot, and on the 21st of December, 1760, started for Pittsburg, leaving Captain Campbell in charge of the station. Thus the French power in Michigan was forever overthrown.

The social condition of the settlers was not much improved by the transfer from the French to the English. Schools were unknown and the instruction of the children continued to be derived from the Catholic priests.

Coin as a circulating medium, was introduced by the English in lieu of peltries, which had been used by the French.

Although the English government had succeeded to the dominion of the northwestern lakes, it did not inherit the friendship of the Algonquin tribes in that quarter. These tribes from the first regarded the whites as intruders, and the smile which played upon the countenance of Pontiac when he first met the detachment of Rogers, only tended to conceal a settled hatred. His professions of friendship to the English were doubtless a matter of policy until he should plot their destruction.

The French had been friends to his race. They had lodged in the same wigwam; drank at the same stream; they had hunted and fought side by side, and were mixed in blood. No sooner, therefore, were the English established on the lakes, than he projected the design of undermining them in this quarter by destroying their forts.

His plan was to attack all the English posts at the same time by stratagem, to massacre the garrisons, take possession of the points, and oppose the advance of the British upon the northwestern waters. He presumed, on good ground, that the success of the Indians in this enterprise, would establish their confidence and combine them in one general confederacy against the English government. His distaste for the English had been greatly augumented by the cold indifference of the traders and soldiers, which contrasted unfavorable with the sociability and kindness of the French. Some of his own tribe, the Ottawas, had been disgraced by blows from the English intruders. As soon as the plan of his policy had been matured, Pontiac called a grand council of warriors at the river Aux Gorce, and there addressed them with great vigor and eloquence. Taking advantage of the superstition which is natural to the Indian character, he related dreams as having occurred to himself and others, to the effect that "they were to drive these dogs in red clothing from the land." The speech of Pontiac had its full effect; for the motives urged, appealed to the pride, interest, superstition and nationality of the savages. Belts and messengers were soon after sent to the Indians along the whole frontier, stretching a thousand miles along the lakes, in order to secure their co-operation. He was joined by six other tribes, and on the 8th of May, 1763, the attack was simultaneously commenced on the forts LeBœuf, Venango, Detroit, Mackinaw, St. Joseph on the St. Joseph river, Pittsburg and Niagara, all of which fell except Pittsburg, Niagara and Detroit. The plan had been so carefully laid as to create no suspicion in the minds of the English. It broke like lightning from a midnight cloud.

Detroit, from its location, was deemed the most important post, as it commanded an extensive region of navigation and trade upon the upper lakes, and stood as a gate to the northwestern waters. The possession of this post wonld break the allegiance of the French inhabitants on the river, and form a chain of operation for the savages from Lake Michigan to

Buffalo and Pittsburg. Pontiac determined to superintend its capture in person. At that time it was garrisoned by one hundred and twenty-two men and eight officers, of whom Major Gladwin was commander. Anchored in front of the fort were two armed vessels, and the fort was protected by three mortars, two six pounders and one three pounder. These were badly mounted and better calculated to terrify the Indians than for substantial defense. Within the limits of the town were also about forty persons connected with the fur trade who were supplied with provisions and arms.

Pontiac's plan for the destruction of the fort exhibited remarkable cunning as well as strategy. He instructed his warriors to cut off their rifles so as to conceal them under their blankets, gain admission to the fort, and at a preconcerted signal, rush upon the troops and open the gate for their companions on the outside, who would stand ready to co-operate with those within. In order to carry his plan into execution he encamped near Detroit and sent word to Major Gladwin that he and his warriors wished to hold a council the next day for the purpose of "brightening the chain of peace."

The council was granted for the 8th of May, 1763. On the evening of the 7th an Indian woman who had been employed by the officers of the post, on coming to return some work she had been doing, lingered around creating the impression that all was not right, and upon being questioned told them they had always been kind and she wished them no harm. After assuring her that any information she might give would not turn to her disadvantage, she gave them the details of the plot. The officers considering it more for the purpose of fright than anything else, put but little confidence in the story; but that night everything was put in readiness in case her prediction should prove true. The next day Pontiac and his warriors were received in the usual manner, and when it came to the point where he was to make the signal, the officers unsheathed their swords and demanded to know why they had come thus armed, at the same time opening one of their blankets, displaying a shot gun. The Indians were taken wholly by surprise. Major Gladwin opened the gate telling them to leave before his young men fell upon and slaughtered them, but as he had promised them protection he would fulfill his word. As soon as the savages were beyond the gate, they gave a yell and fired on the garrison. They then proceeded to the common where an English woman and her two sons lived, whom they fell upon and massacred. The cannibalism of the savages at that time is exhibited in the fact that a respectable Frenchman was requested to repair to their camp and partake of some soup. He complied with the invitation, and after he had eaten, was informed that he had feasted on a part of the English woman. A Frenchman and his family, living three miles up the river, were also butchered with the exception of one. For some time a desultory warfare was kept up by the Indians, firing from behind the buildings in the vicinity of the fort. These were demolished or burned by the order of the commandant of the post, when they retired behind a ridge, sallying out when the opportunity seemed favorable. Major Campbell was much respected by the French and Indians for his kindness, and it became an important object with Pontiac to get this officer into his posession to secure the downfall of the fort, and for this purpose he induced some French residents to seek an interview with the Major, informing him that Pontiac wished him to come to his camp that they might terminate the war and smoke the pipe of peace, and at the same time Pontiac gave the most solemn assurance of his safety. Under this promise, he, in company with a Lieutenant repaired to the camp, where at first they were well received. The crafty chief however did not comply with his promise and the English officers were detained. The Lieutenant shortly after made his escape and returned to the fort in safety. The Major was offered his liberty for the surrender of the fort, but Pontiac's previous treachery had weakened all confidence in his word, and the proposition was spurned with indignation. The captivity of Major Campbell had an unfortunate termination. An Ottawa chief of note had been killed at Mackinaw, and his nephew hastened to Detroit for revenge, where he found Major Campbell and immediately dispatched him with his tomahawk, and fled to Saginaw to escape the vengeance of Pontiac.

The siege of Detroit was uninterruptedly kept up for eleven months with varying success on the part of the besiegers, when it was relieved by General Bradstreet with three thousand men. Twice the effort to relieve them had been made previously.

Once the whole detachment were either killed or taken prisoners by the Indians; the second time they arrived in safety after successfully repulsing the Indians from boarding their vessel, but the reinforcements were so few in number as to prove of no material benefit.

Pontiac's abilities were fully demonstrated duriug the protracted struggle. He issued bills of eredit, made of bark, with a beaver, the *to tem* of his tribe drawn upon them, in exchange for the products of the French. These bills were faithfully redeemed. The neutrality of the French was a drawback to his success, and he did everything in his power to bring them to his side. Councils were called at which he made speeches, relating in glowing style how he and his young men had helped them to defend their country against the English, and accused them of carrying his plans to the enemy. And as a last resort, throwing down a belt and saying to them, "if you are French and with us, take that belt; if not, we declare war against you." But all to no avail; the French stood fast to their oath of allegiance. The armed vessels in the river were another source of annoyance to him, and he determined to burn them. For this purpose the barns of many of the inhabitants were thrown down and made into a raft, and filled with pitch and other combustibles that would burn readily. The whole mass was towed up the river and fired, under the supposition that the stream would carry it down into contact with, and set fire to the vessels. The English, however, were aware of the plan, and had anchored boats above the vessels connected with chains so as to ward off the blazing mass. The plan was successful and the burning rafts floated harmlessly down the river. Upon the arrival of General Bradstreet, it became evident to the Indians that they could not succeed against so heavy a force; they therefore laid down their arms and concluded a treaty of peace. Pontiac, however, stood aloof and took no part in the negotiations, and soon after retired to the Illinois, where he was assassinated by an Indian of the Peoria tribe, about the year 1767, thus ending the career of a most remarkable man.

The Ottawas, Potawotomies and Chippewas made a common cause in avenging his death by waging war with and nearly exterminating the tribe of his murderer.

While these events were passing at Detroit, others of no less importance or destructive in their character were occurring at Mackinaw. They were set in motion by the master mind of Pontiac, who had plotted the overthrow of the other posts on the lakes. At that time the fort at Mackinaw was in the middle of a two acre lot enclosed with cedar pickets. On the bastions were planted two small brass cannon, taken some years before by a party of Canadians in an expedition against the trading post of the Hudson Bay company. The stockade contained about thirty houses, also a chapel, in which mass was regularly held by the priest missionary. The inhabitants derived the principal part of their support from the traders who congregated here on their voyages to and from Montreal. The furs were collected here for transportation from the upper lakes, and outfits prepared for Lake Michigan, Lake Superior, the Mississippi, and the remote Northwest. It contained in 1763 about thirty families. The garrison at that time was composed of ninety-three officers and soldiers; there were also four English merchants at the post.

On the 3d of June a large collection of Indians had gathered in the vicinity of the fort, under various pretexts. As a ruse a game called *baggatiway* was proposed between the Chippewas and Sacs for a high wager. It was played with a bat and ball. Two posts were planted in the ground some distance apart, each party having its post. The game consisted in propelling the ball, which was placed in the center, toward the post of the adversary. The design of the Indians was to throw the ball over the pickets and in a natural manner all rush for it in the heat of the game, thus securing an entrance to the fort. This stratagem was successful. Major Ethington, the commandant, was present at the game, and laid a wager on the side of the Chippewas, while all the garrison who could be induced were drawn outside the pickets for the purpose of weakening the defenses of the fort. In the midst of the game there was an Indian war yell, and the crowd of Indians who had rushed for the ball within the pickets were seen cutting down and scalping those within the fort. The massacre of the garrison, and the destruction of the fort by burning, completed their project. A number of canoes, filled with English traders, arrived about the same time. These were dragged through the water, beaten, and marched by the Indians to the prison lodge. After the fall of the fort, the savages fearing the English and Indians who had not joined in the plot, divided their forces, a part going to the Island of Mackinaw, the remainder to assist Pontiac in the siege of Detroit.

During the whole period of the American Revolution Michigan was in a state of quietude, being composed of a part of the Canadian Territory and far removed from the active scenes of war her people rested in comparative peace. Although serving as a magazine of arms for the savages, and a mart where the price of scalps was paid, it exhibited no prominent events which gave interest and coloring to the page of history, from the fact that it was not the theatre of action. The war which was waged in the Eastern part of the country was, however, brought to a termination by Washington, and the treaty of 1783 included Michigan within the American boundaries. The important ordinance for the organization of the Northwestern Territory was passed in July, 1787. This ordinance has been the basis for all Territorial Governments since that time. It was drawn by Nathan Dane, of Beverly, Massachusetts. The Territory was made into one District, subject to a division at the will of Congress. It was provided that until the free white male inhabitants should amount to five thousand, the government should be vested in a Governor and three Judges, who, as well as Secretary, should be appointed by Congress. The Governor and Judges were empowered to adopt and put in force such laws of the orginal States as might be suited to the circumstances of the District, these laws to be in force until superseded by acts of Congress. The Governor was also vested with the power of dividing the Districts into Counties and Townships, and of appointing civil officers for the same. It was provided that when the free male inhabitants reached five thousand in number, a legislative council should be established. This council was to be composed of five members, who were to hold their office for two years, unless removed by Congress, and were appointed in the following manner: the House of Representatives was authorized to nominate ten persons, each possessed of a freehold of five hundred acres of land, and out of this number Congress was permitted to appoint five as members of the legislative council. The council had power to enact laws, in connection with the General Assembly, and to elect delegates to Congress. In 1798, the Northwestern Territory assumed the second grade of territorial government, and the Territory of Michigan, as afterwards established, comprised one County, that of Wayne. It then sent one Representative to the General Assembly of the Northwestern Territory, then held at Chilicothe, Ohio, and for this purpose the first election was held in Michigan under the American Government. A Court of Common Pleas was established, and the General Court was periodically held at Detroit. In 1802 the peninsular portion of Michigan was attached to Indiana, by an act of Congress which authorized the erection into a State of that portion of the Northwestern Territory which constitutes the State of Ohio. Up to this time the people had paid but little attention to agriculture, but had devoted themselves to the procuring of furs and trading with the Indians; and when we contrast the difference between that time and this, and the improvements that have been made, the change seems almost miraculous.

On January 11th, 1805, by an act of Congress, Michigan was erected into a separate Territory, the Government to be established on the plan which had been prescribed by the ordinance of 1787. William Hull was appointed Governor, Augustus B. Woodward and Frederick Bates Judges of the Territory. On the second Tuesday in July, 1805, the oaths of office were administered to the several officers, and Michigan commenced its governmental operations. This was done, however, under very unfavorable circumstances. On the 11th of June the town of Detroit had been consumed by fire. It at that time covered about two acres of ground, and was very compactly built, with streets but fourteen feet wide, and as a matter of defense the village was environed with strong and solid pickets. The houses being so closely built, and composed of combustible materials, were soon swept away by the conflagration, and when the officers arrived they found the body of the people encamped on the public grounds, while some had taken refuge in the country on the banks of the river.

Judge Woodward drew up a code of laws for the government of the territory, known as the "Woodward code." The administration of justice in the early days of the territory had to conform to the character of the people and appears somewhat amusing at this day of greenback currency. In one case, the defendant was to perform a certain number of day's work, in another, the plaintiff was to deliver a certain number of cords of wood on the bank of the river, as penalties for nonfulfillment of contracts.

In 1804, a land office was established at Detroit, more for the purpose of adjusting titles that had been granted by previous administrations, than for sales; for as yet the Indian title had not yet been sufficiently extinguished to warrant the opening of lands to market.

From the time that the Americans took possession of Michigan until the close of the war of 1812, their possessions were anything but peaceful, surrounded on all sides by Indians acting under the impression that their lands were to be taken from them in case of their success, and urged on by British emissaries, whose object was to repossess the country they had ceded by the treaty of peace at the termination of the Revolution. It was the objeet of the British government to combine all the savage tribes in one grand confederacy for the extermination of the Americans. Even before war was declared, their agents were busy among them distributing presents and giving council. Tecumseh believing the British to be their true friends greatly aided in bringing the Indians to their wishes. Tecumseh is described as a man much after the style of Pontiac, five feet ten inches high, well proportioned, and commanding in his address. He combined the qualities of the statesman and the warrior. His counsels were listened to with respect, both by the Indians and the British. He held under the English government a commission as Brigadier General. He was in no way inflated by the tawdry tinsel that pervades military circles, but confined himself to the dress of his tribe. At one time when he had given important information, he was presented by General Brock with a sash from his own person as a token of honor. Tecumseh handed it to another saying, that he was an older and better warrior than himself. His purposes were unselfish, devoting himself to the benefit of his people, and in no way aggrandizing or turning anything to his own personal benefit. He fell at the memorable battle of the Thames. The war of 1812, fell with great force upon the people of Michigan. Situated on the confines of civilization, and in the immediate vicinity of the strongholds of the enemy, they suffered all the hardships and horrors of border warfare. General Hull, at this time acting Governor of the territory, was clothed with full discretionary power to act as he thought proper, either offensively or defensively. This power was granted because he was supposed to know the character of the country and the nature and strength of the enemy better than any other person, and had served with credit under Washington.

Some blame should be attached to the general government for not notifying the outposts of the declaration of war against Great Brittain at an earlier day, as the enemy was in possession of and acting upon the information sometime before it was known to our officers on the frontier.

For the purpose of defending Michigan and invading Canada, an army of twelve hundred men was drafted in Ohio by order of the President and, collected at Dayton, and this force was considerably augumented by volunteers. This army was divided into three regiments under Colonel's McArthur, Cass and Finelly. To these was added a fourth regiment composed of militia and regulars numbering about three hundred men, under the command of Colonel Miller; the whole force was placed under General Hull.

This army was ordered to immediately repair to Detroit, and started about the middle of June. They had to cut their way through the trackless wilderness and swamps, and after many hardships arrived at the point of destination, on the third of the same month. General Hull had been to Washington for the purpose of removing some of the embarassments in his way, and on his return had dispatched his baggage, documents and disabled soldiers in a vessel *via.* the Malden channel. On her appearance at that point the vessel was captured, and news of the declaration of war first broke upon the astonished crew from the lips of the British as they boarded the American vessel.

For some time after the arrival of the army at Detroit, the time was employed in cleaning up the arms that had become rusted and dirty in their march through the wilderness, and recruiting the men. The army under General Hull was very anxious to attack Malden immediately, as it was known at that time to be in a weak condition but daily expecting reinforcements. This would have been in accordance with the policy of the war department, and the possession of Malden would have been of immense advantage in future campaigns.

Having made arrangements for the expedition, General Hull with his army, crossed over to Sandwich on the 12th of July, and established a fortified camp. Here he issued a proclamation which was from the pen of Colonel Cass, and was of an energetic and impressive character, and backed by the bayonets of his army had the effect of keeping the Canadians and Indians, who were opposed to the American cause, on neutral ground. He also issued an invitation to them to come over to the American side, stating the advantages that would accrue to them under a republican form of government, and many of them availed themselves of the privilege.

On the 17th of July, while Hull was lying at Sandwich in a state of torpidity, a detachment of the enemy was sent to Mackinaw, and the first intimation that Lieutenant Hanks, the commander of the post, received of the declaration of war was the summons to surrender, with the British under the walls of his fort; and as the force under his command numbered but fifty, while the British and Indians numbered over one thousand, his only course was to surrender it.

General Hull delayed making an attack upon Malden until it was reinforced and became inexpedient, and on the 9th of August recrossed the river to

Detroit. His pretext for not making the attack was the want of heavy artillery which he was daily expecting from Detroit, but, as subsequent events show, it was from a want of pluck.

On the 14th of August General Brock, one of the most able and energetic of the British commanders in Canada, arrived at Malden, and on the 15th marched up to Sandwich, and immediately upon his arrival at that point summoned General Hull to surrender. Hull with some spirit refused, and on the 16th Brock crossed over the river under cover of his armed vessels, landing near Springwell, and immediately marched upon the fort. Hull in the meantime called in the troops that had been sent out to harass the enemy in their approach, and soon after hoisted a white flag, in token of surrender. Negotiations immediately commenced. The regular troops were surrendered as prisoners of war, the public property given up, and the militia ordered to return home and not to serve again during the war, unless regularly exchanged.

Thus ended the inglorious campaign of General Hull on the frontier. He was afterward tried before a court martial for treason and cowardice. The court gave a verdict of acquittal on the first count, but condemned and sentenced him to death on the second, at the same time recommending him to the mercy of the President of the United States. His life was spared by the Executive, but he was dishonorably dismissed from the service.

After the capitulation of Detroit, the English established a provisional government over Michigan and left a small force in charge of the post at Detroit. The Indians who had assisted them claimed large rewards for their services, and were permitted to ravage the houses of the defenseless inhabitants, who were compelled to submit to the atrocities of the savages or exile themselves, in self defense, to remote regions.

From the time of Hull's surrender until the decisive victory of Commodore Perry on Lake Erie, Michigan was in a state of unrest. Surrounded on all sides by British troops and their allies, the savages, all communication by water cut off by the British squadron, their condition was anything but enviable. Among the fruits of that brilliant victory, came the opening of communication with the army in Ohio and the dawn of better days for the pioneers.

On the 23d of September General Harrison with his army set out for Malden. On his arrival at Amhurstburg, instead of finding British arms to oppose him, he met the Canadians with their wives and daughters, bearing in their hands emblems of peace, who had assembled to solicit his protection. General Proctor had evacuated Malden after having burned the fort and store houses, and retired to the Thames, about eighty miles from Detroit. The American forces took possession of Detroit and immediately marched in pursuit of Proctor, and the battle of the Thames, in which Proctor was defeated, concluded the brilliant campaign of General Harrison on the Northwestern frontier. This was the most directly effective battle fought during the whole war, so far as Michigan was concerned.

General Proctor had been advised by Tecumseh to make a stand at Malden, but this advice was disregarded and he proceeded to the point above described.

The British troops and Indians numbered about twenty-four hundred, while the American army comprised twenty-seven hundred, of whom one hundred and twenty were regulars, thirty were Indians, and the remainder were militia, infantry and mounted volunteers, armed with rifles and muskets. The victory was decisive. Tecumseh, the grand instigator of the Indians to the assistance of the British, fell in the engagement. Six brass field pieces were recaptured, which had been surrendered by Hull at Detroit, and on two of these were engraved the following inscription: "*Surrendered by Burgoyne at Saratoga.*"

General Harrison, having effected the object of his compaign, left General Cass in command at Detroit and moved down toward the Niagara frontier. The only part of Michigan Territory then remaining in the possession of the British was the Island of Mackinaw. This island is about three miles in diameter, and was then covered with a dense forest, occasionally broken by a small patch of cleared land. On one side was the fort adjoining the village, and on the other a wilderness.

Colonel Crogan and Commodore Sinclair, the former commander of the land forces and the latter in charge of the fleet, set sail in July, 1814, for the purpose of reducing this post; but failed in the attempt, owing to the strength of the defenses and the unfavorable character of the ground over which they had to pass. This post remained in possession of the British until the treaty of peace, February 17th, 1815.

In October, 1813, General Lewis Cass was appointed Governor over the Territory of Michigan. He had served with distinction through the war and seemed in every way well qualified for the position; nor was this confidence misplaced, for to no other one man do the people of Michigan owe so great a debt of gratitude as to Governor Cass. Clear-headed, bold and energetic, he found the country in a state of dilapidation, with morals corrupted by long contact with warfare and its attendant evils, the people demoralized by the devastations of the British and their savage allies—in fact a worse state of affairs could hardly be imagined than existed when he assumed the reins of government. He brought order out of chaos, and immediately began a system of improvements, and prosecuted them with an energy worthy the cause he had undertaken.

The only access to the Territory at that time was through the black swamp, then an almost impassable morass, and the military road along the Detroit river, and this was made almost impassible by the refuse of war strewn along it during the occupation by the British. The interior was one dense wilderness, only inhabited by the Indians and an occasional French trader on the streams. Frenchtown and Detroit were the two principal settlements on the lower peninsula, and these had been nearly destroyed during the war. Governor Cass immediately set about reorganizing the Territory, building up its interests, and forming amicable relations with the Indian tribes.

On the 16th of February, 1819, Congress passed an act for the election of a delegate to Congress from the Territory. As yet no land had been brought into market, from the fact that the Indian titles had not been fully extinguished, consequently there was no inducement for settlers to come in. But in 1819, a treaty at Saginaw was effected, by which a considerable part of the eastern portion of the Territory was ceded and brought into market. This produced a new era in its progress, inciting immigration and settlement by the low price and easy terms of payment, it soon brought into the country a large increase of population, and in 1820 this population had increased to eight thousand eight hundred and ninety-six. A serious drawback had been imposed on the settlement by a report of the commissioners who had been sent out by Congress for the purpose of locating two million acres of land for the soldiers of the war of 1812. They returned without locating, and reported the country to be low, sterile, and filled with swamps.

In 1820 Detroit contained a population of fourteen hundred and fifteen inhabitants, and was then a point of considerable activity and business. The Island of Mackinaw, which was at that time the principal mart of the fur trade, had a population of four hundred and fifty, which was augmented to two thousand at certain intervals, by the accession of *voyageurs*, Indians, and traders, on their return from their hunting and trading expeditions to the forests of the upper lakes. Walk-in-the-water was the only steamboat that plied on the lakes, and this was deemed sufficient to transact all the commercial business of the Territory. This boat made her first trip to Mackinaw in 1819.

On the 24th of May, 1820, Governor Cass started on an exploring expedition to the upper country, which he had determined upon and made preparations for, during the preceding year. The objects were to examine the soil, the number and condition of the Indian tribes, and their character, to investigate the mineralogical resources of the country, especially the copper mines of Lake Superior, to collect the material for a map, to select the site for a garrison at the foot of Lake Superior; and also to perfect treaties with the Indian tribes in that quarter. For that object a memorial had been forwarded to Mr. Calhoun, then Secretary of War, which was favorably received, and the expedition encouraged. An escort of soldiers was furnished, the commanders of the garrisons along the route instructed to facilitate its progress, and a mineralogist, topographical engineer and physician were appointed to assist in carrying out the work.

The expedition was provided with bark canoes manned by Canadian *voyageurs* and Indians. They coursed along the track which, although yet an unbroken wilderness, had nevertheless been made memorable ground by the wars of the savages and the hardships and adventures of the early traders, soldiers and missionaries of the French government.

The disaffection of the Indians on the upper lakes toward the United States, continued to exist in a great degree, and their attachment to the English was fully exhibited during this expedition.

By the treaty of 1795, the United States were entitled to all the land in the Nortwestern Territory which had been granted by the Indians to the French and English governments, and on that ground the American government claimed the concession which had formerly been made to the French at the Sault de St. Marie, through which it had been occupied as a military post.

A council was accordingly held for the purpose of establishing this grant, and the object distinctly stated to the Indians through an interpreter. They were opposed to the proposition of Governor Cass, and endeavored to evade it by denying their knowledge of the original grant; and when the fact was pressed upon their conviction, they exhibited great dissatisfaction and gave a qualified refusal. Some of the chiefs were in favor of allowing the grant, provided it should not be used as a garrison, alleging as a reason, that their young men might prove unruly and kill the cattle, if any should stray away from the post. This was intended and received as a threat, and Governor Cass in answer told them that so far as the establishment of a garrison at the Sault, he would spare them all trouble, for so sure as the sun rose and set, there would be an American garrison at that point, be their decision what it might.

The council on the part of the Indians, was composed of chiefs dressed in costly broadcloths, epaulets, medals, silver ornaments, and feathers of British manufacture, by which it was understood that English diplomacy was controlling their deliberations.

The council was employed several hours in animated discussion, and the last chief who spoke, a Brigadier in the British service, drew his war lance and struck it furiously into the ground, and, pulling it out, kicked away the presents that had been laid before him, and the council broke up in confusion. In a few minutes the British flag was seen flying over the Indian encampment.

Governor Cass immediately ordered his men under arms, and proceeding to the camp with an interpreter, took down the insulting flag, telling them at the same time that that was an indignity they should not be permitted to offer on American soil; that the flag was an emblem of national power; that two standards could not float over the same land, and they were forbidden to raise any but our own, and if they should presume again to attempt it, "the United States would set a strong foot upon their necks and crush them to the earth."

The firmness of the Governor produced the desired effect. In a few minutes the Indian encampment was broken up, they taking to their canoes on the river. The Americans numbered sixty-six men, of whom thirty were regulars, and the savages could muster seventy or eighty well armed warriors. Some time having elapsed and no demonstration on the part of the Indians being made, the soldiers were dismissed to their tents. An overture was soon made by a few of the older chiefs who had not been present at the former council, and in the evening a treaty was concluded, in which they ceded to the United States four miles square on the Sault, reserving to themselves the right to fish in the river and camp on its banks. The calumet having been smoked and the shaking of hands concluded, the signatures of the Indians were obtained to the treaty, for which they were paid on the spot, in blankets, knives, broadcloths and silverware.

In 1818, upon the erection of Illinois into a State, the limits of Michigan were extended by the annexation of all the territory lying north of that State and the State of Indiana.

In 1823, the Territory of Michigan was vested with a more compact form of government by an act of Congress, providing for the establishment of a Legislative Council, which was to consist of nine members. These members were to be appointed by the President of the United States with the consent of the Senate, out of eighteen candidates elected by the people of the territory, and, with the Governor, were vested with the same powers which had been granted by the ordinance of 1787.

On the 7th of June, 1824, the first Legislative Council of Michigan, was held at the Council House, in Detroit. Governor Cass, at that time, delivered his message, in which he briefly reviewed the history of the Territory and its progress, and marked out what he considered a proper line of policy in its existing condition.

With the opening of the Erie canal of New York, in 1825, Michigan received an impetus of immigration, such as she had not known before. This avenue opening up the way to her fertile soil from the remote Atlantic seaboard, emigrants from the sterile and mountainous New England, as well as from the sections intervening, came pouring in, and from this time Michigan properly dated her prosperity.

In 1827, Congress granted the right of electing members of the Legislative Council to the people, and the representation was ordered to be apportioned among the several counties and districts according to their population.

Governor Cass in 1820, at Chicago, effected a treaty with the Indians for the lands south of Grand river, and also another at Carey Mission in 1828, for the remainder of the lands in Michigan, except certain reservations.

In 1830, the population of Michigan had increased to thirty-one thousand six hundred and thirty-nine.

In 1831, Governor Cass resigned his office for the purpose of accepting a seat as Secretary of War in President Jackson's Cabinet, after occupying the important position of Governor of the Territory for eighteen years. During this time his entire energies had been devoted to strengthening the foundations of the prosperity of Michigan and increasing the wealth of the United States by perfecting treaties with the Indians, developing the resources and defining and establishing the legislation of the Territory. He found the country weak from the devastations of war; he left it strong. He had given general satisfaction to the people, in effecting substantial improvements for the benefit of the State. Although endowed with few of the brilliant qualifications of an orator, he possessed the solid and discriminating judgment of a statesman; discreet, sagacious, prudent, politic, he sought only the best good of the Territory.

Governor Cass was succeeded the same year by George B. Porter, a lawyear of Lancaster, Pennsylvania. He was appointed by President Jackson; although not possessing talent, he was acknowledged to be an active and thorough business man. The administration of Governor Porter was marked by no extraordinary measures effecting the condition of Michigan, with the exception of the erection of Wisconsin, which had formerly been attached to it, and the Black Hawk (or Sac) war.

In April, 1834, a census was taken, when it was found that Michigan contained a population of eighty seven thousand two hundred and seventy-three. During this year, the gubernatorial chair was again left vacant by the death of Governor Porter, and Stephen T. Mason, then Secretary of State, succeeded him as Governor, in which capacity he remained until elected by the people in 1836, with the exception of a part of 1835, when the chair was occupied by John S. Horner.

On the 11th of May, 1835, Michigan acting under the ordinance of 1787, which empowered the territories when their population reached sixty thousand, to organize into a State, called a convention at Detroit, framed a constitution and elected State officers. This constitution was rejected by Congress. But a conditional act passed, which in effect was for Michigan to give up the disputed fifteen mile strip, as claimed by Ohio, in accordance with her boundary lines as established on her admission into the Union. Michigan indignantly refused to comply with the provisions of this act, assuming that Congress had no right to dictate terms other than those laid down in the original compact.

In September, 1836, another convention was called at Ann Arbor, for the purpose of considering this act, when it was rejected. Local prejudices sprang up and public feeling was aroused. Some were in favor of coming in on any terms, while others favored staying out until their rights were fully recognized. On the ground of expediency another convention was called on the 17th of December of the same year, when the condition was recognized. The basis of this accession was to secure the benefits of the Union and share in the division of the surplus revenues. The question then arose as to whether this convention was empowered to accede to the terms as imposed by the act of Congress for the admission of Michigan. The President did not deem himself authorized to issue his proclamation on the action of this convention, but determined to lay the whole matter before Congress. This body after a protracted discussion, admitted Michigan as a State, on the 26th of January, 1837. In lieu of the disputed territory, Michigan was granted the Upper Peninsula, which, at that time, was considered of but little value, except for its fisheries and fur trade. The details of the dispute between Ohio and Michigan, in regard to the territory claimed by each, are given at some length in a separate chapter, under the head of the "Toledo War."

The limited space we have to devote to this part of our subject, prevents carrying it farther, although it by no means loses interest at this point, but is well worthy the attention and study of both the student and general reader.

THE TOLEDO WAR.

By the ordinance of 1787 it was laid down that a line running due east and west, touching the most extreme southern point of Lake Michigan, should be the dividing line between the two tiers of States that were to be erected out of the Northwestern Territory. In accordance with this, in 1802 Ohio, by an act of Congress, was admitted as a Territory, but put in her constitution the proviso that if the line drawn due east and west should extend so far south as not to touch Lake Erie, or if it should touch Lake Erie south of the mouth of the Maumee river, then in that case, *with the assent of Congress*, the northern boundary of the State should be the line running from the most extreme southern point of Lake Michigan to the most northernly cape of Maumee bay, and under this provision she was admitted; although by an act of Congress in 1805 admitting Michigan under the original boundaries, it can not be said that Congress assented to the conditions as laid down by Ohio, and in 1807 Ohio instructed her Representatives in Congress to use their influence to obtain the passage of a law defining their northern boundary in accordance with the proviso in their constitution.

In 1812 two lines were run by order of the Surveyor General, one in accordance with the original plan, called the Harris line, and the other to correspond with the Ohio proviso, called the Fulton line. The point with Ohio was to secure the mouth of the Maumee river, then, as has since proved correct, deemed important on account of its commercial location, being at the starting point of the Wabash canal and one of the principal shipping points on Lake Erie.

Michigan continued to exercise jurisdiction over the disputed territory without serious opposition until 1834, although Wood County, soon after its organization in 1820, attempted to control the territory in dispute.

In 1834 Ohio sent a memorial to Congress, setting forth her grievances, and in 1835 passed an act defining the northern limits of William, Henry, and Wood Counties, according to their proviso, all going to show that Michigan up to this time had jurisdiction over the disputed territory. By the same act the Governor was empowered to appoint Commissioners to survey the northern boundary in accordance with the proviso.

The Commissioners undertook the work, but were prevented by the people of Michigan. This brought Ohio to her feet. An extra session of the Legislature was called by the Governor on the 8th of June, 1835, at which the County of Lucas was organized, a considerable portion of which was made up of the disputed territory. This, however, did not quiet the difficulty. In the spring of 1836 two sets of officers were elected, one acting under the laws of Michigan, the other under the laws of Ohio. The Sheriff of Monroe County, at the head of a posse of men, marched in and arrested and carried to Monroe the local officers elected and acting for Ohio. Thereupon Governor Lucas levied troops and encamped at fort Miami, above Toledo. At the same time acting Governor Mason called out the militia of Michigan, and, placing himself at their head, marched to the front. Not finding the enemy, he pushed on and took possession of Toledo.

The Ohio Legislature on the 19th of June, 1835, passed an act raising the sum of three hundred thousand dollars for the purpose of defraying the expense of establishing her northern boundary. About this time two Commissioners, Richard Rush and Colonel Howard, were appointed at Washington for the purpose of settling the difficulties between the belligerents, in which they were successful, giving to Ohio the territory in dispute, and to Michigan, in lieu thereof, the Upper Peninsula, thus ending the controversy of many years standing.

ANCIENT EARTHWORKS.

With the early settlement of this country the discovery was made of a previous settlement by a people long since extinct. The only records remaining of this ancient people, or their habits, are the mounds, earthworks, and relics they have left behind them. That they were an agricultural people seems evident from the fact that these relics are always found on or near the most fertile land the country affords. That they were unlettered, also seems evident, for among all the relics that have been discovered nothing appears to show that they had any written language. And how, when, or for what purpose these mounds were built, will perhaps remain in the future as it has in the past, a mystery beyond the explanation of our most learned, yet a fertile source of speculation for all who may have a taste for delving in the pre-historic age of the country.

Many theories have been advanced by the various authors who have written on the subject, but we find after a careful perusal that they all come to one conclusion, and leave the reader just where he began; and the same mystery enshrouds this ancient people and their works that to the early settlers was inexplicable. Perhaps science in her rapid strides may in the future throw light on this important subject

—4

that will give us an idea of their character and habits.

The earthworks of this county are of two kinds; one the common mounds to be found in nearly every township in the county, and considered the most primitive in their character of any of the earthworks in existance, and a few of what seem to have been pleasure grounds or flower gardens. One of this latter kind was discovered by Squire Edwards on Pokagon prairie, when he came there in 1826. It is described as a low mound of considerable size, with well defined walks radiating from the center in all directions, and in several other parts of the county we have been informed that formations of like character existed in an early day, but, owing to their being located on the most fertile soil, they have been obliterated by the hand of the practical agriculturist.

These seem to be entirely different from the work of the Indians, although deemed by some to be one and the same, but with the Indians, everything was planted in parallel rows, each year planting in the same row and raising the ridge with each successive cultivation, following this system until the land became so exhausted that it would no longer produce remunerative crops, when a new piece was taken alongside and the system repeated, thus giving no correct impression of the extent of their agricultural operations, for by their manner of planting, it may have been carried on for many years, and when it became sodded over with the natural grasses of the country, it looked as though it all might have been under cultivation at one time.

The mounds of this county, in common with nearly all that are found north of the 41st degree of latitude, are of the most primitive character and in no wise compare with those found farther south. Their composition is universally of the surface soil without any admixture of foreign ingredients whatever, and apparently taken from the adjacent locality in such small quantities as to make no appreciable depression, thus creating with some investigators, the impression that it had been brought long distances for the purpose of building these mysterious monuments.

Who the people were that built these works or what was their purpose, is beyond the province of the author of the present day to divine. A number have been opened in different parts of the county, in nearly all of which something has been found: in some bones and rude implements, in others, a coarse kind of crockery ware with traces of charcoal and ashes in the bottom, but nothing in any of them that leads to any satisfactory conclusion.

The Indians have a theory that these mounds were used by their forefathers for two purposes; those having bones in them were monuments of important battles and covered the bones of the braves that fell, while those not having these relics, were used for abode, similar to the dug-outs in use in some parts of the west at the present time. But this does not seem at all likely, for those used for habitation would necessarily have to be hollow on the inside and would not have preserved their round, comely appearance, after the long space of time that has elapsed since their construction.

MICHIGAN INDIANS.

When father Alloues and Dablou first visited Green Bay, in 1670, for the purpose of establishing a mission, they found the country in the possession of a tribe of Pottawatomie Indians. The extent of their possessions or the number of their tribe is not given, but from the important position they afterwards occupied, it is safe to presume that their possessions were wide spread, and their tribe numerous. . This is the first record we have of the existence of this people or their whereabouts.

In 1675 Marquette made the voyage in open boats up the west shore of Lake Michigan, for the purpose of establishing missions among the Indians. He first landed where Chicago now stands, and it being late in the fall, went into winter quarters. On this voyage he was accompanied by Illinois and Potawattomie Indians. This is the first trace of the Potawattomies coming as far south as the extremity of Lake Michigan. How soon after this they left their home on Green Bay to inhabit a more genial clime, or whether the change was made gradually or at once, history does not state. But a portion of them settled on Saginaw bay, others on the banks of the Detroit, and still another portion located on the east shore of Lake Michigan, in the vicinity of the St. Joseph river, while still another portion settled in northern Illinois. The precise dates of these migrations can not be given, but that they were in the vicinity of Detroit and on the St. Joseph river about the middle of the last century, and have not been known at Green Bay in the last hundred years, is recorded. It was a powerful tribe and constituted about one-fourth of the Algonquin confederacy, and was among the last to give up its place to the encroaching white man.

The Algonquin confederacy was one of the most powerful combinations that was ever formed among the Indians of the West, and made its power felt in their alliance with the French against the English under the leadership of Pontiac. The Ottawas, Pottawatomies, and Chippewas were closely related in all their operations, and made common cause in avenging the death of Pontiac, to the extermination of the Illinois, once the most powerful race that inhabited the prairie country. The extermination of the Illinois gave them almost unlimited sway, and their possessions were extended far into Wisconsin on the north, south to the Wabash and east to Lake Erie. The Sac and Fox Indians west of the Mississippi river were their constant enemies and an almost continual warfare was kept up between the two contending parties for the possession of disputed territory.

To what extent the Pottawatomies assisted the British in the war of 1812, is not definitely known, but that some of their young braves did take part against the Americans is a well established fact.

During the Black Hawk war of 1832, as a tribe, they remained loyal to the United States, but it was with great difficulty that the young men could be restrained from participating with the Sacs and Foxes.

When the settlers first came to this county, they found it occupied by three bands of this tribe of Indians, comprising in all, about four hundred. In the western part was the Pokagon family of about two hundred and fifty, occupying the prairie that still bears the chief's name. In the northeast was Weesaw's band, of about one hundred, occupying Little Prairie Ronde, and in the southeast, the Shavehead family of about fifty, with their summer quarters on Baldwin's prairie.

These people were domestic in their habits, following the pursuit of agriculture as well as the chase in obtaining a livelihood. Their farms (or more properly gardens,) were usually in the timber bordering on the prairies. These were fenced against their ponies (the only stock they kept,) by felling the small timber into a windrow on three sides, and on the fourth side, next to the prairie, poles laid in crotches, formed the protection to their crops. The timber within the enclosure was girdled sufficiently to kill it, and the tops cut off thirty or forty feet above the ground. Their mode of cultivation was of the most primitive character, and performed almost wholly by the hoe, from the breaking up of the sod to the cultivation after planting. And each succeeding year the grain was planted on the same spot as the preceding year, and the cultivation continued until it would no longer produce, when another place was selected and the process repeated.

Of their productions, corn was the staple; while pumpkins, potatoes and melons, all of small varieties, were raised in limited quantites. The manner of securing their corn was to thoroughly dry it at harvest time, and store it away in holes in the ground. For this purpose a quantity of bark was peeled each year and kept for ready use, and when it came time for securing the crop, a place was selected in a convenient thicket of brush, the sod carefully removed and placed handy by, while the soil was carried in baskets and thrown in the nearest stream, for the purpose of leaving no trace of their concealed treasures. When the hole was finished, it was filled with dry combustible material and burned out, after which it was lined with bark, the corn put in and covered with the same material, when the sod taken off, would be replaced, making a secure compartment against the elements, as well as against any light-fingered gentry that might be passing that way. How long grain could be kept in this manner, is a matter of conjecture, as with the Indians it seldom rested beyond one winter. But that the period might be and was farther protracted is illustrated by the fact that in the spring of 1827, a squaw and her son came to the house of Baldwin Jenkins, from the north, and opened one of these bins within a few rods of the house, and took out the contents, which was in good condition, the family not having once suspected that the treasure was so near their door.

After securing their crops, the band would start on a hunting expedition, which would occupy the entire winter. The hunting grounds were some distance from the summer quarters, and periodically changed, for the purpose of letting the game accumulate, showing a providence that is rarely accredited to the Indian. In the spring they would repair to their sugar-making ground and occupy the season in making and storing a supply of sweets for the year, after which they would return to their summer residence. The corn was reserved until this time, unless the chase had been unsuccessful, or other untoward circumstances drove them to break in upon their stores.

Of their habits and customs but little new can be said. Their language was expressive and composed of but few words, each of which had numerous meanings, and in talking, was accompanied with gestures as expressive as the language itself. Their marriages were contracted by the parents, without ceremony, the friends came together bringing such presents as were suitable to the standing of the couple. If after living together for a time, they found their temperaments were not compatible, or if from any other cause, they wished to separate, they were free to do so and could be married again to their liking.

Their manner of burial has been commented upon by many writers, and much speculation indulged in upon the subject. The peculiar manner of disposing of the dead, some hung on trees, others in a sitting posture, others in pens, while a few were entombed in troughs hollowed out from the trunks of trees. Some with all their worldly goods surrounding them and a supply of provisions kept by them for a long time, has given rise to many theories on the subject. But with the Indians, these all had a special meaning, and any one of the tribe passing through a strange land could tell the rank, or if the subject had committed any serious crime, or was a noted brave, it was as plain to them as the marble tablet is to us. This is illustrated by the fact that in some of their earlier journeyings around the south end of Lake Michigan, a woman whom they all respected, named Me-mis-no-qua, (brave lady), was taken sick and died, and the last words she said were "here let my people eat." A tight pen was built over her grave, in which was deposited a quantity of dried venison, berries, etc., that any of the tribe coming that way hungry, could stop and eat. This was kept up as long as the tribe continued to travel on that trail.

Many of the early settlers will remember how the Indian babies were strapped to a board—a seemingly inhuman practice—but by them deemed necessary, as they reasoned that to keep the child straight would make straight men, which was the pride of the nation. Any one who has seen their children thus treated, and noted the smiles of the little fellows when the bells tinkled on shaking the board, and the convenience of disposing of them against the wall, or any out of the way place, does not wonder at the mode as practiced by these simple people.

Their manner of disposing of old or decrepit persons, was as summary as effective. Whenever they became useless or could not take care of themselves, they were put out of the way. A case of this kind occurred in the spring of 1830, near the northeast corner of Young's Prairie, where a band had wintered, when the party were ready to move, one old squaw was unable to go along. A committee took her in charge, cut a hole in the ice and deposited her therein, when the band proceeded on its way.

In July, 1829, John Baldwin (for whom Baldwin's prairie was named) had some difficulty with the Indians in regard to a yoke of cattle, which he had bought of them and paid for in whisky. It is claimed by some that a yoke of oxen was bought of the Indians, by others that the Indians shot an ox for Baldwin, crippling him, when Baldwin compelled them to buy the ox, and afterward bought it back and paid for it in whisky as stated. The Indians' ground for complaint was that the whisky was watered so much that it would not make them drunk.

One night, in harvest time, they came after he had gone to bed, armed with clubs, gained admittance and demanded that the matter be made right. Baldwin denied the charges, jumped out of bed and toward the fire-place where he had a stick of timber drying for a scythe snath, which he hoped to get to defend himself with. The Indians anticipated his movement, and were ahead in time to fell him with a club. He called to his son, Joel, a young man sleeping in an adjoining room, for help, who, coming to the outside door, found it guarded by Indians.

He then went in and jumped through a small window between the two rooms, but was caught by the Indians, who pulled his shirt over his head, at the same time assuring him that if he was quiet no harm would befall him. The Indians continued to beat Baldwin until they supposed him dead, after which they drew him into the doorway, and on leaving each one jumped upon his body, at the same time uttering an unearthly yell.

After the Indians left, the young man, with the assistance of the children, got his father onto the bed and found that he still breathed. Leaving him in charge of the children, Joel mounted a horse and aroused the neighbors, little thinking that he would be alive on getting back. But when the neighbors came in, it was found that he still lived. Dr. Loomis, of White Pigeon, was sent for, who dressed his wounds, which were mostly on the head, one side of which was half skinned and the balance badly beaten up.

Baldwin recovered from his injuries, put in a bill against the Indians for damages to the agent and was allowed nearly three thousand dollars, which was taken out of their annuities.

Topennebee was the acknowledged leader or Grand Sachem, and held sway over the various tribes of Pottawatomies of the Northwest. In 1795, as head chief, he signed the treaty which ceded all of Southern Ohio to the United States. His name also appears on various other treaties at different times, in which the cession of lands was made, in Northern Ohio, nearly all of Indiana and Michigan, and parts of Illinois and Wisconsin. His name in the Indian language signifies peacemaker, and from the characteristics of the man it would seem that he merited the appellation.

At the time of the threatened invasion by Black Hawk the Indians were in council near Niles, when Topennebee advised his people to keep on neutral ground, assigning as a reason that they would soon have to remove beyond the Mississippi, and it would be better for them not to take sides with either party. When he was through Op-to-go-me—Half Day—arose and said the reason for such advice as this was that Topennebee was a coward. At this the old chief threw over to him a butcher knife, at the same time bidding him to defend himself. At the first thrust Topennebee drove the knife nearly through his body, and for years a white flag was kept flying over the dead Indian's grave. He in common with the other members of his tribe was removed to the West in 1838.

Pokagon was next in command to Topennebee, and by many was considered the ideal red man of the forest, but by the Indians, in early times, he was held in derision and received his name (signifying rib) from the fact that at the massacre of Chicago he killed a pregnant white woman and cut her under the ribs, extracting the child. His original name was Saqoquinick. He married a daughter of Topennebee's brother, which, with being a good talker, placed him in the position of chief of his band and second in command of the Pottawatomies. His home was on the west side of the prairie that bears his name. He early became a convert to the Catholic faith and adhered to it through life, and set a good example for his band by abstaining from spirituous liquors.

By the treaty at Chicago, in 1833, Pokagon and his band were exempted from being removed beyond the Mississippi in common with the other Indians. His objection to being removed was the fear that they would lose the faith and civilization they had attained, and refused to sign the treaty unless the privilege of remaining was guaranteed him.

When the other Indians were taken away Pokagon purchased a large tract of land in Silver Creek Township, where he remained until his death, in 1841. He gave largely of his possessions to the Church of his faith.

In 1839 Pokagon was taken very sick and thought he was going to die, whereupon he sent for a priest, who on coming, refused to confer absolution unless forty acres of land were deeded to him. This Pokagon acceded to, the priest making out the papers; but upon the recovery of the chief, a short time after, the deed proved not to be for forty acres, but about seven hundred, and a lengthy litigation was necessary to recover it back.

Weesaw, the third in command of the Pottawatomies, occupied the Northeastern portion of the county, making his home in the summer season on the farm now owned by B. G. Buell, Esq., on Little Prairie Ronde. His winter quarters were on the Dowagiac creek, on the farm of Hon. George Newton, where he had wigwams for the twenty families constituting his band. He made sugar in the northwestern portion of the township of Volinia, near the farm of the late Daniel C. Squiers.

Weesaw is described as a man fully six feet high, finely formed. His carriage was proud and erect, and when dressed in his suit of blue broad cloth, of which he was very proud, he made a fine appearance. His favorite mode of dressing, however, was in the true Indian style, and as described by those that saw him, with a large silver ring in his nose, one in each ear, a breast-plate of the same material as large as a pie tin, his leggins adorned with a row of bells, that tinkled at every step, a blue sash, tied around his body, and a turban on his head of the same gay color, all combined to give impression of true Indian grandeur. He had three wives, of whom one was the daughter of Topennebee, and was the favorite, and on marches and important occasions was allowed to take the station nearest him.

Weesaw was a friend of the whites, and always evinced a desire to cultivate their acquaintance and friendship. In 1827, while the surveying party were working north of the big swamp, their packer got lost and could not find them for several days, in which time provisions ran very low and it became necessary to send out two men to procure supplies. Mr. Orlean Putnam and another man were detailed for this purpose, and went to Weesaw's encampment on Little Prairie Ronde to procure the necessary supplies, arriving just at night. On making their wants known, the utmost hospitality was shown them, and immediately the squaws set about preparing food to be taken to the party. They were given a separate tent to lodge in, and at the same time asked to guard the fire arms that were brought to their place, as there was a general drunk among the braves of the band, and a number of times during the night the squaws came and peeped in to see if all was safe. In the morning Weesaw and his favorite wife accompanied the party some distance on their way, assisting them in carrying the provisions. At this time there was no white inhabitant nearer than Pokagon prairie.

In the spring of 1830 or 1831 Weesaw wished to move from his winter quarters to the sugar making ground, but owing to the indisposition of one of his wives, who had been badly hurt in a drunken brawl by an Indian who had with a sharp stick prodded nearly all the joints in her body, making it impossible to move her with their means of conveyance, he came to Jonathan Gard for assistance, and wished him to take his ox team and move her. Mr. Gard fearing that in her critical condition something might happen and blame be attached to him, evaded the chief, by telling him that the oxen were in the woods and he did not know where to find them. To this Weesaw replied, "me find them," and immediately set out in pursuit of the oxen, and on the next morning drove them up. A long sled was prepared, with litter, and the squaw carefully loaded on; but in going through the woods they came to a large log that it was impossible to get around. Mr. Gard improvised a bridge of such small poles as they could pick up, and instructed Weesaw as the sled came to a balance to ease it down, so as not to jar or hurt her. The idea struck him so forcibly that he clapped his hands for joy at its success. The trip was made in safety, but the poor woman, owing to the serious nature of her wounds, lived but a few days after her removal.

Weesaw held, or assumed to hold, for a number of years a grant of three miles square on the south side of Little Prairie Ronde, taking in a portion of Gard's prairie and the creek intervening, but no attention was paid to his claim by the settlers, and about 1832 he removed his band to the western part of Berrien County.

Shavehead and his band of nine families occupied the southeastern part of the county, and a portion of the time wintered east of Young's prairie. This chief received his name from the peculiar manner in which he wore his hair, it being nearly all shaved off, leaving only a lock on top and a small portion on the back of his head, which was trained down behind, giving him a very peculiar as well as savage appearance. He was of a sullen, morose disposition, and always seemed to feel that the settlement of the country by the whites was an intrusion upon the Indian's rightful domain, and treated them accordingly. This was carried so far on several occasions that it came near costing him his life for his impudence and indiscretion. At one time he came to the house of Reuben Pegg, on Young's Prairie, while that gentleman was from home, and demanded of Mrs. P. some tallow to use on his gun, which she told him she did not have. This so enraged him that he threatened her until she was frightened nearly to death. Mr. P. coming home soon after and being informed of what had transpired, cut an ox gad and followed after and overtook the Indian near old Mr. Green's, when he gave him a severe castigation with an admonition to keep scarce in the future. On another occasion as Mr. Savory, of White Pigeon Prairie, was returning home from Carpenter's Mill, where he had been to get a grist ground, his team was stopped in the woods by this Indian, who stepped from behind a tree and took hold of the leaders, at the same time demanding a bag of meal for the privilege of passing through his country. Mr. S. told him to let go of the horses and come and take what meal he wanted, which Shavehead proceeded to do, but hardly got his head over the side of the wagon-box, when it was struck with the butt of the heavy laden whip in the hands of the driver, knocking him senseless to the ground and falling between the forward and back wheels of the wagon, from whence he was dragged by Mr. S. and left lying beside the trail more dead than alive. Many incidents of like nature could be related going to show the character of the man, but these will be sufficient. He never signed any of the treaties releasing the Indian title to the lands, consequently was cut off from their annuities, which perhaps may account for his manner of treating the whites. He died in 1837 or 1838, near Paw Paw, this State. A lake on section 19, of Porter township, commemorates his name.

CAREY MISSION.

The following sketch of the first white settlement in the St. Joseph Valley, (except by the French), is taken from the historical address delivered by the late Judge Bacon, before the Old Settlers' Society, at Niles, in 1869:

"This event so important in the history of the country, and which was in fact the pioneer step in the way of settlement, deserves particular notice. It was barely ten years since the massacre at Chicago, and about the same time after the memorable battle of Tippecanoe, and the disastrous defeat of our army at Brownstown, when this Mission was established. Emigration had in a great measure stopped. Very few dared to venture beyond the older settlements, until he, (McCoy), whose name we have just mentioned, boldly entered into the heart of the Indian country, and began his mission school among the Pottawotomies, who dwelt on the river St. Joseph. The fact was soon made known throughout Indiana and Ohio, and at once adventurers began to prepare to follow the example of the missionary, who had led the way. If McCoy had not founded Carey Mission, Thompson and Kirk might never have crossed the Elkhart.

"The Rev. Isaac McCoy was born June 13th, 1788, near Uniontown, in the State of Pennsylvania. When six years of age, his parents moved to Jefferson county, Kentucky. In October, 1803, he married Miss Christiana Polk, daughter of Captain Charles Polk, of the last named State, and in March, 1804, after having been licensed to preach, he and his wife emigrated to the town of Vincennes, in the State of Indiana, where he began his labors as a missionary among the Indians, and accordingly removed into the neighborhood of their village on Raccoon creek, and there erected a double log cabin and opened his school. His devoted wife was a faithful helper, and she with their seven children followed and shared with him his privations and toils. In 1820 he removed his school to Fort Wayne, and there, for two years, devoted himself to his chosen work, and from thence removed to Carey on the St. Joseph river, as has been stated.

"Permit me now to call your attention for a few moments, to Mrs. McCoy, and to a few incidents in her eventful life. She was born in Shelby county, Kentucky. She was one of four children, who with their mother were captured by the Indians and carried by them to Detroit, and they with other captives were ransomed by British officers and kept for three years.

"At the time, Captain Polk was from home in a scouting party against the Indians. On his return he found his house in ashes and his wife and children gone. He made immediate pursuit, but in vain; the savages made their escape, and he returned not to a home, but to the place where his dwelling had once stood, to mourn their loss.

"At the end of three years, he found his wife and children at Detroit all well. He paid their ransom and brought them back in safety to Kentucky. I cannot speak at this time of the sufferings and terror which attended their capture and captivity by the savages. It can never be fully told, or even imagined. They were seized, hurried off, and compelled to keep up with their captors in their flight.

"After their removal to Fort Wayne, and while their school was in successful operation, Mrs. McCoy knowing that she could not receive such attention as her situation would soon require, deemed it best to return to Fort Harrison, and there remain for a time among her friends.

"Accordingly in June, 1821, she, together with her three youngest children, set out in a canoe to descend the Wabash, to the place last named. The distance was between three and four hundred miles. Mrs. McCoy sat up the first night, and by the light of a fire built on shore, watched her three sleeping children and protected them from the mosquitoes.

"In the month of September following, she returned to Fort Wayne on horseback, carrying in her arms her infant child, not yet two months old. The distance she traveled was about one hundred and eighty miles, and the road lay across and through a new country, much of it was a wilderness and inhabited by savages only. Most of the time she slept in the woods with no shelter but a tent.

"On the 14th of May, 1822, McCoy visited the

Indian villages upon the river St. Joseph. He held a consultation with the chiefs and a site for the mission buildings was selected. He returned to Fort Wayne on the 23d of May, and carried with him three Indian children for the school. On the 9th of October, 1822, Mr. McCoy, with Mr. Jackson and his family, four hired men and some of the oldest Indian boys, in all twenty persons, left Fort Wayne for the purpose of erecting buildings at the Mission Station.

"They brought with them two wagons drawn by oxen, one four horse wagon, and five milch cows. They arrived on the 19th of October, wet with rain, and worn down with fatigue. They immediately began their work, cutting down trees and hauling them onto the ground and fitting them to be laid up into the four walls of a house. McCoy, though not fully recovered from an attack of fever, labored with the men and directed the work.

"On the 11th of November, the buildings were in such a state of forwardness, that McCoy left the party to go on with the work and he set out on his return to Fort Wayne. It was November weather, stormy and cold. He was wet every day with rain, and riding through the wet bushes, and at night slept on the ground, or in a deserted wigwam. The missionary, famishing with hunger and shivering with cold, reached home after a ride of three days.

"Preparations having been made for the final removal, McCoy with his wife and five children, Mr. Dusenbury, an assistant missionary, six laboring men, and eighteen pupils and Indians, making in all thirty-two persons, moved off from Ft. Wayne on the 9th of December, 1822. They were stowed away in three wagons drawn by oxen, and one wagon drawn by four horses. They drove with them fifty fat hogs, and five cows. Beds, bedding, clothing, and provisions were packed in the wagons. Some of the men and boys rode on horse-back, the balance were obliged to plod along on foot. A large tent was carried along, which at night and on very stormy days afforded shelter for the whole party. The weather was cold, and there was three inches of snow on the ground, and ice had already formed in the swamps and on the streams. For many miles the road was through a low level country, having a clay soil, and covered with heavy timber.

"From the very start they could look for nothing but a tedious, comfortless, and wearisome journey; most of the party, too, had been sick with chills and fever, from which they had not as yet fully recovered. Three large rivers had to be crossed. There was neither ferry nor bridge; nor was there a cabin or house on the whole route. Winter had set in. Snow was falling daily, and the mercury was below the freezing point when they bade farewell to Fort Wayne and attempted to ford the St. Marys. The water was deep and the ice was running swiftly, but after hours of struggle and toil, the whole party, with the cattle, got safely over. They made but three miles advance the first day. The snow was carefully removed, a fire built, the tent pitched, beds made on the ground, and the party encamped for the night. They retired early to rest, and arose at four o'clock in the morning and ate breakfast by candle light. This was their custom during the entire journey. Delays and hinderances happened daily. Wagons were broken, which must be repaired, cattle strayed away at night and a whole day was spent in search of them.

"On the night of the 14th they encamped on the bank of the Elkhart. After cutting away the ice they got safely over the river, but not until after a day of hard labor and great exposure.

"Early on the morning of the 17th, McCoy, though very unwell, took two men with him and went ahead of the party ten miles to the St. Joseph and built large fires on each bank, by which they could warm themselves from time to time as the slow and tedious work of crossing was going on. Although the water was deep and the ice running fast, which made the crossing dangerous, yet the party with their effects got safely over, and encamped for the night. They were now eighteen miles from the French trading house at *Parc aux vaches.*

"On the morning of the 18th of December they made a desperate effort, and at night found shelter under the roof of the kind and hospitable Mr. Bertrand. They now were within six miles of the mission house. On the 19th they came to this place (Niles) and forded the river near the foot of Main street, crossing it diagonally, and landing near the rear of the garden of Mr. Colby. In an hour thereafter they reached their home in the woods.

There is a large stream of water which empties

into the St. Joseph, near the present site of Elkhart, which is known as the Christiana creek. It was so named by the missionary in honor of his wife, as they crossed it the 18th of December. If no other monument shall bear her name, this placid stream will in all future time remind the beholder of its namesake, the gentle Christiana McCoy.

When the missionaries arrived at Carey, their stock of flour was almost exhausted. Two wagons drawn by oxen were immediately sent to Ohio, by way of Fort Wayne, to procure a supply. It was hoped that they would return in a month. It was not, however, until the 13th of February that they arrived. The family had been on short allowance for more than four weeks. They had been able to buy from the Indians and French traders only a few bushels of corn, which was boiled and served as bread. It often happened during their six weeks of semi-starvation, that they were reduced to a single bushel of grain, and knew not where to go for more. It, however, did happen, or rather was ordered, that a supply, though a scanty one, should come. They procured a little corn from the traders and natives, and kind old Mr. Bertrand most generously divided his last barrel of flour with the famishing missionaries.

"The following extracts from the journal give a vivid picture of the condition of the family:

"'February 1st. Having eaten up our corn, and having only flour enough for one meal, we sent five of our strongest Indian boys five miles to an Indian trader and borrowed a barrel of flour and a bushel of corn. Our teams were absent and the boys carried it home on their backs. The flour was damaged, nevertheless it was very acceptable to us.'

"'February 7th. Ate our last meal of bread for breakfast, which was so scarce that we had to divide it carefully that every one might have a little. We had saved a few pounds for the small children. We were without milk and they were suffering. An Indian was sent out to try to buy corn. He returned with six quarts, which was all he could procure.'

"'February 8th. Breakfasted upon corn, which we had procured yesterday. Blessed be God, we have not yet suffered for want of food, because our corn is an excellent substitute for bread. But now having eaten our last corn, we can not avoid feeling some uneasiness about the next meal.'

"In this extremity McCoy set out on horse-back, accompanied by an Indian, who was on foot acting as guide, in search of food. He was yet weak from sickness, the snow was deep, and it was extremely cold. He had hardly left the house when an old Pottawatomie widow, who lived near by, having heard of their destitute condition, kindly sent Mrs. McCoy sweet corn enough for a full meal for the whole family. McCoy in the meantime was slowly working his way through the trackless snow, when he accidentally met Mr. Bertrand and made known to him his business. The kind-hearted Frenchman, touched with pity for the starving missionaries, generously divided his own stock of flour and corn, giving them one-half, (Bertrand's own supply was by no means large) and he accompanied the gift with a few words of broken English: 'I got some corn, some flour; I give you half. Suppose you die, I die, too.'

"On the 10th of February, two Indians brought a supply of corn, and a few days afterward, two traders named Rosseau, having heard of their wants, brought them a little flour. In this way they subsisted until the 13th, when the wagons arrived with supplies. They not only brought flour, but brought in addition, two boxes of clothing, which had been sent from Massachusetts. This timely donation was almost as acceptable as food itself to them, who were pinched with cold as well as hunger.

"On the 21st of February, Mr. Johnston Lykins, after an absence of several months, arrived, to the great joy of all. He had at first been employed as a teacher, when the school was established in the Wabash country. He came with the missionaries to Fort Wayne, and was an associate with McCoy. His ability, integrity and christian devotion, eminently fitted him for the work in which he was engaged. He had the entire confidence of McCoy, and was equally with him a principal.

"He remained at Carey until the establishment was broken up, and the success of the Mission was in a great degree attributable to his wise counsel and administrative talent.

"In February, 1828, he married Miss McCoy, the eldest daughter of the missionary. Dr. Lykins is yet living, and now resides at Kansas City, Missouri.

"The winter and spring of 1823 were times of great suffering with the Mission family. Many of them were sick from over-labor, and from exposure and privation. McCoy himself was confined to the house by fever, and Mrs. McCoy was unwell, not having fully recovered from the sickness of the preceding summer.

"There was great activity among all the employes at the Mission in the spring of 1823. The school was in full operation. The daily cares of the household and family were large. It was no trifling matter to look after the never-ending routine of labor in the kitchen, where food was prepared for sixty people. A new farm was to be cleared, fenced, plowed and planted. Various as were the departments of labor, there was order and regularity in all of them.

"In the month of May, 1823, Major Long of the United States army, while on his way to explore the sources of the St. Peters, called with his party at the Mission. In the report which was made of this well-known tour, he mentioned this visit. The following extract is taken from it:

"'The report which we had received of the flattering success which had attended the efforts of the Baptist missionaries on the St. Joseph, induced us to deviate a little from our route, to visit this interesting establishment.

"'The Carey Mission House, so designated in honor of the late Wm. Carey, the indefatigable apostle of Hindostan, is situated about one mile from the river St. Joseph. The establishment was erected by the Baptist Missionary Society in Washington, and is under the superintendence of the Rev. Mr. McCoy; a man whom from all the reports we have heard of him, we should consider as eminently qualified for the important trust committed to him. We regretted that during the time we passed at the Carey Mission House, this gentleman was absent on business connected with the establishment of another missionary settlement, on the Grand river of Michigan, but we saw his wife, who received us in a very hospitable manner, and gave us every opportunity of becoming acquainted with the circumstances of the school.

"'The spot was covered with a very dense forest seven months before the time we visited it, but by the great activity of the Superintendent, he has succeeded in the course of this short time, in building six good log houses, four of which afford comfortable residences for the inmates of the establishment; the fifth is used as a school room, and the sixth forms a commodious blacksmith shop. In addition to this, they have cleared about fifty acres of land, which is nearly all enclosed by a substantial fence. Forty acres have already been plowed and planted with maize, and every step has been taken to place the establishment upon an independent footing.

"'The school consists of from forty to sixty children, and it is contemplated that it will soon be increased to one hundred. The plan adopted appears to be a very judicious one; it is to unite a practical and intellectual education. The boys are instructed in the English language—reading, writing and arithmetic. They are made to attend to the usual occupations of a farm, and perform every operation connected with it, such as plowing, planting, harrowing, &c. In these pursuits, they appear to take great delight. The system being well regulated, they find time for everything.

"'The girls receive the same instruction as the boys, and in addition are taught spinning, knitting, weaving and sewing, both plain and ornamental. They are also made to attend to the pursuits of the dairy, such as milking cows, making butter, etc. All appear to be very happy, and to make as rapid progress as white children of the same age would make. Their principal excellence rests in works of imitation. They write astonishingly well, and many display great natural taste for drawing.

"'The institution receives the countenance of the most respectable among the Indians. There are in the school two of the great grand-children of To-pen-ne-bee, the great hereditary chief of the Pottawatomies. The Indians visit the establishment occasionally and appear well pleased with it. They have a flock of one hundred sheep, and are daily expecting two hundred head of cattle, collected in Tennessee, Ohio and Kentucky.'

"On the 15th of June, a drove of one hundred and twenty-one cattle arrived at Carey. They were a part of the drove of over two hundred spoken of by Major Long, a part of them having been left at Fort Wayne to recruit. The stock was now increased to about one hundred and fifty head. They very soon had sixty cows for their dairy, and large quantities of butter and cheese were made. They had a large stock of all the domestic animals, which are kept on a well conducted and well managed farm. It was commonly reported they had about two hundred head of cattle, about three hundred sheep and an immense herd of swine. The latter subsisted most of the time on nuts and roots, which they found in the woods, and were in fine condition.

"The Mission was now in full operation but had not attained its full growth. New scholars were received, additions made of new missionaries, new teachers and new laborers.

"In November, Miss Fannie Goodridge, of Lexington, Kentucky, arrived, and became a teacher. She was followed, but at a later day, by Miss Wright and Miss Purchase, of Ohio, and by Mr. and Mrs. Polk, of Indiana. The late Major Britton, who died in 1862 at St. Joseph, honored and respected by all that knew him, was among the teachers.

"In October, 1823, Charles Noble, Esq., of Monroe was commissioned by General Lewis Cass, who was then Governor of the Territory of Michigan and also Superintendent of Indian Affairs, to visit the Carey Mission and make a report of its condition. In pursuance of this commission, Mr. Noble came to the mission house and there spent three days in making his examination. The result of this visit and the opinion of that gentleman, are spoken of by General Cass in a letter to McCoy, dated December 1st, in which he said:

"'Your report, and that of Mr. Noble, are entirely satisfactory. The affairs of your agency appear to be in the best condition, and if the experiment is ever successful, I am satisfied you will make it so.'

"Although this year was one of prosperity, and the products of the farm had been as large as could reasonably be expected, still there was a lack of breadstuff at the Mission. It is true they had gathered nine hundred bushels of corn and a large quantity of vegetables, but they had not as yet raised any wheat, and flour was transported in wagons from Ohio. They were in need of clothing and there was a debt of several hundred dollars incurred in the support of the Mission.

"To procure supplies Mr. McCoy left Carey on the 20th of December, and proceeded to Washington, and from thence in February he went to Philadelphia, New York, Boston, and other places, where he made a representation of the condition and wants of the mission. Wherever he went there was a generous response to his appeals. He received large donations of clothing, books, goods, and more than two thousand dollars in money.

"On the 25th of May he embarked at Buffalo, on a schooner bound for Detroit, and the mouth of the river St. Joseph. He had on board, besides boxes of clothing and goods, one hundred barrels of flour, twenty-four barrels of salt, and thirty bushels of wheat for seed. He left the vessel at Detroit and came across the country on horse-back, arriving at Carey on the 11th of June. He found all well and the work going on prosperously. In his long absence of five months, Dr. Lykins and Mrs. McCoy had managed with ability the affairs of the mission. Their stock of flour was again almost exhausted, and none could be obtained until the arrival of the vessel at the mouth of the river. What occurred at this time is thus stated in the journal:

"'In my absence the labors of the missionaries have been greater than they were able to sustain. Laudably ambitious to keep all matters moving forward, and to prevent retrogression in any department, they have toiled beyond their strength. Mrs. McCoy's health was very poor, and her spirits were more depressed than I ever knew them.

"'I found them on a short allowance of bread. On the 16th we had exhausted all our flour and meal, excepting a few pounds reserved for the small children and the sick. All except myself were in good spirits in regard to food, hourly expecting the arrival of the vessel. I feared that contrary winds or other hinderances might cause us to suffer, but concealed my anxiety. On the 18th we had only corn enough for one day, but our merciful God was still near us.

"'The harbor at which the vessel would stop was without inhabitant, and we had sent two of our Indian pupils to build and keep up a fire at the place, in order that the smoke by being seen from the vessel might point out the place of landing. The boys were directed to open a barrel of flour immediately on the landing of the vessel, and hasten to us, a distance of twenty-five miles, with what they could bring. On the evening of the 18th, to our great joy, and mine in particular, one of the young men arrived with a mule packed with flour. We brought our property from the lake to the station upon the river in pirogues. From that time forward the mission did not suffer for bread, nor did our pecuniary wants ever again become so great as they had been.'

"The Mission was prosperous during the next two years. The number of scholars increased. The farm was greatly enlarged. More than two hundred acres were enclosed with substantial fences. About three hundred bushels of wheat were harvested in 1824 and in 1825, a flouring mill was erected which was worked by horse power. This was the first mill built west of Tecumseh or Ann Arbor. It was most necessary for the comfort and convenience of the Mission. Prior to this they ground corn on a hand mill, which required the constant labor of one man to make sufficient meal for daily consumption.

"The condition of the Mission and its influence upon the natives of the surrounding country is clearly stated by the late John L. Lieb, Esq., of Detroit, the government agent, whose duty it was, among other things, to visit annually the Indian schools within the bounds of the Michigan superintendency. He visited the Carey Mission in August, 1826, and made his report to General Cass, from which the following extracts are made:

"'On the 15th of August, I proceeded to the Carey establishment on the St. Joseph, where I arrived on the 21st, and was much gratified with the

—6

improvement in all its departments. It is a world in miniature, and presents the most cheerful and consoling appearance. It has become a familiar resort of the natives, and from the benefits derived from it in various shapes, they begin to feel a dependence on, and resource in it at all times, and especially in difficult and trying occasions. There is not a day, I may say hardly an hour, in which new faces were not to be seen.

"'The smithery affords them incalculable facilities and is constantly filled with applicants for some essential service. It is a touching spectacle to see them, at the time of prayer, fall in with the members of the institution, which they do spontaneously and cheerfully, and with a certain animation depicted on their countenances, exhibiting their internal satisfaction.

"'There are at present seventy scholars, forty-two males and twenty-eight females, in various stages of improvemnt. Eight of the alumni of this institution who have completed the first rudiments of education, have been transferred to academies in New Jersey and New York. Two of the boys are learning the trades of blacksmithing and shoemaking. The remainder of sufficient size are employed occasionally on the farm. The girls are engaged in spinning, knitting, and weaving. The loom has produced one hundred and eighty-five yards of cloth this year. Two hundred and three acres are now enclosed by fences, of which fifteen are in wheat, fifty in Indian corn, eight in potatoes and other vegetable products. The residue is appropriated to pasture.

"'There have been added to the buildings since my last visit, a house and a most excellent grist mill, worked by horse power. The usefulness of this mill can scarcely be appreciated, as there is no other of any kind within one hundred miles at least of the establishment, and here as benevolence is the preponderating principle, all the surrounding population is benefited.

"'Numerous Indian families have since my last visit settled themselves around, and have from the encouragement, countenance, and assistance of the missionary family, made considerable progress in agriculture; indeed a whole village has been formed within six miles of it, under its benevolent auspices and fostering care. I visited it to witness myself the change in their condition. To good fences, with which many of their grounds are enclosed, succeed domestic animals. You now see oxen, cows, and swine grazing around their dwellings without danger of destroying their crops. Here are the strongest evidences of their improvement, and not the least of the benefits arising from the neighborhood of this blessed abode of the virtuous inmates of Carey. It is not alone in the immediate neighborhood that the efforts of the missionary exertions are felt. In distant places, near the mouth of the St. Joseph, and at Grand River, the most surprising changes have taken place. Strong and effective enclosures are made and making, and stock acquired; and at the latter place the missionary family have erected spacious buildings, including a school-house, and improved some land.

"'I was visited by numerous chiefs of known and approved influence over their tribes, who came to express their satisfaction at the establishment and inviting me to a conference with them.'

"In September, 1827, a treaty with the Indians was held at Carey. The commissioners on the part of the United States were Governor Cass and General Tipton, and Judge Leib of Detroit was Secretary of the commission. The Mission had now attained its full growth and blazed forth in all its splendor. While negotiations for the treaty were pending, the commissioners examined carefully into the management of the institution, and most cordially approved it.

"It was known from the very beginning that the Carey Mission must fall before the white men who would immigrate to the country. The Indian title to the land would soon be extinguished and then it would be purchased by actual settlers. The white man and the Indian could not live side by side until the latter should be civilized and made equal to the former. Accordingly preparations were being made at the Mission for bringing it to a close, and its removal beyond the western boundary of the Territory of Missouri. It was not fully wound up until the year 1830.

"The founder of Carey was a man of great energy and untiring perseverence; affable, generous, and a sincere Christian, he made friends wherever he was known. He died at Louisville, Kentucky, in 1846. Mrs. McCoy, his most amiable and devoted wife, died in Jackson County, Missouri, at the house of her son, J. C. McCoy."

PIONEER LIFE.

CABIN BUILDING.

The first thing to which the early settler gave his attention, on arriving at his destination in the new country, was a habitation for himself and family. In some instances the man would come on the season before and prepare the necessary shelter, but in most cases the family all moved together, using the large covered wagon which had conveyed them on their journey, for a place of abode until a cabin of logs could be erected. A location was usually selected behind a belt of timber, and near a spring, or running stream, thus securing protection from the elements and a supply of that very important article, water, at one and the same time. First in order came the clearing of a suitable plat of ground for the cabin. This done, logs of a proper size and length were cut for the body of the building and hauled together. Thus far the man could get along alone, or with such assistance as his sons or hired man could render, but in order to raise the building the assistance of the neighbors for perhaps a half dozen miles around was solicited. If the day was generally known on which the raising was to be done, no invitation was necessary, as the friendliness and generosity of the early settlers was of such a spontaneous nature that all that was needed was to have it known that a new comer was in want of help and it was speedily forthcoming. Many instances are reported of strife between parties as to who should be the first on the ground—some coming long before daylight, perhaps only to find several of their neighbors there before them—and at earliest dawn the business of putting up the habitation commenced.

First, the two side logs were placed on suitable blocks—or if the proprietor was particular to have it substantial, stones were used instead—notches were cut along for the sleepers to rest in, which were round poles faced on one side with an ax, and the four best "corner men" took their places.

The post of "corner man" was one of no minor distinction, and to be successful he must not only be skilled in the use of an ax, but have a mechanical eye as well, and be able to make a joint every time, as it was of the utmost importance to avoid rolling the log back and forth.

The men were then divided into two parties, each choosing a captain, and took their respective stations at either end of the log to be put in place. As soon as the building had risen to a height to make it necessary, the skid and crotch were brought into requisition, the former formed by placing long straight poles from which the bark had been peeled, with one end resting on the building, the other on the ground, and on these the logs were rolled up to the "corner men." The crotch was cut from a sapling three or four inches through, having a natural fork at a suitable distance to make it the right length to reach the top of the building. The fork was secured by winding with hickory withes, which had first been run through the fire to toughen them. A two-inch auger-hole was bored at right angles with the fork near the butt end, in this was placed a pin three or four feet long, to push up by, forming an implement that was very effective in raising the logs to their places. Many times the excitement would rise to the highest pitch, especially if there was a supply of whisky on hand—which was quite common on these occasions—each party striving to push their end of the log up first. In some instances, so much force was used as to throw the corner men from their positions when the log came against the building.

The hickory withe can hardly be appreciated in this day of ropes, tools and machinery, but then it was of the utmost importance. The pioneer on starting to the woods, or on a journey, always carried an ax, and with this he would cut roads, build a bridge or mend his wagon, as the case might be or circumstances require. A broken axle-tree was of no uncommon occurrence, and with the ax alone, he would mend his vehicle by cutting a pole and tying it fast to the axle-tree with withes, and proceed on his journey. The tools required in building a house were an ax, saw, and auger, and with these the pioneer would do the whole job; in fact, he seemingly needed no others.

The cabin being built up to the height considered

necessary—which was usually that of the tallest member of the family—notches were cut along in the two side logs, to admit poles laid in crosswise for joists. When up to the square, the two end logs were extended over about a foot each way, for the purpose of receiving a log to rest the first tier of shakes against; and the building of the gable ends commenced, a system of architecture much easier to take in with the eye than describe on paper.

The lack of lumber and the absence of machinery for manufacturing it, made it necessary to do everything with such material as was at hand; hence the system of "cobbing" as it was termed, by which it was meant the forming of the gable ends with logs, which were cut of suitable lengths, each pair being shorter as the work progressed upward, and sloped off to form the pitch of the roof. With each pair of end logs, a pole ran lengthwise of the building, for the shakes to rest upon, taking the place or answering the purpose of rafters in more modern architecture.

When the ends had been brought to a peak the roofing commenced. While one party was engaged in putting up the building, another would be busy preparing material for the roof, which consisted wholly of shakes and poles; the former were made from some rifty, free-splitting timber—usually white or red oak—cut three feet long and split from four to eight inches wide and one inch thick. These were laid in double courses, the first course resting on the logs spoken of above, as forming the top of the square, and which sometimes were hewn out in the form of troughs, thus answering the double purpose of supports for the shakes and conductors for the rain water.

After the first course of shakes had been laid, two or three short blocks were placed on the roof, one end resting against the trough or log that held the lower end of the shakes, the "weight-pole" against the other; the "weight-pole" answering the double purpose of holding one tier of shakes down and making a base for the next tier above. This process was continued until the roof was complete, the last tier of shakes projecting over at the comb six or eight inches in the opposite direction to that from which the prevailing winds came, to prevent storms from beating under; and, so far as rain was concerned, no shingle or slate roof could have afforded better protection—the only drawback being that in the winter season fine snow would find its way through the cracks, and not unfrequently would the pioneer family find, on rising in the morning, an inch or more of snow on their beds; not a very pleasant state of affairs to contemplate in this day of air-tight houses, but one which was then looked upon as a matter of necessity and the situation accepted accordingly.

When the cabin was up and covered, the assistance of the neighbors was no longer needed, and the pioneer proceeded to finish off the building without the aid of architect or joiner.

The first thing now to be considered was an entrance way, for as yet the building stood entire, without an opening in it—if we except the numerous cracks between the logs. In putting up the building, two notches large enough to admit the point of a saw, had been made where the door was designed to be. From these he sawed down in two parallel lines sufficiently far apart for the width of the door. Half way down it would frequently be of double width, to admit of a window being placed beside the door. When the logs were cut out of the way, "cheek pieces" were prepared by splitting out timbers the suitable length and width and hewing them to a uniform thickness, and if an extra nice job was wanted, a drawing knife would be used to finish up with. These were pinned to the ends of the logs, forming a casing and support.

The place for the window was cased up in the same manner, and if the proprietor possessed glass enough to fill a six light sash, he was considered very fortunate; if not, oiled or greased paper was used as a substitute. The light coming through this semi-transparent material could hardly be said to equal that transmitted by the best French plate glass, yet it answered its day and purpose.

Upon the door the pride and ingenuity of the proprietor was fully displayed, as the finish of this, so far as looks went, was considered of more importance than any other part of the house. Planks, or boards, were split from some soft-wood tree, the preference being always given to the basswood, as the second growth of this timber splits very straight and even, requiring less work to bring it to the required thickness than any other. Battens or cross-pieces were prepared in the same way, then the whole was pinned together in a manner that looked as though they were preparing a habitation for their great-grand-children instead of a temporary abode.

The hinges for hanging were formed by making two eyes of wood, six or eight inches long, with one end large enough to admit of an auger hole through it, the other brought down into the form of a pin and driven into a hole bored into the logs of the house. Two cleats were then pinned to the door, projecting over at one end with holes through them to correspond with those in the eyes, a round stick whittled out with a knot on one end to keep it from dropping too far through, the whole being put together, the hanging was complete, a structure not to be wafted by every gentle breeze, or damaged by the undue slamming of any unruly member of the family.

The latch was made of a thin piece of board, an inch and a half wide and hung at the back end on a pin, working through a slot in another piece fastened to the door and into a catch fastened to the door-cheek, and if any nails were to be had they were used in these finer parts, to hold the small pieces, catch, etc., but if they were not to be had the whole was put together with pins. The latch was worked from the outside by a string, one end of which was fastened to the latch inside and passed through a hole above; and all that had to be done at night to make everything secure, was to pull the string through on the inside. The favorite material for the string was well tanned deer or woodchuck skin, but if these were not at hand, from a bunch of tow—of which there was an ample supply in every thrifty household—the lady of the house would readily twist a cord for this or any like purpose.

"The latch-string always out," is a time-honored synonym for hospitality, which originated from the habit, as the country developed, of some keeping the string on the inside and attending to the callers at the door, instead of allowing the visitor to come in at his pleasure.

The next thing to claim attention was the fire-place, and the character of the man would be as much exhibited in this as in any other part. If he was from the South, or his associations had been with Southern people, his chimney would be fashioned after the manner of that section. That is, a large opening perhaps eight feet long, would be cut out in the end of the building, and the fire-place and chimney built wholly on the outside. This doubtless originated from the fact that in the genial climate in which he was raised or educated, the warmth of the building was not taken into consideration, but rather an avoidance of it, while people from the East who were accustomed to the rigors of a Northern climate, would take the opposite view, and build the chimney on the inside, thus securing all the warmth possible. If the chimney was to be built on the outside, after cutting away sufficient space in the wall, saplings six or eight inches through were taken and split in two, and of these a three-sided crib was built up to the height of a man's head, the fourth side being the inside of the house, and upon the crib rested the stick chimney.

Many different compounds were used in making the jambs and hearths, nearly every one having a receipt which they considered the very best. The great difficulty to overcome being the tendency of the jambs to crumble, and the hearths to sweep out into basin-like cavities, and finally to entirely disappear under the vigorous use of the splint broom wielded by the good mothers and daughters of that day.

It must be borne in mind that there were no brick to be had in the country and something must be used as a substitute, and this brought the ingenuity and experience of the settlers into requisition. One of the methods was to mix the clay with sweet milk, another to put in a quantity of unleached ashes, cut straw, etc., but sooner or later they would all need repairs.

When the compound was determined upon and the mortar mixed, an excavation would be made a foot or eighteen inches deep and this filled with the prepared mortar and pounded down solid with a heavy wooden maul made for the purpose. The jambs were made of the same material. Sometimes a form was made by building a crib on the inside of the outer one, leaving a space the thickness of the jamb to be built, this was filled with mortar and pounded in. When it became dry a fire was built and the inside frame burned out, but the more usual plan was to build the jambs up with stiff mortar, forming them by the eye, and extending them up to where the chimney commenced.

The chimney was built of sticks and mud. The

sticks were split about an inch and a half wide and half an inch think, and laid up house fashion. The plaster, which consisted of a mortar made of clay and fine cut straw, was put on as the work·advanced upward. It would seem remarkable that the whole mass did not burn up the first time a fire was built, but fires were of no more frequent occurrence then than now. This may be accounted for, in a measure, by the constant vigilance in the care of the fire, the last duty of the housewife before going to bed was to look up the chimney to see that all was safe.

The cabin up, covered, and chimney built, next in order was the floor, which also must be made from the material at hand. No lumber-yard to order from, nor planing and matching machines to make the flooring ready for the joiner, but the nearest free-splitting tree was selected and cut into lengths from six to eight feet long, then split as wide as the tree would make, and from two to four inches thick, and the degree of precision with which a good ax-man would split a plank to the required thickness would surprise a novice.

To face one side of these planks, or puncheons, it was almost absolutely necessary to have the use of a broad-ax; a tool not to be found in the kit of every pioneer, and the loan of one from a neighbor forty miles distant, was of no uncommon occurrence.

It is related that during the first season of the settlement of Little Prairie Ronde (1829), while the neighbors were together putting up a cabin for one of their number, another hovel which had been built temporarily of rails and poles, to protect the owner's household goods from the elements, took fire from the smouldering embers of a burnt brush-heap near by, and consumed or spoiled the only saw and auger in the settlement, a calamity that was almost irreparable.

The puncheons, as the floor slabs were termed, were hewed on one side as smoothly as possible, and the underside sized at the ends, and laid on the sleepers, forming a floor that for strength and durability would hardly be excelled. Upon the manner in which the floor was kept rested each housewife's reputation, and the "floor clean enough to eat a dinner off from" was the height of woman's ambition in that line. The floor usually extended only about two-thirds the distance from the back end of the building, the remainder being mother earth.

Chinking or filling up the crack between the logs, came next. Chinks were usually made from the hearts of the bolts left in making the shakes for the roof. These were placed in the cracks, thin edge out, and held in place by pins, thus making an even surface on the inside, while the outside was daubed from the nearest clay-bank, and the habitation was complete, and for comfort it is not to be looked upon with disdain, or an unfavorable comparison made with the better class of buildings in use by our citizens now.

From this sketch of cabin building it might be inferred that it was always carried along in regular order until completion, but in point of fact it frequently took the whole season at different intervals to complete the structure, as other important duties came along in succession interfering with the continuous work on the building, and it was more than likely that the last job in the fall would be to make the cabin comfortable for winter.

FURNITURE AND FIXTURES.

The furniture was made from the same general material as the house, and the same hands were employed in its manufacture. A broom was one of the first requisites. This was made from a small hickory sapling, by commencing at the butt end of the stick and running the splints, which were started with a knife, upward, until they were long enough for the brush of the broom. This was continued as long as the stick would run, when the small heart was sawed off, the splints turned back and the upper end run in the same manner, commencing far enough up to make the length of splint required, and when down to the proper size for a handle, the balance of the stick was finished up to correspond, and with a tow string to hold the splints together, the implement was complete, and as effective as it was simple in construction. Simple as the operation is of making a broom of this kind would seem, it was attended with some risk, and a man (J. S. Shaw) in the north part of the county lost the sight of an eye in the manufacture of one, by a younger brother running against his elbow just at the time of raising a splint.

A "lug pole" was placed across the chimney on which to hang the hooks to hold the pots for cooking purposes. The hooks were made of small crotches cut from saplings, with a pin in one end to hang the pot on, the crotch hanging on the lug pole. A number of these hooks of different lengths, to suit the several sized pots, or the fire used under them, were necessary. When not in use they were pushed to one side to be out of the way of the fire.

The wooden hooks were superseded by trammels, as soon as the country was supplied with blacksmiths. These consisted of a bar of iron with a hook on one end, which hung on the lug pole, and numerous holes in the face in which was fitted an adjustable hook running through an eye at the bottom of the bar, making a very convenient arrangement, and considered at the time one of the greatest improvements of the age. This again was superseded by the crane, when the country became sufficiently populated to warrant the making of brick, as before these came into use, there was no way of holding the crane in position. This was an improvement that was considered to leave nothing more to be desired in that line. As yet the cook-stove had not entered the fertile brains of Yankee inventors, and when they were brought into use, they were looked upon by many with prejudice, as few housewives could be made to believe that anything could equal the Dutch oven for cooking purposes.

The dresser (cup-board) was made by boring two parallel rows of holes in the logs, up and down, and inserting wooden pins, whereon the shelves, made from split puncheons and smoothed down to a uniform thickness, were laid, and if any newspapers had been brought from the old home, or could be

—7

procured, they were held sacred to add the finishing touches to the dresser; being cut into notched strips and pasted on the edges of the shelves, and finally the whole was covered with a calico curtain, making a neat and not uncomely affair.

The one-posted bedstead has long been noted as one of the requirements of early housekeeping; but how it was constructed is a mystery to the younger portion of our present citizens, as cabinet-makers followed close in the wake of the early settlers, and soon furnished a more light and elegant, if not a more commodious article of furniture.

In the primitive, or one-posted bedstead, the post was first made of the required size, shape, etc., and two holes bored through it at right angles at the proper height for the base, and two more in the walls of the house to correspond with these, one in the side log and one in the end log; and in each of these a pole was inserted reaching to the hole in the post, forming the side and foot rails to the bedstead. A row of holes was now made in the side logs of the house at the same distance from the floor as the others, in each of which was inserted the end of a short pole, the opposite end resting on the side rail and serving the purpose of cords or slats. The great drawback to this style of furniture was, that being made in the corner of the house, it was not movable; but when the whole was completed and had received the finishing touches of the housewife, in curtains of snowy white linen or cotton of home manufacture—sometimes reaching from ceiling to floor—with white counterpane and pillow-slips of the same material and manufacture, just peeping forth, showing a glimpse of the comforts within, it formed a sleeping place by no means to be despised.

The bed curtains, or drapery, performed quite an important part in more ways than one. The house having no partitions, the one room necessarily serving as kitchen, parlor, dining-room, sleeping-room, closet, etc., to a person of delicate nerves it might seem rather embarrassing to retire in the same room in which many others, perhaps of different sexes, were to abide for the night, especially if such person chanced to be a "school ma'am," on her weekly tour of "boarding round." This unpleasantness, however, was greatly abridged by the aforenamed curtains or screens; and the dexterity and neatness with which the lady members of the family there performed their daily changes of attire, without the aid of dressing-case or mirror, would be quite astonishing to a modern belle.

The storage, too, that the mysterious corner "under the bed" furnished, was one of the arts of primitive housekeeping, as nearly everything from a farming implement to a jar of sweetmeats, or a feather bed, could be produced from this commodious receptacle.

Seats were also made of puncheons, some in the form of stools, with three legs, others in the form of benches, from four to eight feet long, having two legs at each end. Holes were made in the lower side of the slabs in a slanting direction, so that, when in an upright position, the legs would project out farther than the body, thus giving them a firm foundation. The legs were made from poles of the right size, cut off and driven into the auger-holes; and when drawn around the fire of hickory logs of an evening, the grand-mother having the post of honor in the warmest corner and the less important members of the family arranged according to distinction, ending, perhaps, with a baby, in a sap trough for a cradle, in the opposite corner, formed a picture of domestic happiness pleasant to contemplate.

Hung from the ceiling in front of the fire was the family lamp, formed at the nearest blacksmith shop from a piece of iron in the form of a dish, with a pitcher nose on one side, in which a cotton wick was laid. The material burned was usually hog's lard, though a frequent substitute was coon's or woodchuck's fat. In some seasons when shack (acorns and beechnuts) was plenty, these animals became very fat and furnished an abundance of this useful article. For a light to run around with, a candle or "slut" was used, made from bee's wax, of which an ample supply was furnished by the forest as well as that sweetest of luxuries, honey. For a mould in which to run the candles, an elder was sometimes hollowed out, but the more common way was to make them into "sluts." This was done by commencing with the wick, which was made large and long, then after heating the bee's wax by the fire until it was soft, it was scraped off with a knife and put on in layers until of the required size. This made a light, not very stylish in appearance, but, like many other things of those times, answering its purpose.

COOKING UTENSILS.

To prepare the staple food, bread, for the family, required the talent and ingenuity of the housewife in an eminent degree. One of the necessary accompaniments of pioneer housekeeping was the bake kettle, or Dutch oven, holding half a bushel and standing on legs three inches high, (made of cast iron, with a tight fitting cover of the same material.) This formed an implement of no mean pretensions, and in this was not only the bread, biscuit, and johnny-cake baked, but the roast of venison and beef, or the spare-rib of pork made ready for the table, and to use it successfully required a skill of no common order.

The favorite plan of using it was to have a large fire of hard wood logs pretty well burned down, so as to furnish an ample supply of live coals. A heap of these was formed on the hearth, in which the oven was partially embedded with its contents, and on the top was piled another quantity of coals to furnish heat to the upper side, and when the slow, measured tick of the wall sweep clock indicated that the precise time during which the contents should remain in its repository had expired—the housewife in the meantime busying herself about the cares of the morning—out would be rolled the golden loaf, as tempting and appetizing as the heart could wish.

This may seem a little primitive, but still more so was the ash cake, prepared when the bake kettle was not at hand. It was prepared in the same manner as the short cake of modern times ; a place was swept clean on the hearth, the cake laid down and covered lightly with cold ashes and then with hot ashes and live coals, the whole patted down smoothly with a wooden shovel, and when it cracked once it was patted down again—the rule for its being done was when it cracked a second time—and for a palatable piece of bread, especially if the youthful appetite was whetted up to the proper pitch by a long fast, perhaps occasioned by being late from mill, nothing made in after years approaches it.

Another favorite kind of bread, more especially prepared for hunters and those going on long journeys, was made by mixing corn meal and water with fat pork cut in small squares and distributed through the mass, and baked in a large "pone," as it was called, sometimes six or eight inches through; when used it was cut in slices and toasted before the fire, which brought out the qualities of the pork, answering the purpose of shortening and flavoring.

After the bake kettle came the reflector, made of tin, in which a great many kinds of cooking were accomplised by placing it before the fire, and cooking by radiation of heat. This was succeeded by the out oven, which has been improved and remains in vogue to the present day. In early times it was constructed of clay mixed in mortar, in which was put a quantity of cut straw. It was built on a platform of poles laid on crotches driven into the ground. A form of sand was them made around it, on which the mortar was spread. When it was sufficiently dried the sand was taken out and thoroughly burned, forming almost as good and permanent a structure as though made of brick.

The material for bread making had also to be manufactured at home in a great measure, as, for a number of years after the first settlement of the County, no mills were within reach of the settlers, except small hand mills and the horse mill at the mission. And even after mills were built, the bad state of the roads, especially in the winter season, made the hand method of manufacturing a necessity.

For this purpose a hard wood log, three feet long and eighteen or twenty inches through, was selected, set on end and burned out in the form of a mortar, an iron wedge driven into a sapling formed a pestle; and in these primitive implements the breadstuff was manufactured. A quantity of shelled corn was thrown in at a time and pounded until it became fine enough to use, when it was sifted, the finer portions being used for making bread, aud the coarser for making hominy. This work was usually performed during evenings and stormy days by the male portion of the family.

DOMESTIC MANUFACTURES.

Clothing, bedding, and many other household articles were also manufactured at home from materials grown on the farm. Of these, flax and wool formed the principal bases, while cotton was used to some extent. Flax was grown, rotted, broken, scutched, hetcheled, spun, and in some cases woven at home, as well as manufactured into garments, towels, sheets, pillow cases, &c., for the family. Wool, also, after being carded, was spun, dyed and woven by our foremothers of precious memory.

In the manufacture of flax, after being grown and pulled, it was rotted by covering it with water, or spreading on the ground, when it was broken with a heavy hand machine made for the purpose, then scutched with a broad wooden knife, taking off the woody portion from the fiber; it was then ready for the hetchel. This was an implement made of a piece of board in which were driven a quantity of sharp steel teeth, four inches long, and through these the flax was drawn, separating the coarser tow from the flax.

The tow by being carded into bats could be spun on the large wheel, and was manufactured into tow linen and used chiefly for men's summer wear. The flax, from its finer texture, had to be spun on a little wheel, and required a good degree of skill to manipulate it properly. The little wheel, with its distaff and flyers, is among the things of the past. The flyers were the especial terror of the little folks, looking so fascinating as they swiftly thundered around, but woe unto the fingers that came within their magic circle. The flax, after being spun, was woven into linen and used for towels, table-cloths, grain bags, and many other household articles.

For the winter season woolen goods were made, from wool or wool and cotton combined. If of all wool, it was spun and colored at home, and in many instances, woven also. The portion designed for women's wear was woven into flannel, and if an extra finish was desired, it was taken to the woolen mill and pressed, and in this case it was also colored at the mill. Full cloth was made of all wool, and after being woven was taken to the mill, colored, fulled, and finished. This was used for the men's wear.

But by far the greater portion of the goods used was manufactured at home, of cotton and wool combined in different proportions, according to the use it was designed for. Linsey was made of cotton warp and woolen filling, in equal proportions, and used for dresses, skirts, and sometimes aprons. Jean was made by using a fine cotton warp, and in such manner that the filling nearly covered it, making a thick, firm cloth, strong and durable, which was used in common every-day wear by both men and boys.

Shoe making was mostly done by itinerant mechanics, traveling from house to house with a kit of tools on their backs, which was termed "whipping the cat." Their shop would be in the common living room of the family, and their offices commenced usually with the older members of the family and continued down until all were shod. If a miss fit was made for the one designed, it was passed on to the next in order and another trial made. Shoes were almost universally worn by both sexes, boots being considered too extravagant for common people. In some cases the farmer or some one of his sons learned enough of the trade to make their own ware, thus saving the expense of hiring the itinerant. Leather was manufactured at the country tan-yards, and the universal custom was to have it tanned on shares, the tanner cutting the hides in two and tanning one half for the other.

Wash basins were almost unknown, and the ablutions were performed by members of the family taking turns in pouring on water from a cup or basin for each other, or if the family had a guest, some one of the number was detailed for this purpose. A gentleman living in the northern part of the county and carrying a high military title, ignored all assistance and waited upon himself, by holding the cup between his teeth while he washed his hands, and then passing it from one hand to the other while he washed his face.

The lack of cultivated fruit was one of the most severe privations that the pioneers had to undergo, coming as they did from lands of plenty, and many substitutes were made use of. Among these were the blackberry, strawberry, raspberry, cranberry, and wild crabapple, all natives of the country, and growing spontaneous in large quantities. The berries were dried, or preserved in sugar, while the apples were buried in holes through the winter—which had the effect of extracting much of the extreme tartness that they had when first picked—and then made into sauce.

Pumpkins also entered largely into common use in various ways; large quantities were dried for pie-making, and about the first thing that would attract the stranger's attention on entering a cabin would be the poles hung near the ceiling covered with rings of pumpkin in the process of drying. Pumpkin butter was also a staple article the year round.

This was made from the juice which was extracted from a portion of the crop that had been allowed to freeze and thaw, then boiled down and thickened with the better portion that had been preserved from frost. Another process was to boil that part intended for cider instead of freezing it, and use it in the same way as by the previous process.

AGRICULTURAL IMPLEMENTS.

The first implement needed in tilling the soil was a plow, the irons for which were either brought with the pioneer from his old home, or manufactured at the country blacksmith's shop, consisting of an iron land side and share combined; the balance of the plow was made of wood, fashioned by the farmer, and called a "bull plow." With this he would break the new ground or turn the stubble as the case might be, and it was considered an effective and complete implement. In fact, for a number of years after the introduction of cast iron plows they were looked upon with distrust by many, who thought they were conducive to the growth of June grass, which at that time was considered the bane of the farmer.

That they were not equal to the best polished steel or chilled iron of the present time, no one will question, but at the same time they formed a basis for something better, and many improvements were made even in these, and the Baker pattern—the first successful cast plow manufactured in this county—was devised from a wooden plow that William Jones carried on horseback from Barron Lake, in Howard township, to Young's Prairie.

The shovel plow was the only implement of the cultivator kind, and for many years was used almost exclusively in the cultivation of corn and other similar crops. It consisted of an iron shovel and wooden stock similar to those in use at the present time.

The wooden harrow was used to bring the ground into proper tilth for seeding. and was composed of a wooden frame, wooden teeth, and a wooden hitching bar, and might be strictly called a wooden implement.

For harvesting wheat and other small grains, the hand sickle was used and continued in use until 1835 as a regular implement, and for a number of years after in very heavy or lodged grain. It was superseded by the grain cradle. The cutting of grain with a hand sickle was a slow, tedious operation, requiring a good hand to cut an acre a day.

In 1845 the grain cradle had a competitor in the market, in the form of a Hussey reaper. It was brought in by B. Hathaway, of Little Prairie Ronde, in that year, and has continued in active service nearly every harvest since that time, and will do creditable work yet. As it came from the manufactory it was a heavy, cumbrous affair with wooden wheels and a pair of thills similar to those used on drays at the present time, in which the horses were driven tandem fashion. But it was remodeled by the owner and adapted to practical use.

After harvesting, the grain was stacked, and threshed on the ground. In threshing, either a flail was used to pound it out by hand, or it was trodden out by horses and cattle. The stacks were placed in the form of a circle with sufficient space left in the middle for a threshing ground. When threshed it was winnowed with a sheet, two men taking hold of either end and giving it a waving motion, while a third threw up the grain and chaff from a basket; the air put in motion by the sheet blew away the chaff, while the grain fell in a pile.

CASS COUNTY.

Cass County was named in honor of Governor Lewis Cass, who served the people of Michigan so long and faithfully in her Territorial career. It is bounded on the south by the State of Indiana, on the west by Berrien County, on the north by Van Buren County, and on the east by St. Joseph County.

Its soil is composed of three distinct varieties, and numerous sub-varieties. The prairie soil is of a black, sticky, tenacious character, underlaid with a sub-soil of sand and gravel. Its productiveness is universally accredited, and the test of fifty years of constant cultivation verifies the prediction of the early settlers that it was of the best.

The heavy timber soil is of a gravelly nature, intermixed with sand and clay in proportions varying with different localities. That it is a good soil, is evidenced by the heavy growth of timber it formerly produced, which had to be removed before it could be cultivated.

The soil of the openings is of several varieties, from heavy clay to light soil. In the earlier days of the settlement of the County, much prejudice existed in the minds of the settlers against this portion of the soil, as it was considered too light for agricultural purposes. But time, the great leveler of all human errors, has demonstrated that it is equal, if not superior, to much land that was considered of better quality.

The prairie portion of the County was settled first, requiring less labor to bring it under subjection than that covered with heavy timber. All that was necessary was to have a good strong team and plow, to commence operations with almost the same facility that could be had in an older settled country. Corn was planted the first season between the furrows, and needed no further attention until harvesting, frequently yielding from forty to sixty bushels of grain per acre. When preparing for wheat, the sod was broken before harvest, and let lie until seeding time, when the seed grain was harrowed in.

The original sod on the prairies was of a very tough nature, the wild grass roots, although penetrating to the depth of but a few inches, required a strong team and plow to break them up. The first plowing was not usually over four inches deep, or just deep enough to get below the grass roots, and the furrows were thrown up into kinks to give the elements a chance to hasten the decay of the sod.

The labor of clearing up the timbered land was immense, the primeval forests requiring to be chopped off, cut up, logged and burned, a job much easier said than done; but after clearing off the cultivation was very easy, if we except the many roots that were in the way.

Logging was usually done by "bees," or by exchanging work. If by a "bee," the neighbors for several miles around were invited, and it partook more of the nature of a frolic than the actual hard work that it was. If by exchange, it was made a matter of business, and the day's work punctually returned. In the earlier settlement the logs were rolled by hand, especially by the immigrants from Ohio and the South, the heavier ones turned together, and the smaller carried on hand-spikes and laid on top; but with the advent of Eastern people came the use of cattle in drawing the logs together, where they could be rolled up by hand.

The openings, although presenting the appearance of an immense plain, where a coach and four could be driven without interruption, were, nevertheless, not without their drawbacks. The practice of the Indians was to burn the land over every fall, which had the effect of keeping not only the annual vegetation burned off, but the grubs also. The grubs thus treated were formed into immense "stools," as they were termed, although the tops were hardly perceptible, and when the land was to be broken up for cultivation, it required a team of from four to nine yoke of cattle, and a plow of corresponding strength. The breaking was done by men who followed it for a business. After breaking, it was comparatively a light matter to bring the land under cultivation.

The County is watered by the St. Joseph River,

the Christianna Creek, both branches of the Dowagiac, and numerous other smaller creeks, lakes, &c. The St. Joseph touches on the south east corner of the County, and cuts off about two and one-half sections of land.

The Christiànna Creek, which was named by the Rev. Isaac McCoy in honor of his wife, rises in Penn Township, and flows south through Calvin, Jefferson and Ontwa, emptying into the St. Joseph near Elkhart, Ind. It is a rapid stream and affords a good water power, which has been improved at Vandalia, Wright's Mills, Redfield's Mills and Adamsville.

The north branch of the Dowagiac rises in Van Buren County, and flows to the southwest, entering this county in Wayne Township, through which it runs into Silver Creek, thence into Pokagon, where it is joined by the south branch, and empties into the St. Joseph River, in Berrien County, near Niles. It is a slow running, sluggish stream, and affords no water power.

The south branch of the Dowagiac rises in Marcellus Township, and runs through Volinia and La Grange, and enters the north branch on the line between the Townships of Silver Creek and Pokagon. It is a rapid running stream and affords ample power for driving machinery, which has been improved nearly its entire length. The name Dowagiac is of Indian origin, and signifies fishing-water.

The first settlement in the county was made on Pokagon prairie, in the fall of 1825, by U. Putnam, Baldwin Jenkins, Squire Thompson, Abram Townsend, and Israel Markam and son.

In 1826 this settlement was augmented by Ira Putnam and family and Lewis Edwards, Sr., who came on and raised a crop, but did not move until the succeeding year. There was also a settlement made by Ezra Beardsley, on the prairie that still bears his name, and in 1827 this was increased by the two Meachams, George Crawford, and ——— Sage.

By an act of the Territorial Legislature, approved April 12th, 1827, all the Territory lying west of Lenawee County, to which the Indian titles had been extinguished by the treaty of Chicago, was organized into one Township, under the name of St. Joseph, and attached to Lenawee County for judicial purposes. An election was also ordered to be held at the house of Timothy Smith. Where this Smith lived is not given, but probably on White Pigeon prairie. We have no means of knowing what was done under this organization, as the records of Lenawee County were burned a number of years ago.

In 1828 settlements were made on McKenney's, La Grange, Young's, and Baldwin's prairies. Ford's mill, the first in Southwestern Michigan, was started in the spring of this year. Although in what is now Berrien County, it was of great importance to the settlers of this county, as there was not another mill for grinding grain by water power within one hundred miles.

In 1829 a settlement was made on Little Prairie Ronde, and in November 5th, of the same year, by an act of the Territorial Legislature, Cass County was organized and divided into four Townhips, Pokagon, La Grange, Penn, and Ontwa, composed as follows: Pokagon to consist of what is now Silver Creek, Pokagon, and the north half of Howard Townships, and an election was ordered to be held at the house of Baldwin Jenkins. Wayne, LaGrange, and the north half of Jefferson Townships were organized under the name of La Grange, with an election to be held at the house of Isaac Shurte. The Townships of Penn, Volinia, Marcellus, Newberg, the north half of North Porter, and the north halt of Calvin were organized under the name of Penn Township, and an election appointed at the house of Martin Shields.

The Townships of Milton, Ontwa, Mason, South Porter, and the south half of North Porter, Calvin, Jefferson, and Howard were organized under the name of Ontwa Township, and an election ordered at the house of Ezra Beardsley.

Also, by the same act, Van Buren County was organized into one Township, under the name of La Fayette, and attached to Penn Township, of this County, and some of the first officers of that Township were residents of Van Buren County.

Berrien County was also organized into one Township, that of Niles, and attached to Pokagon for judicial purposes. Although it would seem that the local government was ready to run, there is no record of any election being held in the spring of 1830.

The most important events of this year,—1829—aside from the organization of the County, were the land sales, which at that time were held at Monroe. The United States law required that every piece of land should be put up at public auction, after which, if not bid off, it was subject to private entry at one dollar and twenty-five cents per acre. To avoid competition and running the risk of losing what improvements the settlers had made, each one quietly kept his own counsel, and after the land had been offered, made application and received his certificate.

In after years, when land speculation became rife, it was a great game with "land sharks" to lie in wait around the land offices and if by hook or crook they could get the description of a desirable location, it was nabbed before the settler could get in. This game, however, had its drawbacks, and there are a number of pieces of land in the county still in the name of the original owner, entirely worthless. This was brought about by the settlers becoming aware of their sharp practices and being prepared for them by having the description of some worthless tract to which they gave them a clue.

In this year entries of land were made in Penn, Pokagon, La Grange, Howard, Ontwa, Milton, North and South Porter, and Calvin Townships. The Carpenter mill, on the Christianna Creek, just below where Vandalia now stands, was built that year, and although a crude structure, it was of great importance to the settlers and the first mill in the county. A hollow log served the purpose of a forebay. Mr. Carpenter sold out in a few years, and said, on leaving, that he was "determined to build a good mill if it cost him a hundred dollars."

In 1830 settlements were made at Geneva and Whitmanville, and entries of land made in Jefferson, Mason, and Volinia Townships.

On the 4th day of October, 1831, the first Board of Supervisors for Cass County met at the house of Ezra Beardsley (now Edwardsburg) but, owing to the absence of one member, they adjourned to the 17th of the same month, when the following members were present: John Agard of Penn, Othui Beardsley of Ontwa, James Kavanaugh of LaGrange, and Squire Thompson of Pokagon. An organization was effected by electing John Agard Chairman and A. H. Redfield Clerk. The assessed valuation of the different Townships as equalized by the Board was as follows: Pokagon, $23,364; amount of tax levied, $113.52. LaGrange, $23,321; amount of tax levied, $116.60. Penn, $37,643; amount of tax levied, $188.21. Ontwa, $33,634; amount of tax levied, $188.21. The Board at this meeting passed a resolution offering a bounty of two dollars for the scalps of large wolves and one dollar for prairie wolves and pups. In this year Edwardsburg and Cassopolis were laid out, and entries of land made in Wayne Township.

On the third Monday in January, 1832, the Board met at the same place, but for the want of a quorum no business was done, except to adjourn to the 5th of March, when Kavanaugh and Thompson met and ordered the clerk to notify the other Supervisors to meet at the house of Abram Tietsort, on the 31st of March, to settle with the Treasurer.

At this meeting, Squire Thompson was elected Chairman, when they adjourned to the house of Ira B. Henderson in Cassopolis. A resolution was passed to build a jail, the dimensions of which were to be 15 by 30 feet, one story high, with a partition through the middle, to be built of hewn logs one foot square, to have two windows and two doors, and costing not to exceed three hundred and fifty dollars. But it would seem that the building was not put up in accordance with this resolution, for again we find in '33 another entry to the same effect.

By the numerous resolutions passed, instructing their agent to proceed against a number of residents of Cassopolis for non-payment of subscriptions, it seems that the building was not put up entirely at the expense of the county. This building still stands on a lot now owned by Charles Kingsbury.

In the latter part of April, 1832, the startling news came that Black Hawk had crossed the Mississippi, and had commenced a hostile invasion of the United States. His ravages among the frontier settlements of Wisconsin, and the defeat of a party of over two hundred and fifty Americans, spread the greatest alarm throughout the country, and rolled back the tide of emigration then moving westward.

The report that reached this county was that the Sacs and Foxes were marching upon Chicago, and that all the western settlements were in imminent danger. To this general report were added individual accounts of the most exaggerated character, in some instances that they were joined by the Pottawatomies and had already burned Chicago and were marching eastward with the torch and tomahawk, devastating the country, and slaughtering the inhabitants. Many settlers, especially in the south part of the county, left at the first report, taking whatever availables they could, and leaving the balance.

The presence of several thousand Pottawatomies on the reserve near Niles tended to increase the uneasiness of the people of the surrounding country. Couriers were sent to all the settlements to call out the Militia, and excitement reigned supreme. Many rumors were circulated of the slaughter and butchery going on, volunteers came in rapidly, armed with such implements of warfare as they individually possessed.

General Williams arrived at Niles in a few days from Detroit and took command, and several companies were organized in Berrien, Cass, and Kalamazoo Counties, and marched to Niles expecting to find the Indians in hostile array. Darius Brown was quartermaster, with headquarters at Niles. He seized all the flour in the warehouses at St. Joseph, Berrien, and Niles, for the use of the army, and a large oven was built to bake it into bread.

The excitement which prevailed seems rather amusing at this time, since the hostile Indians did not come within one hundred miles of Chicago. But when we consider that the country was filled with Indians, only kept in subjection by the fear of a superior force, and that on the slightest provocation they might have risen and exterminated the infant settlements, the fears of the settlers do not appear to have been wholly groundless.

Not finding the enemies they looked for, the excitement soon began to subside, and the troops to disperse. General Williams however was anxious to go on to Chicago, but as the militia refused to go out of the State, he called for volunteers. Two companies were made up, one each from Berrien and Cass Counties, and these two companies formed the brigade that marched under General Williams. Captain Benjamin Finch commanded the Berrien County troops, and Captain Gardner those from Cass County. A. Huston was Colonel, David Wilson; Major, Dr. E. Winslow; and William B. Beeson were Surgeon and assistant Surgeon.

The chief authority rested with the rank and file, who, while encamped on Door prairie, superseded Colonel Huston for his haughty, overbearing manner, electing Colonel Edwards to the position. Major Wilson, was also sent home for similar reasons, and George Hoffman elected in his place. The brigade went as far as Chicago, and a few advanced a short distance beyond, when they returned home thoroughly disgusted with the whole experience.

The war ended without serious loss of life or property, but had the effect of stopping all immigration for that season, and comparatively few of our pioneers date their settlement from that year. The principal settlements of the County at that time were on Beardsley's, Pokagon, LaGrange, McKenney's, Little Prairie Ronde, and Young's Prairies, all of which sent their quotas to the seat of war.

In this season the first vessel built in Cass County was constructed by Captain Barnard and his son,

Dr. Barnard, now of Berrien Springs. It was of about fifteen tons burden, and built on La Grange prairie. After being finished, it was drawn on a wagon to the St. Joseph river and launched. The first trip to Chicago and back was made in three days, and cleared to the owners two hundred and fifty dollars. For a number of years it was used in the trade between St. Joseph and Chicago.

The winter of 1832–33 was remarkably mild and pleasant. On New Year's day buds were started, grass greened, bees and house-flies were busy, and wild flowers bloomed in the forest.

In 1833 the Board was increased by a member from each of the towns of Jefferson, Porter, and Volinia, which had been organized since the last meeting. In this year a room was rented of Eber Root, at the rate of one dollar and fifty cents per day, for the use of Courts and the Board of Supervisors.

In 1834 Howard Township was represented for the first time. The Prosecuting Attorney's salary was fixed at seventy dollars per annum. Samuel Marrs informed the Board that, as Justice of the Peace, he had collected from three persons two dollars each, for Sabbath breaking, and was ready to pay over the money to their order.

The year 1835 is one long to be remembered, on account of the frost which occurred on the 21st of June of that year, which blighted nearly every green thing. Corn was up, and in some instances worked over once, when the frost came and cut it closely to the ground, but, where let alone, it came on again and made a partial crop. Wheat was just coming into blossom and was almost wholly killed. Not enough was left for seed, and farmers had to go as far as Big Prairie and La Porte to procure seed wheat, and frequently were obliged to work and pay for it after they got there. What wheat was left by the frost was made "sick," and could not be eaten, and corn and buckwheat were used largely as a substitute for bread making material.*

In this year Calvin was represented on the Board of Supervisors for the first time. At the October session it was resolved to build a building, for county purposes, twenty-four by thirty-four feet square, and ten feet high, to be divided into three rooms, at a cost not exceeding four hundred and fifty dollars, and the contract was awarded to Joseph Harper.

In 1836 an addition to the Board of Supervisors was made by members from Wayne and Mason Townships, which had been organized since the last meeting. At the October session a bill was allowed in favor of George Fosdick for thirty dollars, for a lock to the jail; also an order made to procure a nine-plate stove for the Court House. In September of this year, James Newton and James O'Dell were elected to attend the Constitutional Convention at Ann Arbor.

On November 7th and 8th, of the same year, an election for county officers was held, with the following result:

*There is some variety of recollection as to whether this frost occurred on the 20th or 21st of June. I have fixed the date from a diary kept by Alexander Copley during that year.

James O'Dell and William Burk, Representatives.

John T. Adams, Judge of Probate.

James Kavanaugh and R. V. Crane, Associate Judges.

M. V. Hunter, Sheriff.

William Arrison, Register of Deeds.

Henley C. Lybrook, County Clerk.

Eber Root, Treasurer.

John Woolman, Surveyor.

S. P. Kingsley and John Shaw, Coroners.

On December 8th, of the same year, Edwin A. Bridges, Jacob Silver, Joseph Smith, and Abiel Silver were elected to attend the Constitutional Convention at Ann Arbor.

This was the first election for county officers, previous to which they were appointed by the Governor, as also were the Justices of the Peace. Of the county officers previous to this election, or their doings, we have to depend upon men's memories for information, as the records are very meager and vague. The result of the best research we have been able to make is as follows:

Joseph L. Jacks was the first County Clerk, appointed July 31st, 1830, and was sworn into office by Baldwin Jenkins, then an Associate Justice, on the 4th day of September. Mr. Jacks served about two years and was succeeded by Martin C. Whitman, and he by Henley C. Lybrook.

George Meacham was the first Sheriff, appointed probably in 1830, who served about two years and was succeeded by Henry Fowler, and he by Eber Root, who served until the time of the election.

The first Register of Probate was Thomas McKenney, who was succeeded by Thomas H. Edwards, and Edwards was succeeded by E. B. Sherman, who served with the title of Judge until after the election.

The first Register of Deeds was T. H. Edwards, who acted in the double capacity of Register of Deeds and Probate. He was succeeded by Alex. H. Redfield who served until the election.

E. B. Sherman was the first Prosecuting Attorney, and Circuit Court Commissioner, also District Surveyor, which offices he held all, or nearly all, of the time from the organization of the county until the election in 1836.

Andrew Grubb was the first Treasurer, appointed in 1831, and was succeeded by Jacob Silver, who served until the election—H. C. Lybrook acting as Deputy.

In 1837 Silver Creek, having been organized, was represented on the Board of Supervisors. The County officers elected this year were as follows:

Joel Brown, Associate Judge.

H. B. Dunning, Probate Judge.

Joseph Harper, County Treasurer.

David Crane, Coronor.

In 1838 Newberg was represented on the Board of Supervisors, but, owing to a change from the Supervisor system to that of County Commissioners, no business was done by the Board this year. At the election in November, David Hopkins, Henry Jones, and James W. Griffin were elected County Commissioners.

Myron Strong, Associate Judge.

Joseph Harper, Register of Deeds.

H. C. Lybrook, County Clerk.

M. V. Hunter, Sheriff.

Isaac Sears, County Treasurer.

J. C. Saxton, Surveyor.

J. G. Beeson and L. Chapin, Coroners.

In 1839, William Burk was elected County Commissioner in place of David Hopkins. James Newton and Henry Coleman were elected representatives, and Alexander Copley, Coroner. In August of this year, the County Commissioners entered into a contract with Jacob Silver, A. H. Redfield, Joseph Harper, A. Kingsbury and Darius Shaw, to build the present Court House. The terms were six thousand dollars, two thousand of which was to be paid in cash in one and two years, the remainder in village lots, which had been donated by the proprietors in consideration of the location of the county seat at Cassopolis.

In 1840, Myron Strong and V. C. Smith were elected Representatives.

Thomas T. Glenn and John Barney, Associate Judges.

C. Shanahan, Probate Judge.

James O'Dell, County Commissioner.

H. B. Dunning, County Clerk.

Joseph Harper, Register of Deeds.

Amos Fulton, County Treasurer.

W. G. Beckwith, Sheriff.

Henry Walton, Surveyor.

John Shaw and Marcus Peck, Coroners.

In 1841 William H. Bacon was elected County Commissioner.

S. F. Anderson and F. C. Arnold, Representatives for Cass and VanBuren Counties.

In 1842, S. F. Anderson and John Andrews were elected Representatives for Cass and VanBuren Counties.

James L. Glenn, Sheriff.

H. C. Lybrook, Clerk.

D. M. Howell, Register of Deeds.

Asa Kingsbury, Treasurer.

David P. Ward, Surveyor.

P. Horton and M. Rudd, Coronors.

In July of this year, the system of County Commissioners was discontinued, and the Supervisor system reinstated. Milton had been organized and was represented this year.

By an act of the Legislature, approved in April, 1841, it was required "that the several battalions of State Militia should rendezvous for inspection, drill service, and martial exercise, in each county, between the first days of May and November of each year."

Pursuant to this, in the latter part of October, 1842, all the able bodied white male citizens of Cass County, between the ages of eighteen and forty-five, were notified to rendezvous at Cassopolis for the purposes set forth in the act.

The day proved exceedingly unfavorable, being cold and inclement with a mingled fall of rain and snow. Still nearly one thousand sturdy yeomen assembled on the public square to receive their first lessons in the art of national defense.

They were as motley a crew as ever perplexed a drill sergeant, with shoes and without, with coats and hats, and without either. Some of them armed with rifles and shot-guns, but the majority with clubs, broom-sticks, and cornstalks. There was nothing uniform about them—excepting variety. They hardly realized Falstaff's description of his tarterdemalions, with "a shirt and a half to the whole company"; but their appearance was nearer to that than soldierly.

The only names of officers which have been preserved, are, Colonel, James L. Glenn; Lieutenant Colonel, Asa Kingsbury, and Major, Joseph Smith; and to these were added a rabble of Captains, Lieutenants, Sergeants, and Corporals, from nearly every township in the county.

As far as we have been able to learn, Major Smith was the only officer who had ever been exposed to the innoculation of military tactics and discipline, he having previously served in the Ohio militia; but no one man could avert the confusion worse confounded, which was created by the accumulated ignorance of his confreres, and although he strove with Napoleonic energy to stem the tide and evolve order out of chaos, he was at last compelled to retire vanquished from the field.

The "martial exercise" developed into the broadest burlesque on the art of war, and its glaring absurdity was evident to officers and men alike.

The instructors proving totally unqualified to teach, and the pupils soon being in no mood to receive instruction, resort was had to an exercise in which honors were easy and responsibilities equal.

Informal but effective requisitions being made upon the officers, whisky in barrels was rolled out on the public square and each Captain required to provide a pail and tin cups for the use of his company.

The fun soon grew fast and furious. Friendly wrestling gave place to bellicose fisticuffs. Political and neighborhood quarrels were put in a way for adjustment, "bloody noses and cracked crowns" became the order of the day, and the first and only military training(?) in the history of Cass County terminated in a general debauch.

In 1843 James W. Griffin and Philotus Hayden were elected Representatives for Cass and Van Buren Counties. R. J. Huyck and James Taylor, Coroners.

In 1844 James Shaw and John Andrews were elected Representatives for Cass and Van Buren Counties.

W. G. Beckwith, Sheriff.

George Sherwood, Clerk.

D. M. Howell, Register of Deeds.

Asa Kingsbury, Treasurer.

Clifford Shanahan, Judge of Probate.

S. F. Anderson and William H. Bacon, Associate Judges.

David P. Ward, County Surveyor.

Charles P. Drew and Caleb Calkins, Coroners.

In 1845 James L. Glenn and Josiah Andrews were elected Representatives for Cass and Berrien Counties.

In 1846 James L. Glenn and James Shaw were elected Representatives for Cass County.

James N. Chipman, County Judge.

Mitchell Robinson, Second County Judge.

Barak Mead, Sheriff.

George Sherwood, County Clerk.

D. M. Howell, Register of Deeds.

Joshua C. Lofland, Treasurer.

David P. Ward, County Surveyor.

Peter Shaffer and Isaac Hull, Coroners.

In 1847 G. B. Turner and Milo Powell were elected Representatives.

During this year occurred, perhaps, the most exciting episode in the history of the county, viz.: the seizure and successful rescue of nine fugitive slaves, owned in Bourbon County, Kentucky.

These slaves belonged to personal friends of Henry Clay, and the pressure brought to bear by their owners had great influence in shaping his course and action on the Fugitive Slave Bill of 1850, which, in turn, was among the chief exciting causes of our civil war. The "Michigan riots" were cited by him in detail in Congress, and proved of great service in securing the passage of the bill.

Under these circumstances it has seemed advisable to allow sufficient space in this work for a detailed statement of this celebrated raid, and a separate chapter has been set apart for the purpose.

The facts collated have been gathered from all available sources, and carefully sifted and arranged, and in the main can be relied upon as correct; but unavoidable errors in details may have been com-

—9

mitted, owing to the wide dissimilarity of recollection of the few living actors in this drama, which is largely due to their antagonistic political views.

Party politics ran high at that time and partisan prejudices were extreme, and it is not strange that, after a lapse of twenty-nine years, each should remember disputed data as he then wished them to be. There are no official records extant of this case. The Justice's docket and Commissioner's record for that year are not to be found. Whether they were accidently lost, or maliciously destroyed by the parties whose interests they would have prejudiced, is, and will probably always remain, a mystery. The files are complete up to and succeeding 1847, but for that year they are wanting.

For the facts embodied in the sketches of the Underground Railroad, we are largely indebted to Erastus Hussey, of Battle Creek, and Dr. Thomas, of Schoolcraft, who were both active workers in the cause, and for the details of the raid to George B. Turner, Jefferson Osborn, D. M. Howell, Jordon P. Osborn, Joseph Harper, E. B. Sherman, and many other actors and witnesses.

THE KENTUCKY RAID.

During the decade following the election of Harrison, in 1840, there flourished in its greatest vigor and usefulness that "organized Christianity" known as the Underground Railroad.

Two divisions of this road, viz., the "Quaker line," starting on free soil from the Ohio river, and the "Illinois line," from St. Louis, formed a junction in Cass County and pursued a common course to Canada.

The first of these was in effective operation as early as 1840, but was loosely worked and frequently failed in its object by allowing its passengers to be seized and returned to slavery. It was simply a chain of Quaker settlements extending through Indiana, at all of which fugitive slaves were harbored, fed and directed on their way; but there was no arrangement for providing local guides, and usually the conductor who started with the convoy from the South accompanied them as far as Cass County, Michigan.

The Illinois line, established by John Cross in 1842, was thoroughly organized and equipped, and never met with any accidents so far as we can learn. Its stations were from ten to twenty miles apart, and each station agent was informed only as to the name and location of the agent ahead of him, and neither knew or sought to know aught of those behind.

Regular conductors plied between stations and were always ready, provided with fleet horses and covered wagons, to forward the hunted chattels toward the sheltering protection of the British flag. The password was in the form of a question by the conductor, "Can you furnish entertainment for myself and another person?"

There were two stations in Cass County, kept by Stephen Bogue and Zachariah Shugert, the latter acting also as conductor. They received fugitives from E. McIlvain, agent at Niles, per —— Elliot, conductor, and forwarded them either to William Wheeler at Flowerfield, or Dr. Nathan M. Thomas at Schoolcraft.

Wright Modlin and William Jones (who enjoyed the *sobriquet* of "Nigger Bill") lived in this county and were actively engaged in "nigger running" from Kentucky via the Quaker line.

Some idea of the amount of business transacted by these two lines in six or eight years (for after the organization of the Free Soil party in '48 they were abandoned as unnecessary) may be obtained from the statement of Erastus Hussey, the agent at Battle Creek, who estimates that at least fifteen hundred runaway slaves, representing a million and a half of value, were fed and forwarded by him. Dr. Thomas of Schoolcraft, who divided his hospitality with C. Bird of Pavillion, assisted at least one thousand to escape from "free America."

"The woolly head in the cellar" was no myth to these brave zealots, who risked their property, their liberty, and sometimes even their lives in obedience to their Master's injunction to "Let the oppressed go free."

At first the slave running was done entirely by night, and the utmost precautions taken to escape observation; but as time went on and public sentiment became largely in sympathy with the fugitives, they were carried from station to station in broad daylight, and finally they became so emboldened by immunity as to settle down to labor and residence in the free States, but always clustering around their friends, the Quakers, for protection.

In 1846 it is estimated that there were one hundred runaway slaves in Cass County, mostly in Penn and Calvin Townships in what were known as the East and Osborn settlements, and, unlike some of their successors and descendants, they were honest, industrious and sturdy pioneers who sought to create homes of their own for themselves and families.

A large proportion of the refugees were from Bourbon County, Kentucky, which, by the continued exertions of Modlin, Jones and others of their ilk, was being rapidly depleted of slaves.

During the early part of the winter of 1846-7 an association of Bourbon County planters was formed at Covington, Kentucky, for the purpose of pursuing and returning to their lawful owners the servants that had been "stolen by the rascally Abolitionists."

This organization was similar in its form and workings to the societies for the prosecution and punishment of horse stealing in vogue at the present day.

A few weeks after the formation of this protection league a young Kentuckian entered the law office of Charles E. Stewart of Kalamazoo, ostensibly as a student, but in reality to spy out the land and locate the wandering property.

Under the name of Carpenter he visited the colored settlements in Calhoun and Cass Counties, and, representing himself to be an Abolitionist from Worcester County, Massachusetts, he was warmly received and afforded every facility for the execution of his real mission.

The first result of this movement was the attempted kidnapping of the Crosswhite family at Marshall, Calhoun County, by a party of Kentuckians under the leadership of one Francis Troutman, who claimed to have inherited them as a part of the estate of his grandfather.

They were foiled by the resolute defense made by Adam Crosswhite and his neighbors, who turned out some two hundred strong to resist the slave-hunters.

Upon their return home they detailed their defeat to their friends, and the utmost indignation and excitement was aroused. Mass meetings were held, and, as the tale of their wrongs and the outrages of the Abolitionists lost nothing by repetition, "the Southern heart was fired," and a memorial prepared to the Legislature setting forth their grievances was promptly met by an appropriation of money by the State which was thought to be sufficient "to secure the observance of the laws of the United States" in fanatical Michigan.

Suit was commenced in the United States Court at Detroit against Charles T. Gerham (late United States Minister at the Hague), Dr. O. C. Comstock, and Jarvis Hurd, to recover the value of the slaves and exemplary damages. These gentlemen seem to have been selected rather on account of their social position and pecuniary responsibility than for any especial prominence during the so-called riot.

The trial began in the latter part of 1847, and lasted three weeks. The jury disagreed. The second trial was in 1848, during the Presidential canvass between Generals Cass and Taylor. Party feeling ran high, and the defendants were convicted and required to pay one thousand nine hundred dollars and costs.

This amount was raised by subscription, by a Detroit merchant, a stranger to the defendants, who headed the list with one hundred dollars. That merchant has been heard from since. His name was Zachariah Chandler.

About the first of August, 1847, a party of thirteen men arrived at Battle Creek. They were provided with good teams and covered wagons, and had evidently traveled a long distance. They put up at the hotel, and some of their number represented themselves to be salesmen for an improved washing machine. Under pretext of showing their wares, they proceeded to visit the houses of the negroes in and around the village; but before night, Erastus Hussey, always on the *qui vive* when any danger threatened his proteges, discovered their true character and designs.

He went at once to the hotel, and, assembling the company in the bar-room, charged them with being slave hunters, and notified them to leave town at once, as the people there had firmly determined that no fugiture should ever be returned to bondage from that neighborhood, and he could not be answerable for the consequences if their presence and purposes should become generally known.

The Kentuckians, cowed by the resolute earnestness of this "fighting Quaker," took counsel of their fears and quietly but speedily left the village, which knew them, or their kind, no more forever.

Immediately upon their departure, Mr. H. wrote to Zachariah Shugert and Stephen Bogue, of this county, advising them of what had transpired and notifying them to warn the colored people and their friends to be on the watch for a similar attempt to be made here, but, owing to the irregularity of the mail service, these letters were not received in time to prevent the mischief.

After leaving Battle Creek, the party proceeded southward into Indiana, and finally rendezvoused at Bristol. On the night of the third day they recrossed the St. Joseph at that point, and, crossing Porter Township, came to a halt in the woods, near the south line of Calvin. Here they left their wagons, as too cumbrous and liable to excite alarm, and, dividing into small parties, prepared to make a descent upon the different settlements in Penn and Calvin, as nearly as might be, at the same time.

They were provided with complete maps of the roads and descriptions of the houses where their chattels were to be found, furnished by Carpenter, and designed to seize the negroes, hurry them back to the wagons and escape over the line into Indiana before a general alarm could be given or a rescue attempted. They preferred proving their property (if they should be compelled to do so at all) before an Indiana Justice and under the practice of that State.

The first arrests were made at Josiah Osborn's, where an old man and his two sons were seized, handcuffed in bed, and taken out on the highway.

No resistance was offered by the negroes or their friends, but the alarm spread like wildfire throughout the neighborhood.

At the East settlement four were taken, one of them a wench belonging to —— Stevens, a Baptist preacher, being secured by strategy. She was in a cabin apart from the rest, and being alarmed by the noise incident to the capture of the others, fled, leaving her picanninny on the bed. The Rev. S. discovered the baby, and, coarsely saying, "If you want a cow you can tole her with her calf," shouldered it and started for the road, whereupon the mother rushed from her place of concealment and was secured.

Moses Bristow, who lived in a log hut on the farm of Stephen Bogue, offered the only resistence of the night—being summoned by his master he refused to follow him and was struck down with the butt of a riding whip, cutting his ear and the side of his head severely.

The party who made the arrests at Osborn's waited some time for their friends who had been sent to the other localities, but, as the night wore away, and the free Negroes and Abolitionists gathered around them with no friendly mien, they moved northward to meet their associates, followed by some trusty men who only waited an opportunity to strike.

In the neighborhood of O'Dell's mill the parties came together and were speedily surrounded by an excited mob of citizens armed with rifles, shot-guns, straw cutters, axes, clubs and whatever other weapons chance threw in their way, who resolutely opposed their southward progress.

A parley was had, high words and threats exchanged, weapons drawn, and a bloody riot seemed imminent; but, fortunately, more moderate counsels prevailed and the Kentuckians agreed to go to Cassopolis and submit their case and proofs to the resident Justice.

The leading spirit in this rencounter was "Nigger Bill" Jones, who, after disarming one of the raiders who drew a revolver on him, and forcing the Rev. Stevens to carry the picanniny, and another of the party to relinquish his horse in favor of a wench, was shackled, at his own request, with a slave, and so remained until after the party reached Cassopolis.

The cortege that arrived in Cassopolis, about nine o'clock, was composed of the thirteen Kentuckians, nine slaves, and a promiscuous following of about two hundred persons. Prominent in the procession were the Rev. Stevens, who bestrode a black horse with a negro baby cuddled close to his breast, and "Nigger Bill" Jones, manacled to a negro.

Immediately upon their arrival on the public square, they secured the services of George B. Turner, then a rising young lawyer, who advised them that the rendition of their slaves from Cass County was simply impossible in the then excited condition of the public mind; and that the best they could do would be to note the pecuniarily responsible parties, who might obstruct or hinder the execution of the law, and look to them for damages.

The slaves were hurriedly taken to the north room in the second story of Baldwin's tavern, and a guard placed at the door.

The preliminary steps were immediately instituted to prove ownership and recover property, and a writ of restitution applied for before D. M. Howell, Justice of the Peace, in accordance with the law of 1793.

Messrs. E. S. Smith and James Sullivan appeared for the fugitives, and succeeded in obtaining an adjournment of three days.

Only nine names of the raiding party have been preserved, and these by oral tradition, viz.: C. B. Rust, James Scott, G. W. Brazier, Thornton Timlenlake, John L. Graves (Sheriff of Bourbon County), Bristow, Rev. A. Stevens, Buckner, and Lemon. They were all gentlemen of the true Southern type, and slave-holders.

Immediately upon securing the adjournment, Mr. Bristow was arrested upon a charge of assault and battery. Four of his associates were taken for trespass upon the premises of Josiah Osborn, and the whole party, excepting Graves, who was unknown to the Abolitionists, were arrested upon a general charge of kidnapping. Their bail was fixed by the Justice at two thousand six hundred dollars. Asa Kingsbury, Amos Dow, and Daniel McIntosh were offered and accepted as securities.

At this time there were only fifty-two Abolition voters in Cass County, but the difference in the enumeration of the Whig and Democratic parties was so slight that they (the Abolitionists) held the ballance of power, and were respected accordingly.

Taking advantage of the absence of A. H. Redfield, Circuit Court Commissioner of the county, the friends of the fugitives sent a courier to Niles, post haste, and secured the attendance of James Brown, an attorney, to assist Messrs. Sullivan and Smith, and E. McIlvain, Circuit Commissioner of Berrien County.

Upon the arrival of McIlvain, a writ of *habeas corpus* was sworn out, requiring the Kentuckians to show cause why the fugitives should not be discharged from custody. This occurred on the third day after the arrests. In the meantime the bloody warfare had waxed hot, and hotter, but prudent counsels having prevailed with the Kentuckians, no serious fracas had occurred.

The hearing upon the *habeas corpus* came on Monday, and Commissioner McIlvain decided the case adversely to the Kentuckians, on the ground that there was no certified copy of the statutes of Kentucky offered in evidence showing the legal existence of slavery in that State.

Immediately upon the decision of McIlvain the Negroes were taken in charge by their friends and hurried to the farm of Ishmael Lee, where a party of fifty-two runaway slaves was made up, put in charge of Zachariah Shugert and started toward Canada. This party included probably all the fugitives from Bourbon County.

All of the criminal proceeding against the Kentuckians were then dropped, their object having been attained, and they were permitted to gather up their remaining property and depart to their Kentucky homes.

The year following suits were commenced by the owners of the slaves against D. T. Nicholson, Stephen Bogue, Josiah Osborn, Ishmael Lee, Zachariah Shugert, Jefferson Osborn, Ebenezer McIlvain, and William Jones in the District Court of the United States held in Detroit. Abner Pratt, of Marshall, was attorney for the plaintiffs, and Jacob M. Howard, of Detroit, for the defendants. The first trial resulted in a disagreement of the jury. Several adjournments were had from time to time, and finally, in 1851, D. T. Nicholson, one of the most wealthy of the defendants, compromised with Pratt by paying him, for the Kentuckians, $2,755.

It is somewhat satisfactory to know that this money was absorbed by Pratt, and that neither the slave-owners nor their attorney, Mr. Turner, ever received one dollar of it.

The Quakers refused all offers of compromise from principle, terming such payments "blood money," but they liberally assisted Mr. Nicholson in his payment. Their individual expenses in the case were about one thousand dollars apiece.

Innumerable incidents and episodes occurred during this trial, but our space is too limited for their mention.

In 1849 Cyrus Bacon and George B. Turner were elected Representatives.

Freeman Tuttle, Sheriff.

George Sherwood, Clerk.

D. M. Howell, Register of Deeds.

Joshua Lofland, Treasurer.

C. Shanahan, Probate Judge.

Milo Powell and James W. Griffin, Associate Judges.

Charles G. Banks, Surveyor.

D. Histed and Joseph Smith, Coroners.

In this year the Michigan Central Railroad was completed to Niles, and a grand excursion to that place from Detroit and intermediate points took place.

This work was undertaken by the Territory in 1834, when a survey was made from Detroit to St. Joseph, which was designed to be the terminus, and the preliminary work was begun. It continued under the State management until 1846, when it was completed as far west as Kalamazoo. In its construction under the State management, the old-fashioned strap rails were used; and as a financial experiment, was decidedly unsuccessful, consequently it was sold out to the present company on its completion to Kalamazoo.

With characteristic energy the completion of the road was undertaken by this new company, and instead of making St. Joseph the western terminus, they veered farther to the south, making New Buffalo their western terminus, and to this change of base is Cass County indebted for her first, and up to a few years ago, her only railroad.

At about the same time of the building of the Central the Michigan Southern & Northern Indiana Railroad was pushing its way westward. Although not touching our County it was, nevertheless, of great importance, as it furnished a market for a good portion of the south half of the County.

The peculiar manner in which these two roads run—the Central cutting off the northwest corner of the County, and the Southern running just south of our boundery line—while they furnished us a market of convenient access, they at the same time aided in building up towns and manufactories to which we were tributary, and a large amount of the prosperity of Niles, South Bend, Mishawaka, Elkhart and Three Rivers, from their peculiar location, is due to the trade of Cass County. But with the Air Line running east and west nearly through the centre of the County, and the Chicago & Lake Huron Railroad, running from the southwest to the northeast, directly across the centre of the County, nothing is left to be desired in the way of railroads, unless it should be a line running directly north and south.

In 1849 Pleasant Norton and Ezekiel C. Smith were elected Representatives.

In 1850 James Sullivan, George Redfield and Mitchell Robinson were elected members of the State Constitutional Convention; George Sherwood and Wm. L. Clyborne to the Legislature; Cyrus Bacon and John S. Brown, Judge and second Judge.

James Sullivan, Prosecuting Attorney.

Andrew Wood, Sheriff.

Henry R. Close, Treasurer.

D. M. Howell, Register of Deeds.

William Sears, County Clerk.

David P. Ward, County Surveyor.

H. Linsey and J. Powell, Coroners.

In 1852 Jesse G. Beeson was chosen Senator; E. J. Bonine and Pleasant Norton, Representatives.

W. G. Beckwith, Sheriff.

D. M. Howell, Register of Deeds.

Henry Tiesort, Treasurer.

E. B. Warner, County Clerk.

C. Shanahan, Probate Judge.

H. H. Coolidge, Prosecuting Attorney.

David P. Ward, Surveyor.

H. Linsey and Wm. Merritt, Coroners.

In 1854 James Sullivan was elected Senator; Franklin Brownell and Urial Enos, Representatives.

Joseph Harper, Sheriff.

E. B. Warner, County Clerk.

A. J. Smith, Prosecuting Attorney.

A. E. Peck, Register of Deeds.

Jefferson Osborn, Treasurer.

Amos Smith, Surveyor.

A. Lamb and Geo. Newton, Coroners.

In 1856 Alonzo Garwood was elected Senator; B. W. Schermerhorn and Edwin Sutton, Representatives.

Joseph N. Marshall, Sheriff.

C. Shanahan, Probate Judge.

A. E. Peck, Register of Deeds.

Jefferson Osborn, Treasurer.

Benjamin F. Rutter, County Clerk.

A. J. Smith, Prosecuting Attorney.

Amos Smith, Surveyor.

Ira Wilsey and John Silver, Coroners.

In 1858 George Meacham was elected Senator; George Newton and E. W. Reynolds, Representatives.

Joseph N. Marshall, Sheriff.

A. E. Peck, Register of Deeds.

William W. Peck, Treasurer.

Charles G. Lewis, County Clerk.

A. J. Smith, Prosecuting Attorney.

Amos Smith, Surveyor.

G. C. Jones and Jesse G. Beeson, Coroners.

In 1860 Gilman C. Jones was elected Senator; E. H. Jones and E. Shanahan, Representatives.

B. W. Schermerhorn, Sheriff.

C. Shanahan, Probate Judge.

Charles G. Lewis, County Clerk.

A. E. Peck, Register of Deeds.

Ira Brownell, Treasurer.

A. J. Smith, Prosecuting Attorney.

H. O. Banks, Surveyor.

R. K. Charles and E. W. Reynolds, Coroners.

In 1861 came the war cry, sounding from the Atlantic to the Pacific, and from the Gulf of Mexico to the Straits of Mackinac, arousing the patriotic of the nation to its defense, and the part that Cass County acted in this great war for the safety of the nation is detailed in a separate chapter devoted to that purpose.

In 1862 Emmons Buell was elected Senator; H. B. Denman and Levi Aldrich, Representatives.

William K. Palmer, Sheriff.

Ira Brownell, County Clerk.

J. K. Ritter, County Treasurer.

C. W. Clisbee, Prosecuting Attorney.

Amos Smith, Surveyor.

J. N. Marshall and E. Shanahan, Coroners.

In 1864 Levi Aldrich was elected Senator; Lucius Keeler and A. B. Copley, Representatives.

William K. Palmer, Sheriff.

M. T. Garvey, Probate Judge.

Ira Brownell, County Clerk.

William L. Jakways, Register of Deeds.

J. K. Ritter, Treasurer.

A. J. Smith, Prosecuting Attorney.

H. O. Banks, Surveyor.

J. M. Spencer and C. W. Clisbee, Coroners.

In 1866 C. W. Clisbee was elected Senator; H. B. Wells and L. D. Osborn, Representatives.

Z. Aldrich, Sheriff.

W. L. Jakways, Register of Deeds.

Charles L. Morton, County Clerk.

I. Z. Edwards, County Treasurer.

A. J. Smith, Prosecuting Attorney.

H. O. Banks, Surveyor.

G. C. Jones and J. G. Beeson, Coroners.

In 1868 Amos Smith was elected Senator; U. Putnam, Jr. and James Ashley, Representatives.

William P. Bennett, Probate Judge.

Z. Aldrich, Sheriff.

Charles L. Morton, County Clerk.

Joel Cowgill, Register of Deeds.

I. Z. Edwards, Treasurer.

George Miller, Prosecuting Attorney.

H. O. Banks, Surveyor.

G. C. Jones and L. Aldrich, Coroners.

In 1870 U. Putnam, Jr., was elected Senator; A. B. Copley and John F. Coulter, Representatives.

Levi J. Reynolds, Sheriff.

Charles L. Morton, County Clerk.

Joel Cowgill, Register of Deeds.

Anson L. Dunn, Treasurer.

William G. Howard, Prosecuting Attorney.

John C. Bradt, Surveyor.

G. S. Howard and C. F. Smith, Coroners.

In 1872 A. C. Prutzman was elected Senator for Cass and St. Joseph Counties; A. Robertson and Thomas O'Dell, Representatives.

William P. Bennett, Probate Judge.

William J. Merwin, Sheriff.

Charles L. Morton, County Clerk.

Henry L. Barney, Register of Deeds.

Spafford Tryon, Prosecuting Attorney.

Anson L. Dunn, County Treasurer.

John C. Bradt, Surveyor.

John Hain, Jr., and H. H. Bidwell, Coroners.

In 1874 M. T. Garvey was elected Senator for Cass and St. Joseph Counties; John Struble and John B. Sweetland, Representatives.

J. Boyd Thomas, Sheriff.

Charles L. Morton, County Clerk.

Henry L. Barney, Register of Deeds.

M. L. Howell, Prosecuting Attorney.

Hiram S. Hadsell, County Treasurer.

Austin A. Bramer, County Surveyor.

H. J. Webb and W. K. Palmer, Coroners.

MARCELLUS.

Marcellus was named by Judge Littlejohn, who at the time of its organization was a member of the Legislature. It was the design of the citizens to call it Cambria, and this name was sent in with the petition praying for the organization; but, owing to there being another Township of that name in the State, Mr. Anderson, our Representative at that time, consented to the name as already stated.

The first entry of land made in this Township, was in October, 1832, on section thirty-four, by John Bair. The next was by Daniel Driskel, on section thirty-six, in October, 1833, who also made an entry on section thirty-five, in August, 1834. These were the only entries made in the first three years.

In 1835 entries were made by D. Duncan, J. Clark, Thomas Armstrong, George Poe, A. J. Poe, F. Girton, J. Grenell, M. Rudd, S. Hutchings, W. D. Jones, and John Orr. In 1836 entries were made by Joseph Bair, Greer McElvain, Joel G. Goff,

Harvey Gregory, T. Mosher, M. P. Blanchard, Josephus Gard, Joseph Haight, John Goff, John A. Jacobs, E. T. Jacobs, John C. Beebee, John Huyck, E. Holly, James Kilgore, and U. Williams.

The first settler in the Township was Joseph Haight, who settled on the west side of the Township, in the summer of 1836, and was probably the only settler in that year.

In 1837 Joseph Bair and the widow Goff, with her sons, commenced to make a farms, and in 1838 Daniel G. Rouse and others settled in the Township.

The Township was organized and an election held on the 16th of June, 1843, at the house of Daniel G. Rouse. At this election there were eighteen votes cast. Daniel G. Rouse was elected Supervisor, Guerdon R. Beebee Treasurer, and Ephraim Huyatt Clerk.

Owing to its isolated location and great distance from markets, this Township for many years was considered anything but a desirable location for a home, consequently it was far behind in settlement and improvement, and was the last Township organized in the County, previous to which it had been attached to Volinia Township. But with the advent of the Peninsular Railroad in the winter of 1870–71, running as it does from northeast to southwest, nearly across the center of the Township, affairs assumed a different aspect, and it is safe to say that no Township in the County has kept pace in improvements with her since that date.

In 1845 Mr. Rouse started an ashery and sold goods, which he continued for two years, and was succeeded by the Carroll Brothers. Afterward Fred Patrick traded in merchandise. These were the first merchants of the Township.

In 1840 Savage, Rouse, Beebee, and the two Huycks built the first school-house, on Rouse's land, and Delia Huyck taught the first school in 1840–41.

In the fall of 1840 Alfred Paine was out hunting and shot a turkey which lodged in the top of a tall tree. He determined to climb and get it; when about forty feet from the ground he became dizzy and fell breaking one arm in two places, one leg in two places, between the knee and hip, and two ribs. When found, the bone of his leg was driven into the ground from four to six inches. The neighbors made a litter and carried him home. Dr. Chatfield, of Little Prairie Ronde, was sent for to set the broken limbs, which was done, but, by some carelessness on the part of the patient, the leg was broken again. Dr. Thomas, of Schoolcraft, was sent for to repair it, and after thirteen months in which time several pieces of bone worked out, Mr. Paine got well.

Marcellus village, situated nearly at the geographical centre of the Township, was laid out April 9th, 1870, by George W. Jones, Leander Bridge, Maria Snyder and George R. Roach. Its growth has been rapid. The buildings are of a substantial character, and everything would seem to indicate it as an important commercial point in the near future. It has a population of about five hundred, of as intelligent and enterprising citizens as can be found anywhere.

It has two churches, the Evangelical and Methodist, the latter a fine brick building approaching completion; a two story brick school house, employing two teachers; a Masonic Lodge, an Odd Fellows' Lodge, a Grange of the Patrons of Husbandry, and a Lodge of Good Templars.

It has three dry goods, three grocery, two drug, one hardware, one furniture, and three milliner stores; three blacksmith shops, two wagon shops, one tailor shop, two harness shops, two meat markets, two tin shops, two hotels, one bakery, one eating house, four practicing physicians, two lawyers, two Justices of the Peace, and one printing press which issues a weekly paper called *The Messenger*; there are two stave factories, one planing mill and a sash and blind factory combined, one cooper shop and one steam saw mill.

There is about $21,300 invested in merchandise, doing an annual business of $62,500, and nearly $46,000 invested in manufactories, mills, &c. The following are the principal Township officers that have been elected since the organization of the Township down to the present time:

DATE.	SUPERVISORS.	TREASURERS.	TOWN CLERKS.
1843	Daniel G. Rouse.	G. R. Beebe.	Ephraim Huyatt.
1844	Daniel G. Rouse.	Joseph Bair.	Ephraim Huyatt.
1845	E. C. Goff.	Joseph Bair.	O. C. Lumbard.
1846	E. C. Goff.	J. B. Lutes.	O. C. Lumbard.
1847	Joseph Haight.	Joseph Bair.	William L. Wolfe.
1848	Daniel G. Rouse.	Joseph Bair.	Henry McQuigg.
1849	Daniel G. Rouse.	Joseph Bair.	Henry McQuigg.
1850	Daniel G. Rouse.	E. Comstock.	Henry McQuigg.
1851	Henry McQuigg.	E. Comstock.	O. Blanchard.
1852	Henry McQuigg.	Mathew Gibson.	O. Blanchard,

DATE.	SUPERVISORS.	TREASUREES.	TOWN CLERK.
1853	Henry McQuigg.	*Thadeus Oaks.	J. B. Lutes.
1854	Henry W. Bly.	Leander Bridge.	J. B. Lutes.
1855	William P. Bennett.	F. Patrick.	William L. Wolfe.
1856	William P. Bennett.	F. Patrick.	J. B. Lutes.
1857	H. Dykeman.	F. Patrick.	J. B. Lutes.
1858	William P. Bennett.	R. R. Beebe.	W. O. Mathews.
1859	M. E. Messenger.	D. T. Baldwin.	W. O. Mathews.
1860	William P. Bennett.	D. T. Baldwin.	H. Dykeman.
1861	William P. Bennett.	John Manning.	J. B. Lutes.
1862	William P. Bennett.	John Manning.	H. J. Ohls.
1863	William P. Bennett.	W. O. Mathews.	C. O. Vose.
1864	William P. Bennett.	J. M. Housington.	C. O. Vose.
1865	John C. Bradt.	W. O. Mathews.	C. O. Vose.
1866	John C. Bradt.	John Manning	Gideon Beebe.
1867	William P. Bennett.	John Manning.	C. O. Vose.
1868	William P. Bennett.	John Manning.	H. J. Ohls.
1869	John C. Bradt.	John Manning.	H. J. Ohls.
1870	John C. Bradt.	John Manning.	H. J. Ohls.
1871	John C. Bradt.	Jonn Manning.	H. J. Ohls.
1872	Thomas McKee.	John Manning.	G. M. D. Clemment.
1873	John C. Bradt.	John Manning.	H. J. Ohls.
1874	A. F. Caul.	John Manning.	H. J. Olhs.
1875	A. F. Caul.	John Manning.	S. D. Perry.

*R. R. Beebe, appointed to fill vancancy.

VOLINIA.

This Township was originally called Volhynia, after a province in Poland, and for a number of years it was spelled with *hy*, but, by common consent, these letters were dropped and an *i* substituted. To Josephus Gard belongs the honor of naming the Township.

The first settlement in this Township was made on the 27th of March, 1829, by Samuel Morris, who settled on section one, (now the farm of Elias Morris). He was accompanied by his brother, Dolphin Morris, and Henry D. Swift, who settled in Van Buren County. Three days later Johnathan Gard, Samuel Rich and Elijah Goble came, the former settling on what is known as Gard's Prairie, and the two latter on the west side of Little Prairie Ronde. Both parties came under the guidance of Squire Thompson, of Pokagon Prairie. Jacob Morelan and Jacob Charles came the same season. In 1830 William Tietsort, Josephus Gard, John Curray and the two brothers, Samuel and Alexander

Fulton, arrived. In 1831 Obed Bunker, William Griffis and John Shaw came, and in 1832 David Crane, James Newton, Levi Lawrence and Amos Huff.

In 1830 the first entries of land were made in this Township by Johnathan Gard, Jacob Morelan, Samuel Fulton, Samuel and John Morris, Jacob Charles, Josephus Gard and Samuel Rich. In 1831 entries were made by Samuel Morris, Elijah and John B. Goble, Jacob Charles, Christanna Gantt, Christanna Charles, John Shaw, John Curray, Alexander Copley, Levi Lawrence, Johnathan Gard, David Crane, Daniel C. Squier and William Griffis. In 1832 entries were made by Samuel Morris, John S. Barry, William Griffis, Josephus Gard, Alexander Fulton, Alexander Copley, William Tietsort and James Newton. In 1833 Samuel and John Morris, William Squier, Joel C. and Elijah W. Wright, John B. Gard, Amos Huff, Henry Myers, Isaac and Peter Huff, made entries of land.

The first school house in the Township was known as the Crane school house, built in the spring of 1833, and the first school was taught that season by Michael V. V. Crane.

The first weddings in the Township were those of David Curry and Alexander Fulton to Sarah and Elizabeth, daughters of Josephus Gard. Both couples were married by the same ceremony, in the spring of 1832.

The first birth was that of John H. Rich, October 21st, 1829. The midwife on this occasion was Mrs. McKenney, of McKenney's Prairie, who was brought on the back of an almost unbroken three year old colt a distance of about fifteen miles.

The first saw mill in the Township was built in the summer of 1835, by Alexander Copley, where Nicholsville now stands, and was started on December 20th of that year. The irons for this mill were cast at Mishawaka, Indiana.

In 1833 the Township was organized and an election held at the house of Josephus Gard, July 8th, previous to which it belonged to Penn Township. In 1834 the road district comprised this Township and Van Buren County, which was attached for judicial purposes; and in that season men living on Little Prairie Ronde were obliged to work out their tax on the big swamp near where Lawton now stands. It would seem that the pathmaster was rather exacting, as he required the men to be on hand in season for a day's work, thus necessitating a start long before daylight with a well filled haversack containing the day's rations.

The first store in the Township was kept by James Herron, a little distance north of where Charleston now stands. It was commenced in 1836. In 1837 Morris & Cliffton opened a store in Charleston, and Huych & Daniels commenced selling goods at Volinia (Huycktown).

In 1836 Charleston, on Little Prairie Ronde, was laid out by Jacob Morelan, Jacob Charles, Alexander and Samuel Fulton, and David Fenton, comprising thirty-two lots.

In September of the same year Volinia was laid out by Levi Lawrence, David Hopkins, Obed Bunker, and John Shaw, and comprised fifty-five lots and a public square. Charleston, for a number of years previous to the completion of the Central Railroad, flourished with all the splendor of a Western metropolis. A line of stages passed through daily from Kalamazoo to Niles, and everything seemed to indicate that it was the coming town; but alas for human foresight, she and her sister, Volinia, only remain in the memory of their citizens, and a few scattered houses mark the places where formerly all was hurry and bustle.

In 1837 a carpenter in the employ of David Hopkins, by the name of Smith, who was in the habit of getting intoxicated, was drowned in Bunker Lake. At the time of the accident he was partially under the influence of liquor, and wished to go to Charleston to get another supply, a distance of three miles. He tried to get some of the family to take him across the lake in a boat, but they, knowing his condition, refused to assist him, whereupon he determined to go alone. When near the opposite shore from the house, the canoe upset, and that was the last that was ever seen of him. Some men, fishing on another part of the lake, saw the canoe empty and went to look for him, and for several days the whole neighborhood searched for the missing man; but a hat lying in the bottom of the canoe was all the indication that there ever had been a man there. He left a wife and family in the State of New York.

In 1849 a wagon road was built across the swamp to the railroad, thus giving an outlet for the farm products, previous to which they were teamed to Niles, St. Joseph, or Paw Paw.

About the year 1851 Harry George built the first grist mill in the Township, which continues to do good service yet. Shortly after building the mill he sold it to the Nichols Brothers and put up a store, which was burned in the winter of 1854, since which time C. L. Wilkins, H. T. Wing, A. Goff, and others have carried on merchantile traffic at Nicholsville, until the present firms, who commenced about twelve years ago.

It now contains a population of about one hundred, two general stores, one blacksmith shop, one cooper shop, one wagon shop, one shoe shop, one veneer and basket factory, one tannery, one grist mill, one steam saw mill, one hotel, two physicians, one lawyer, and one carpenter and joiner.

Volinia contains a population of about fifty, has one grist mill, one general store, blacksmith shop, etc. These, with a small portion of Wakelee, are the villages, past and present, of the Township.

The Volinia Farmers' Club was organized in November, 1865, and has maintained its organization ever since, holding meetings for discussion during the winter months, and sheep-shearings, implement trials, and fairs during the summer and fall months. Its present officers are:

President, B. G. Buell.

Vice Presidents, M. J. Gard, W. R. Kirby, John Huff.

Secretary, H. S. Rogers.

Treasurer, John Struble.

The only meeting-house in the Township is that of the colored Methodists, built in 1873.

The Town Hall, built this last summer (1875) is an ornament and credit to the Township.

The following are the principal Township officers elected since the organization of the Township down to the present time:

DATE.	SUPERVISORS.	TREASURERS.	TOWN CLERKS.
1833	James Newton.	*	David Crane.
1834	James Newton.	*	David Crane.
1835	James Newton.	*	Daniel C. Squier.
1836	James Newton.	*	Daniel C. Squier.
1837	David Hopkins.	James Huff.	Daniel C. Squier.
1838	Hubbell Warner.	James Huff.	Daniel C. Squier.
1839		*	Daniel C. Squier.
1840		*	Daniel C. Squier.
1841		*	Daniel C. Squier.
1842	Hubbell Warner.	Joseph Goodspeed.	Daniel C. Squier.
1843	Hubbell Warner.	Hubbell Warner.	Daniel C. Squier.
1844	Hubbell Warner.	Joseph Goodspeed.	R. J. Huyck.
1845	Joseph Warner.	Joseph Goodspeed.	R. J. Huyck.
1846	David Hopkins.	Joseph Goodspeed.	R. J. Huyck.
1847	David Hopkins.	Joseph Goodspeed.	R. J. Huyck.
1848	David Hopkins.	Joseph Goodspeed.	R. J. Huyck.
1849	James Fulton.	Joseph Goodspeed.	R. J. Huyck.
1850	James Fulton.	Joseph Goodspeed.	R. J. Huyck.
1851	George Newton.	Peter Sturr.	R. J. Huyck.
1852	George Newton.	Peter Sturr.	R. J. Huyck.
1853	Hubbell Warner.	Peter Sturr.	R. J. Huyck.
1854	Hubbell Warner.	Peter Sturr.	M. J. Gard.
1855	Emmos Buell.	Peter Sturr.	M. J. Gard.
1856	Alexander B. Copley.	W. L. Dixon.	M. J. Gard.
1857	Alexander B. Copley.	W. L. Dixon.	Joseph Warner.
1858	Alexander B. Copley.	W. L. Dixon.	R. J. Huyck.
1859	Milton J. Gard.	W. L. Dixon.	P. W. Southworth.
1860	Milton J. Gard.	W. L. Dixon.	H. T. Wing.
1861	W. L. Dixon.	W. L. Goodspeed.	P. W. Southworth.
1862	W. L. Dixon.	W. L. Goodspeed.	P. W. Southworth.
1863	W. L. Dixon.	W. L. Goodspeed.	E. S. Parker.
1864	A. B. Copley.	John Huff.	P. W. Southworth.
1865	Milton J. Gard.	John Huff.	P. W. Southworth.
1866	Milton J. Gard.	John Huff.	R. J. Huyck.
1867	A. B. Copley.	John Huff.	J. M. Goodspeed.
1868	John Huff.	L. H. Warner.	J. M. Goodspeed.
1869	John Huff.	L. H. Warner.	C. E. Goodenough.
1870	John Huff.	L. H. Warner.	I. N. Gard.
1871	John Struble.	L. H. Warner.	J. N. Root.
1872	A. B. Copley.	L. H. Warner.	G. W. Gard.
1873	John Struble.	L. H. Warner.	J. N. Root.
1874	John Kirby.	E. C. Goodspeed.	S. L. George.
1875	John Kirby.	E. C. Goodspeed.	S. L. George.

*No record of who was elected.

WAYNE.

This Township was named by Cornelius Higgins in honor of General Anthony Wayne.

Just when the first settlement of this Township was made or who the first settler was I have been unable to determine. It probably occurred in the fall of 1831 or the spring of '32, and Jacob Zimmerman, Elijah W. and Joel C. Wright, Cornelius Higgins, and Jesse Green, were among the first settlers. In 1835 the following in addition to the above named were here: Laporte, Johnstone, the two Hurtles, Ferrell Weaver, Crane, Eck, Meranville and Keys. In 1836 James Kirkwood came, and in 1837 the Gage settlement was made.

The first entries of land were made in 1831 by Josiah Johnson, Dennis Wright and Horace Butler.

In 1832 entries were made by William Griffis, Cornelius Higgins and Jacob Zimmerman. In 1833 Samuel Squires, John Lanman, Jessė Green, David Huff, A. Gunckel, J. C. Wright, John Cays and William Huff, made entries. In 1834 entries were made by R. V. V. Crane, A. Weaver, A. Bond, H. Lansing, John Clark, William Huff, Levi Hall, Susannah Griffis, J. D. Meranville, J. C. Wright, C. Higgins, E. W. Wright, F. Hurtle, William Ferrell, J. Hurtle, Henry Gee, S. Squiers and John Fox, and in 1835 by J. Zimmerman, J. Tucker, S. H. Henderson, James Thompson, E. Boughton, G. Goodman, S. R. Henderson, J. Green, J. Thompson, William Ferrell, J. P. Wiley, Goodman and Cresson, H. Barney, J. Hurtle, J. Smith, J. Hall, R. Bly, D. Runkle, H. Barney, Jr., J. Shookman, S. H. Dobler, J. A. Barney and S. Ball.

The Township was organized in the winter of 1834-5, and the first election held on the 5th of April following, at the house of Elijah W. Wright. Abraham Weaver was chosen Moderator, and R. V. V. Crane clerk of the election. At this election Cornelius Higgins was chosen Supervisor; R. V. V. Crane, Clerk; Ezekiel Wright, Collector; Elijah W. Wright, Jacob Zimmerman and Abraham Weaver, Commissioners of Highways; Jesse Green and Josiah Johnson, Directors of the poor; Elijah W. Wright, Joel C. Wright and Abram Weaver, Assessors; Ezekiel Wright, Costable; David Eck and Jacob Zimmerman, Overseers of Highways; Isaac Thompson and Jacob Hurtle, Fence-viewers; Frederick Hurtle, Pound-master; R. V. V. Crane,

C. Higgins and William Ferrell, Trustees of the school section.

The first school house was built in the fall of 1836, in the eastern part of the Township, and known as the Higgin's school house. It was built by subscription, or rather joint labor, the patrons living in the towns of Wayne and Volinia. George Newton taught the first school in this house in the winter following its building.

The Methodists were the first religious denomination to hold meetings, and have held their preeminence ever since. The first minister was Van Order, who organized a society about the year 1840. At first meetings were held at private houses and school houses, but about the year 1844, the "Old Church" was built which stood until 1872 when the present fine edifice took its place. This denomination also have another society and church, known as the North Wayne Methodist Church.

In 1838 the first road across the Dowagiac Swamp was partially built, and completed the next year. This crossing was of the utmost importance as it was on the direct route from all the northeastern part of the County to St. Joseph, then the most important shipping market within reach of this section.

In 1839 John and Stephen Clark built a tannery near where Glenwood now stands, which was the third tannery in the County, and was in operation for about twenty-five years, or until the bark used in tanning was exhausted. They also carried on most of the time shoe and glove making in connection with their tannery.

The ancient town of Venice, situated in that part of the Township, where Dowagiac now stands, was a "paper town" laid out by Orlando Crane, in August 1836, and known only by name and record at the County Seat. The only requirement at that time, to start a town, was to survey a plat and go on the market and sell lots, and frequently the expense of surveying was dispensed with, and it was only platted—hence the name of paper towns by which they were generally known. The wonder is that purchasers could be found for such mythical property, but when we consider that the Country was overrun with men on the lookout for speculation, it is easily accounted for. The agents for these towns were to be met at all the principal distributing points where the immigrants congregated, with finely engraved plats and a plausible story of the superior advantages of the various embryo cities they represented.

In the winter of 1874-5 Craig Sharp, an enterprising lumberman, purchased a large tract, near Tiesort's Station, on the Central Railroad, and put a small army of men at work clearing up the land. In January 1875 he recorded a plat of the village of Glenwood, located upon his purchase, at the Register's office. The venture proved financially disastrous to Mr. Sharp, but the village remains and contains about one hundred inhabitants, a Disciple Church, one general store, a saw and grist mill, blacksmith shop, &c. It is the only village wholly within the Township; Dowagiac, which is situated in the corners of four Townships, will be described hereafter. The following are the principal Township officers that have served from the organization to the present time:

DATE.	SUPERVISORS.	TREASURERS.	TOWN CLERKS.
1835	Cornelius Higgins.	Elijah W. Wright.	R. V. V. Crane.
1836	Cornelius Higgins.	Joseph Crane.	R. V. V. Crane.
1837	Abram Weaver.	Joel C. Wright.	R. V. V. Crane.
1838	Abram Weaver.	Joel C. Wright.	R. V. V. Crane.
1839		Abram Weaver.	R. V. V. Crane.
1840		Henry Barney, Jr.	S. B. Clark.
1841		Henry Barney, Jr.	S. B. Clark.
1842	Abram Weaver.	William G. Wiley.	R. V. V. Crane.
1843	Cyrus Gage.	S. B. Clark.	R. V. V. Crane.
1844	John S. Gage.	W. H. Atwood.	Joseph Crane.
1845	John S. Gage.	William Ferrel.	P. B. Gage.
1846	Joel C. Wright.	William Ferrel.	J. A. Barney.
1847	Ebenezer Gage.	D. M. Heazlet.	R. V. V. Crane.
1848	Ebenezer Gage.	Micajah Ludlow.	R. V. V. Crane.
1849	William G. Wiley.	D. M. Heazlet.	R. V. V. Crane.
1850	William G. Wiley.	P. B. White.	R. V. V. Crane.
1851	M. V. Hunter.	James Kirkwood.	R. V. V. Crane.
1852	M. V. Hunter.	James Kirkwood.	William H. Hall.
1853	M. V. Hunter.	James Kirkwood.	William H. Hall.
1854	John W. Trotter.	James Kirkwood.	William G. Wiley.
1855	Ebenezer Gage.	James Kirkwood.	A. S. Haskin.
1856	Ebenezer Gage.	James Kirkwood.	Arthur Graham.
1857	Sylvanus Henderson.	*	*
1858	Sylvanus Henderson.	*	*
1859	Sylvanus Henderson.	*	*
1860	H. B. Wells.	*	*
1861	H. B. Wells.	*	*
1862	H. B. Wells.	*	*
1863	H. B. Wells.	*	*
1864	H. B. Wells.	*	*
1865	H. B. Wells.	W. Wells, Jr.	A. Huntington.
1866	Israel Ball.	G. W. Amsden.	L. C. Howard.
1867	Israel Ball.	P. B. White.	Samuel Johnson.
1868	Israel Ball.	P. B. White.	Samuel Johnson.
1869	Israel Ball.	Robert Carr.	Samuel Johnson.
1870	William O. Van Hise.	O. H. Butrick.	Samuel Johnson.
1871	F. O. Van Antwerp.	John Crawford.	Samuel Johnson.
1872	Samuel Johnson.	A. H. Mason.	Charles W. Bigelow.
1873	H. H. Taylor.	Wesley Ely.	Charles W. Bigelow.
1874	H. B. Wells.	Wesley Ely.	Charles W. Bigelow.
1875	Samuel Johnson.	Wesley Ely.	Charles W. Bigelow.

*No record of who was elected.

SILVER CREEK.

This Township derived its name from a stream which emanates from Magician Lake, a part of which was formerly called Silver Lake, from its silvery color, caused by a coating of light colored marl on the bottom.

The first settler in this Township was James McDaniel, who settled on the land now owned by Mr. Foster, and commenced to build the saw mill, since known as the Barney, and now the Foster mill, which was the first mill built in the Township. Mr. McDaniel came in either in the season of 1834 or 1835.

Iu the season of 1836 Jacob A. Suits came in, and at this time there were but three other settlers in the Township, viz: McDaniel, John. Barney and Daniel Van Horn. Mr. Suit's cabin being the fourth one built. In 1837 and '38 the Township settled up very fast; during this time the Deweys and Woolman made the first settlement in the western part of the Township.

In 1839 William Gilbert settled on Indian Lake (then called Woolman's lake) and in 1840 Daniel Blish located in the southwestern part of the Township.

The first entry of land in the Township was made by James McDaniel, on sections one and two, December 16th, 1834, and the only entry made in that year. In 1835 entries were made by James Raymond and J. VanHorn on section one; A. Middlebrook, John Barney, and L. A. Spaulding on two and three; William McKay on three; Gardner Scott, H. Dresser, L. Guitean, Jr., and W. H. Keeler on four; A. Dorr on five and eight; Henry Dewey on eight; James Hall on nine and ten; J. B. Reddick and I. S. Stone on eleven; J. McDaniel, William St. Clair, and H. Harwood on twelve; John Barney and James Allen on fifteen; J. Ridenour, A. Middlebrook, and Reuben Wright on twenty; J. L. Parent on twenty-one; John Woolman on twenty-nine and thirty-one; J. Ridenour and John Woolman, Sr. on thirty-two, and F. Veeder on section thirty-five.

In 1836 entries were made in different parts of the Township by W. Mendenhall, R. J. Wells, W. B. Wade, Samuel Pletcher, D. Gardner, B. R. Wood, S. Morton, E. Corning, R. Brant, Z. Jarvis, Charles Glover, J. Sallee, P. B. Dunning, J. Harwood, James Allen, William Brooks, J. A. Suits, S. Treat, B. McConnell, E. H. Keeler, H. D. Bostwick, B.

Jenkins, G. Kennel, Joseph Wells, I. W. Duckett, Joseph Mills, A. Jenkins, M. B. McKenney, E. Gleason, George Kimmel, H. Dodge, J. Bertrand, J. Perkins, Jacob Silver, T. Husted, James Dixon and seven hundred and fifty acres by Pokagon.

Owing to the swamp on the Dowagiac Creek the first settlers were put to great inconvenience to arrive at their destination from the south side, and the only means of reaching the Township were by the way of Jenkins' bridge, in Pokagon, and thence through a trackless wilderness almost impassable for teams, or by the way of Paw Paw, necessitating a travel of nearly forty miles.

In February 1838 John G. A. Barney came, and bought land in this Township, but, owing to the impassable condition of the swamp, had to remain in Wayne until the following winter, when it was frozen sufficiently to allow him to pass over with an ox team, which was probably the first team that ever crossed the big swamp between Paw Paw and Sumnerville.

On the arrival of Mr. Barney the mill spoken of was pushed on to completion, and in 1843 John Barney erected a furniture manufactory on the creek at which the various articles of furniture, for household use, were made, also spinning wheels, then an article of every day use. John G. A. Barney also sold goods and was the first merchant in the Township. The first school house was built in the season of 1838 or '39, on the land now owned by E. B. Godfrey, and the first school was taught by Mr. Copley, of Little Prairie Ronde. The first grist mill was built by Mr. Hoyt, nearly twenty years ago. Among the first ministers that preached to the people of this Township were Luther Humphrey and Father McCool. The first postoffice was kept by James Allen and afterwards by J. G. A. Barney.

By the stipulations of the treaty at Carey Mission, in 1828, Pokagon and his band were exempted from being removed beyond the Mississippi, in common with the other Indians of South Western Michigan; and in 1836 they made an entry of a large tract of land in this Township. Although the title was vested in Pokagon, many other Indians had assisted in furnishing funds for the purchase, and these were allotted plots of from five acres upwards, in proportion to the amount put in, and settled on them, but upon the advent of PETE, Pokagon's oldest son, who succeeded the old chief, they were indiscriminately ousted. In the early settlement of the Township the Indians numbered about three hundred, but by the treachery of PETE, in driving them from their homes and other causes beyond the ken of man, they have dwindled down to a mere handful, and what was a prosperous family forty years ago is now a ragged remnant of poor Mr. Lo.

Pokagon gave largely to the Catholic Church, of which he was a devoted member. In 1840 he built the first church in the Township. In the building he was much troubled, as a good deal of prejudice existed among the whites against this denomination, and they would not turn out to help him to raise his log structure, and the Indians did not possess sufficient ingenuity to erect the building. In this dilemma he went to John G. A. Barney and related his troubles, Mr. Barney, on hearing his tale of woe, told him to get his logs together and he would come and assist him. This pleased the old chief very much and he went at the preparation vigorously. When all ready Mr. Barney and his three hired men went to assist him. They found that Pokagon had sent to Niles and procured a jug of whiskey for their use, while the Indians were treated to a plentiful supply of sweetened water, Mr. Barney asked him, on going to get a drink, if he thought they would drink what was not fit for an Indian, and at the same time turned the whiskey jug bottom side up, spilling the contents on the ground. The old log church has been superseded by a commodious frame structure, which, from its elevated location, is a landmark for many miles around. Attached to the church is a frame house for the use of the priest. There is, besides the Indians, a large Irish population devoted to this faith.

The Methodists have a fine house of worship, erected in 1868, on section twenty-one. There is also a Christian house of worship on section seventeen.

The Patrons of Husbandry have an organization in prosperous working condition in this township, which was organized in December, 1873.

There is no village or postoffice in the Township, if we except a portion of Dowagiac, in the southeast corner.

The Township was organized in 1837, and at the first election but fifteen votes were cast. The following are the principal officers that have been elected since the organization:

DATE.	SUPERVISORS.	TREASURERS.	TOWN CLERKS.
1837	Timothy Treat.	†	James Allen.
1838	P. B. Dunning.	†	James Allen.
1839		†	James Allen.
1840		†	James Allen.
1841		†	John Woolman, Jr.
1842	John Woolman, Jr.	†	†
1843	John Woolman, Jr.	†	†
1844	John G. A. Barney.	†	†
1845	John G. A. Barney.	†	†
1846	Daniel Blish.	†	†
1847	Daniel Blish.	†	†
1848	Daniel Blish.	†	†
1849	Daniel Blish.	†	†
1850	Daniel Blish.	†	†
1851	Daniel Blish.	P. Hamilton.	J. C. Harrington.
1852	Daniel Blish.	D. M. Heazlet.	E. M. Bird.
1853	Daniel Blish.	D. M. Heazlet.	Eli W. Beach.
1854	B. W. Schermerhorn.	E. H. Foster.	William D. McCool.
1855	B. W. Schermerhorn.	J. S. Becraft.	William Arbour.
1856	B. W. Schermerhorn.	B. F. Bell.	A. Harwood.
1857	Gilman C. Jones.	William Fowler.	A. Harwood.
1858	Gilman C. Jones.	Nathan Dewey.	N. B. Hollister.
1859	B. W. Schermerhorn.	L. R. Brown.	H. Michael.
1860	B. W. Schermerhorn.	L. R. Brown.	H. Michael.
1861	Justus Gage.	M. Cory.	H. C. Jones.
1862	Daniel Blish.	M. Cory.	H. C. Jones.
1863	Daniel Blish.	R. Watson.	H. C. Jones.
1864	B. W. Schermerhorn.	R. Watson.	H. Michael.
1865	G. C. Jones.	R. Watson.	H. Michael.
1866	William M. Frost.	T. T. Stebbins.	J. D. Taylor.
1867	William M. Frost.	H. Michael.	J. D. Taylor.
1868	William K. Palmer.	T. T. Stebbins.	J. D. Taylor.
1869	William M. Frost.	D. Henderson.	J. D. Taylor.
1870	William K. Palmer.	J. D. Taylor.	H. Michael.
1871	William K. Palmer.	H. Micnael.	B. L. Dewey.
1872	William K. Palmer.	Myron Stark.	H. Michael.
1873	G. Conkling.	Myron Stark.	E. E. Armstrong.
1874	Arthur Smith.	D. McOmber.	E. L. Jones.
1875	Arthur Smith.	Enoch Jessup.	Henry Michael.

†No record as to who was elected.

NEWBERG.

This Township was named by Surveyor John C. Saxton, in honor of a town in Ohio of which he cherished pleasant memories.

John Bair and family, who settled on section thirty-four in 1831, were the first white inhabitants. Daniel Driskel settled on section thirty-five in 1833. In 1835 George Poe settled on section twenty-two. In 1837 John Grennell, Samuel Hutchings, William Jones, William Allen and Spencer Nicholson made purchases and commenced to make improvements.

Of the earliest settlers only three are now residents of the Township, viz.: William D. Edson, Samuel Hutchings, and Barker F. Rudd.

The first school was taught by Anson Nicholson in a small log cabin on section thirty-two in 1837.

The village of Newberg, situated on the south bank of Lilly Lake, was laid out in May, 1837, by Spencer Nicholson, and comprised ninety lots. Of this embryo city nothing remains to mark its location, excepting the record of its survey and platting at the County seat. The Township was organized in the winter of 1837 and '38 and the first election was held in the spring of 1838.

The first minister of the Gospel was Elder Martin, of Penn Township, of the close communion Baptist persuasion.

The first regular Baptist Church of Newburg was organized June 8th, 1841, they have a house of worship but when it was built we could not learn. It is the only church in the Township.

The first entry of land was made in 1832 by John Bair, on section thirty-four, which was the only entry made in that year. In 1833 an entry was made on section thirty-six by Daniel Driskel, also in 1834 he made an entry on section thirty-five. In 1835 entries were make by John Orr, William D. Jones, Samuel Hutchings, Felix Girton, John Grenell, Marverick Rudd, Thomas Armstrong, George Poe and A. J. Poe. In 1836 entries were made by M. P. Lampson, Chauncey Wood, A. Chapin, Henry Ladd, William Meek, Jr., Robert Meek, Marcus Sherrill, Alexander Allen, William Hamilton, John S. Barry, Thomas Charlton, Ira Warren, George Poe, Norman Smith, R. B. Brody, Notsil Bair, Joseph Grenell, Roger Wilson, Hugh Brody, Abram Hutchings, H. Whittier, John Grenell, Silas Grenell, Spencer Nicholson, Marverick Rudd, Lewis Powell, L. Evenhart, B. F. Rudd, Warren Patchin, Marvin Hannah, Jeremiah Rudd, William Wilson, Hazen Whittier, John Bair, William Jones, Daniel Driskel,

Otis Murdock, Abram Mowyer, Alva Pine and Alexander H. Weatherwax.

The first white child born in the Township was Harriet A. Bair, now the wife of Leander Bridge of Marcellus.

In the summer of 1838 Horace Nicholson lost his life under the following circumstances: He had shot and wounded a deer, which plunged into the lake and swam across. Young Nicholson hurried to the bank of the lake where an old canoe was moored. The canoe was leaky and unsafe, but in the hurry and excitement of the moment he allowed his zeal to overcome his prudence and ventured out in the rotten craft, intending to paddle across the lake before it would fill and sink, but the water gained on him so fast that it went down before half way across. He was a good swimmer, but from his reduced condition, caused by a recent attack of the fever and ague, he was unable to make much headway and sank to be seen no more. At the time of the accident his father and mother were on the bank of the lake and saw their son go down but were unable to render him any aid. Their anguish may be imagined, but it is beyond the power of pen to describe. Although the lake was searched and raked for days, by parties of men from the neighborhood, his body was never found, with the exception of the skeleton of one leg, enclosed in an old boot, which was hooked up by some fishermen a year or two afterward.

On the night of the 18th of June, 1858, near the the site of the present village of Jones' Crossing, occurred the most terrible tragedy in the history of the Township, if not of the County.

Wm. D. Jones, who, it will be remembered, settled on the north side of Bair Lake in 1835, was one of the oldest and best citizens in the neighborhood, prominent for individual enterprise and public spirit.

He had remained upon his original location, gradually enlarging its boundaries as his means of profitably improving it increased, had seen the wilderness develop into fruitful farms, and its solitude replaced by a populous community, and was preparing to replace the rude log cabin of his earlier manhood with a substantial brick dwelling in which to pass his declining years.

The building was enclosed, the exterior completed and he contemplated with satisfaction his new home which he was fated never to occupy.

On the night above mentioned the family retired to rest as usual, Mr. J. and two carpenters, who were employed on the building, sleeping in the second story, while his wife—then an invalid—with her daughter and grand-daughter occupied the first floor.

At about eleven o'clock a fire broke out in a frame kitchen which was attached to the old house, and the dense smoke aroused the carpenters to a sense of their danger.

Loudly giving the alarm they hastened down stairs, but the daughter had arisen before their descent and rushed through the burning kitchen out to the well, leaving the doors wide open. This furnished a draft, and the flames swept through into the main part, cutting off the escape of the men in that direction. They hurried to the front door only to find it fastened, beyond their undoing, but fortunately they chanced upon an ax with which they battered it down and secured their escape from the most horrible of all forms of death.

They at once ran around to the window near Mrs. J.'s bed and broke it in to attempt her rescue, but this only furnished the fire fiend a new weapon and they were beaten back by the flames, and, with the daughter and grand-child, were obliged to stand helplessly by, impotent witnesses of the holocaust.

The old gentleman had, on the first alarm, followed them to the bottom of the stairs, but was there overcome by the smoke and perished.

The grand-daughter was asleep at the time and never knew how she left the house—the first seen of her she was in the road running and screaming, but entirely frenzied by the terrible spectacle.

At the time of the disaster their only son, E. H. Jones, was absent at Elkhart and was summoned by telegraph only to find his home in ruins.

The completion of the Air Line Railroad, which runs through the south tier of sections in the Township, gave it new vigor and the growth and improvement since that time has been rapid and substantial. Previous to this their markets were at Decatur, Three Rivers and Constantine, and so far distant as to make it a detriment to the settlement. Within the Township are the villages of Corey, on the extreme east side; Jones' Crossing, on section thirty-four, and Dyer, on section thirty-three.

Corey contains one general store, one blacksmith

shop, and ten dwelling houses, with a population of about fifty inhabitants. The shipment of wheat in 1874 was about fifteen thousand bushels and other produce in proportion. The village was surveyed and laid out on the 4th day of April, 1872, by Amanda Weatherwax, proprietoress.

At Jones' Crossing there are two general stores, one drug store, one steam saw mill, two blacksmith shops, one shoe and harness shop, and two practicing physicians. It is claimed that there is annually shipped from this point seventy-five thousand bushels of wheat, besides other produce, lumber, etc. E. H. Jones is the proprietor of the village, but neither the plat nor the date of survey have yet been recorded.

Dyer is only a stopping place for the accommadation of passenger traffic, and has no business enterprises as yet worthy of note.

The following are the principal Township officers that have been elected since the organization of the Township down to the present time:

DATE.	SUPERVISORS.	TREASUREES.	TOWN CLERK.
1838	James Aldrich.	*	Isaac Sprague.
1839		*	George Poe.
1840		Ira Warren.	W. D. Easton.
1841		Ira Warren.	W. D. Easton.
1842	Hiram Harwood.	Andrew Stetler.	W. D. Easton.
1843	Hiram Harwood.	Julius E. Nicholson.	W. D. Easton.
1844	Hiram Harwood.	Ira Sprague.	W. D. Easton.
1845	Hiram Harwood.	Ira Warren.	W. D. Easton.
1846	Barker F. Rudd.	George F. Jones.	Julius Nicholson.
1847	Barker F. Rudd.	A. S. Munger.	Julius Nicholson.
1848	Barker F. Rudd.	A. S. Munger.	Julius Nicholson.
1849	Barker F. Rudd.	A. S. Munger.	Julius Nicholson.
1850	Hiram Harwood.	A. S. May.	William D. Easton.
1851	Barker F. Rudd.	Ira Warren.	T. V. Bogert.
1852	J. M. Chapman.	J. Grenell.	T. V. Bogert.
1853	J. M. Chapman.	J. Grenell.	William D. Easton.
1854	J. M. Chapman.	J. Grenell.	William D. Easton.

*No record of who was elected.

DATE.	SUPERVISORS.	TREASURERS.	TOWN CLERKS.
1855	S. Harwood.	James Churchill.	E. H. Jones.
1856	S. Harwood.	James Churchill.	E. H. Jones.
1857	Edward H. Jones.	J. Grenell.	Silas Harwood.
1858	Edward H. Jones.	J. Grenell.	Silas Harwood.
1859	James Chapman.	J. Grenell.	O. C. Gillett.
1860	Barker F. Rudd.	Sullivan Cook.	O. C. Gillett.
1861	Silas Harwood.	Hazen W. Brown.	O. C. Gillett.
1862	Silas Harwood.	Nathan Harwood.	O. C. Gillett.
1863	James Chapman.	Silas Harwood.	Eli Hathaway.
1864	James Chapman.	H. A. Crego.	A. L. Dunn.
1865	J. M. Chapman.	H. A. Crego.	Eli Hathaway.
1866	J. M. Chapman.	M. F. Burney.	A. L. Dunn.
1867	J. M. Chapman.	A. L. Dunn.	Horace Francis.
1868	J. M. Chapman.	A. L. Dunn.	Sylvester Mihill.
1869	Anson L. Dunn.	H. A. Crego.	John B. Warner.
1870	Anson L. Dunn.	H. A. Crego.	John B. Warner.
1871	J. M. Chapman.	N. Harwood.	H. A. Crego.
1872	W. H. Pemberton.	N. Harwood.	F. M. Dodge.
1873	Silas Harwood.	J. S. Thompkins.	F. M. Dodge.
1874	J. S. Tompkins.	W. H. Pemberton.	F. M. Dodge.
1875	N. Harwood.	W. H. Pemberton.	F. M. Dodge.

PENN.

This Township was named after William Penn, the celebrated founder of Pennsylvania, who was also a noted Quaker or Friend, and as there was a large number of this denomination among the early settlers it was named by them.

The first settlement was made on Young's Prairie in the season of 1828. The prairie was named by Nathan Youngs after himself, when the surveying party, with which he was connected in the capacity of "slyper," was running out the land in 1827.

The first settlers were one Hinkley, who settled on the farm now owned by James E. Bonine, another named Whitehead, and Thomas England; but as none of them made entries of land or any improvement, with the exception perhaps of a log cabin each, the details of their settlement would be uninteresting. They were what were generally denominated "squatters," and sold out their improvements at the first opportunity. The Hinkley claim was sold for fifty dollars.

In 1829 the following settlers were among those that commenced to make farms: George Jones and his four sons, Charles, Henry, Nathan, and George Jr., John Price, John Rinehart and his four sons, Jacob, Lewis, John, and Abraham, William McClary, Martin Shields, Stephen Bogue, Mr. McIntosh and his three sons, Daniel, Duncan and William, and a number of others whose names we have mislaid.

According to the records Martin Shields made an entry of land on the 11th of March, 1829, and, if correct, this was the first entry made in the County. But this is probably a mistake, as the general land sales for this County were not held until the 16th of June in that year. In the same year entries were made by George Jones on sections seventeen, eighteen, twenty, twenty-eight and thirty; George Jones Jr. on eight and twenty-one; Henry White on nine; William McClary on eighteen; William Justice on eighteen; John Nicholson, Charles Jones and Jacob Miller on nineteen; Martin Shields, Isaac Commons, John Nicholson and Charles Jones on twenty; John N. Donald and Thomas England on twenty-one; John Rinehart on twenty-seven and twenty-eight; Samuel Boyles on twenty-eight; Daniel McIntosh, Boyles & McIntosh, and Stephen Bogue on section thirty.

In 1830 entries were made in various parts of the Township by William McClary, Ezra Hinkley, John Price, George Jones, Benjamin Bogue, Joseph Frakes, D. McIntosh, E. S. Sibley, A. I. McClary, Henry H. Fowler, Jesse Gardner, and Jonathan Donnel.

In 1831 David Brooks, William McClary, Ezra

Hinckley, Thomas England, Lewis Boon, Charles Jones, Stephen Bogue, Robert Clark, H. L. and A. C. Stewart, Alexander Anderson and William McIntosh made entries, and in the years of 1832–33 entries were made made by Thomas Kirk, Job Wright, John Townsend, Martin Harless, Thomas O'Dell, and James Kelsey.

In 1828 the first gristmill in the County was built by Mr. Carpenter on the Christianna Creek, just below where Vandalia now stands. It was a rude log structure, with a hollow log for a forebay, and nearly all its parts were of the same rude character, but answered the purpose for which it was built, and was a great convenience to the people for many miles around. The burs and irons for this mill were brought from Ohio on wagons drawn by oxen. In 1832 the property was bought by James O'Dell and run by him for a number of years.

In 1831 or 1832 John Donnel built a distillery a short distance east of where Vandalia now stands, and for a number of years this institution furnished stimulant to the inhabitants of the country around, which was then considered as necessary as bread and butter.

The Township was organized by an act of the Territorial Legislature, dated November 5th, 1829, and an election ordered at the house of Martin Shields. The Township at this time comprised what is now Marcellus, Volinia, Newberg, Penn, the north half of North Porter, and the north half of Calvin Townships. Although ordered to hold an election by the Legislature, the records do not indicate that such was the case until the spring of 1831.

In the spring of 1830 John Agard arrived at what has since been known as Geneva, but was then an almost unbroken wilderness, with a stock of goods. He was accompanied by Ira Nash, who acted in the capacity of clerk. This was the second store in the County—that of Mr. Edwards, at Edwardsburg, having preceded it. The goods for this store were brought out from Detroit with ox teams, by Daniel McIntosh and George Meacham, who each owned a large breaking team.

In 1831 Dr. Henry H. Fowler settled at Geneva and commenced the practice of medicine, and was the first physician in this part of the County. He was also interested in the prospective village, being one of the proprietors and the principal worker in manipulating for the location of the County seat at that point. The village was laid out in this year by E. S. Silsby, H. L. and A. C. Stewart, H. L. Fowler and Abner Kelsey, but was not placed upon record until April, 1832. It was named by Mr. Fowler after a village of the same name in the State of New York.

The question of the location of the County seat was agitated to a considerable extent, and it is said that some of the Commissioners appointed by the Governor and sent on for the purpose of locating it, when the spot was determined upon, withheld information of their decision one day, and in the meantime sent an agent to the Land Office and entered the land upon which the future seat of justice should be located. This course of procedure naturally gave rise to dissatisfaction, and by some manipulation another set of Commissioners were appointed, who gave the prize to Cassopolis. But, notwithstanding its loss of the County seat, Geneva flourished for a number of years with true Western grandeur.

In the fall of 1830 Nathan Baker opened a blacksmith shop, and in 1833 or '34 commenced the manufacture of cast plows, which was the first furnace in the County. The iron used in the blacksmith shop and foundry was brought in wagons from Ohio.

Soon after Mr. Baker, his son-in-law, John White, came, who was also a blacksmith, and worked at the business with his father-in-law. Their business proved a decided success, and its development kept pace with the growth and wants of the country. For nearly twenty years the "Baker Plow" was the only one in use in the County, excepting the "Bull Plow," which it superseded. They added, also, in time the manufacture of cultivators, shovel-plows, and other argicultural implements.

Upon the decline of Geneva, the shops were moved to Cassopolis, and formed a leading feature of her prosperity. Some of these plows are in use to-day, and still prove capable of doing good service.

In 1832 Mr. Agard was succeeded by Ira Nash, who carried on business for a number of years. Daniel and Abner Kelsey also sold goods for a time. A tailor by the name of King followed his ovocation. Nelson Shields worked at cabinet making, and William Williams at carpenter work.

After the location of the County seat at Cassopo

lis, the village gradually declined, until there was nothing that the eye could detect as ever pertaining to the once prosperous place. It is now known as Diamond Lake station, one of the most popular summer resorts in Southwestern Michigan, and rapidly growing in public favor.

In the winter of 1832–33, Lewis Rinehart, wife and infant son, made a visit to his father-in-law's, Mr. Frakes, then living east of Big Prairie. When returning home toward night they were overtaken by a severe snow storm. Their track lay through a wilderness, marked only by the blazed trees. Mr. L. urged his horses forward to their utmost strength, knowing that if darkness overtook them, they would not be able to follow the dim path. When within three or four miles of home it became so dark and the snow so deep they could not proceed farther that night. Hitching his team, he cleared away the snow from around a low, branchy tree, where he deposited the wife with her infant child, then but three weeks old, covering them with all the blankets they had with them, while he paced the ground during the entire night to keep himself warm. In the morning he found that he was but a few rods from the track, but the snow was nearly breast deep to the horses, and this had to be broken down by him before the team could get through. The child that was sheltered that cold night under a forest tree, is now an enterprising builder at Union, in this County.

On the 11th of October, 1845, an Anti-Slavery Society of Friends was formed on Young's Prairie, and Zachariah Shugart, Ishmael Lee, and Samuel Thomas were elected Trustees.

On the 3d of January, 1851, Stephen Bogue and Charles P. Ball laid out the village of Vandalia, and about the same time built the grist mill that has done service ever since. Asa Kingsbury was the first merchant to sell goods in the place. A. J. Smith and George Wells were his salesmen. T. J. Wilcox was the first postmaster. Dr. A. L. Thorp was the first practicing physician, in which capacity he still remains. A. Sigerfoos was the first blacksmith.

The village was incorporated by the last Legislature, and now contains a population of about five hundred. It now has two dry goods stores, one clothing and boot and shoe house, one hardware store, three grocery and provision stores, two drug stores, two meat markets, one machine shop and foundry, with planing mill attached, four blacksmith shops, one wagon shop, two hotels, one milliner store, one furniture store and cabinet shop, a handle factory, with planing and saw mill combined, a Disciple Church, a public hall, one of the finest school buildings, for a town of the size, in the State, three physicians, a private bank, a Masonic and Odd Fellows' Lodge, a Grange of the Patrons of Husbandry, one broom manufactory, one cooper shop that employs five men, one tin shop, and one livery barn.

Jamestown, on the line of the Chicago & Lake Huron Railroad, was laid out November 12th, 1869, by Isaac James. It now contains two general stores, a blacksmith shop, cooper and wagon shop, with a population of about one hundred. A large amount of grain, stock, and other products are shipped from this point annually.

That part of Wakelee that contains the store is also within the boundaries of this Township. This village, which is situated in the corners of Penn, Newberg, Marcellus, and Volinia, was laid out in 1871 by Levi Garwood, and in 1873 an addition was made by George W. Jones and Orson Rudd. It now contains a population of about one hundred and fifty, one general store, one hotel, one steam saw mill, and the usual number of mechanics' shops, etc. A large amount of wood and lumber is shipped from this point, also wheat and other farm products.

On the east side of Young's Prairie there is a Society of Friends, who have a house of worship with regular meetings. The following are the principal officers elected since the organization of the Township:

DATE.	SUPERVISORS.	TREASURERS.	TOWN CLERKS.
1831	John Agard.	Hardy Langston.	Ira Nash.
1832	James Odell.	Samuel Hunter.	Ira Nash.
1833	James Odell.	Samuel Hunter.	Ira Nash.
1834	James Odell.	*Daniel McIntosh.	Ira Nash.
1835	James Odell.	Thomas E. Odell.	Ira Nash.
1836	James Odell.	Daniel McIntosh, Jr.	Ira Nash.
1837	Alpheus Ireland.	Daniel McIntosh, Jr.	Ira Nash.
1838	Daniel Kelsey.	A. R. Lamb.	Ira Nash.
1839		A. R. Lamb.	Ira Nash.
1840		Samuel Alexander.	Ira Nash.
1841		John W. Odell.	Ira Nash.
1842	Ira Kelsey.	Stephen Rudd.	Allen W. Davis.
1843	Ira Kelsey.	Stephen Rudd.	Allen W. Davis.
1844	Ira Kelsey.	Stephen Rudd.	Allen W. Davis.
1845	Ira Kelsey.	Stephen Rudd.	Elias Carrier.
1846	Elias Carrier.	Stephen Rudd.	Ira Kelsey.
1847	Elias Carrier.	Stephen Rudd.	Allen W. Davis.
1848	Elias Carrier.	Stephen Rudd.	Allen W. Davis.
1849	Isaac Seely.	R. S. Pemberton.	Elias Carrier.
1850	Alpheus Ireland.	R. S. Pemberton.	George D. Jones.

*H. H. Fowler was elected in October.

DATE.	SUPERVISORS.	TREASURERS.	TOWN CLERKS.
1851	Alpheus Ireland.	Stephen Rudd.	George D. Jones.
1852	R. Pemberton.	J. E. Nicholson.	George D. Jones.
1853	Barker F. Rudd.	Edward Talbot.	John Hurd.
1854	R. Pemberton.	Edward Talbot.	John Hurd.
1855	R. S. Pemberton.	M. Rudd.	J. B. McIntosh.
1856	George D. Jones.	M. Rudd.	A. L. Thorp.
1857	George D. Jones.	John Alexander.	A. L. Thorp.
1858	Georgo D. Jones.	John Alexander.	A. L. Thorp.
1859	E. Alexander.	John Alexander.	J. E. Nicholson.
1860	Amos Smith.	J. S. East.	William H. Sullivan.
1861	R. S. Pemberton.	G. W. Jones.	William H. Sullivan.
1862	E. C. Collins.	J. W. Odell.	N. Monroe.
1863	C. C. Nelson.	A. W. Davis.	A. J. Foster.
1864	Nathan Jones.	A. W. Davis.	A. L. Thorp.
1865	Nathan Jones.	A. W. Davis.	A. L. Thorp.
1866	Amos Smith.	R. S. Pemberton.	†G. Clendennen.
1867	Amos Smith.	R. S. Pemberton.	H. C. Walker.
1868	R. S. Pemberton.	W. H. H. Pemberton.	H. Francis.
1869	John Alexander.	W. H. H. Pemberton.	A. L. Thorp.
1870	John Alexander.	John A. Jones.	A. L. Thorp.
1871	John Alexander.	John A. Jones.	A. L. Thorp.
1872	John Alexander.	John A. Jones.	W. E. Bogue.
1873	John Alexander.	William E. Bogue.	A. L. Thorp.
1874	John Alexander.	William E. Bogue.	A. L. Thorp.
1875	J. H. Stamp.	C. F. Smith.	J. W. Bartlett.

†And A. L. Thorp.

LA GRANGE.

This Township, and the prairie of the same name, were named by Abram Townsend, after the home of Lafayette in France. For a number of years after the first settlement the prairie, that is now known as La Grange, was called Townsend's Prairie.

The first settlement of this Township was made in the spring of 1828 by Abram Townsend, and his son Gamaliel, John Lybrook, James Dickson, Abram Loux, Lawrence Kavanaugh and Thomas McKenney, for whom McKenney's Prairie was named.

In 1829 the Wrights, John Ritter, Isaac Shurte, David Brady, John and Thomas Simpson and others made entries and commenced settlement.

The first entries of land were made in 1829 by James Dickson, on section eight; Isaac Shurte, on fifteen; Thomas McKenney, on seventeen; John and Thomas Simpson, on eighteen; Abram Loux, on twenty; Abram Townsend and Dennis Wright, on twenty-one; John Ritter and John Lybrook, on twenty-two; R. Wilson, on twenty-eight; Squire Thompson, on ten, and David Brady, on twenty-one.

In 1830 entries were made by Renniston and Hart, Frederick Richhart, Y. and Z. J. Griffin, A. Colvin, Isaac Dewey, George Jones, Wm. McClary, Samuel Shurte, James Dickson, M. J. McKenney, John Jones, Henry Dewey, William Garwood, Lawrence Kavanaugh, E. Simpson, M. C. Whitman, John and Thomas Simpson, L. G. Earle, Robert Wilson, David Brady, Shurte and Putnam, H. Lybrook, Sally Ritter, D. McClary, George Jones, A. V. Tietsort, Abram Tietsort, Thomas Vanderhoof, Abram Huff, James Pettigrew, John Hain, John Lybrook, A. Tietsort, Jr., and H. L. Fowler.

In 1831 entries were made by G. Nixon, J. D. Meranville, M. C. Whitman, E. Simpson, Thomas McKenney, David Brady, William McClary, R. C. Clark, Jr., O. Johnson, Charles and Henry Hass, E. B. Sherman, Abram Tietsort, Thomas Vanderhoof, J. R. Coats, A. and C. Huff, J. Pettigrew, Thomas Were, Margaret Pettigrew, J. M. McPherson, J. W. Roberson, G. Townsend, D. T. Nicholson, and Thomas Clark.

The first marriage in the Township was in 1829, and the contracting parties were James Kavanaugh and Ama Townsend.

The first school was taught by Miss Jane Brown, a sister of Gamaliel Townsend's first wife, in a log cabin on the farm of Abram Townsend.

M. C. Whitman was the first merchant, his store

was on the northwest corner of section sixteen, and commenced in 1830. He afterwards moved over and established himself on the land of Abram Townsend, and in 1831 moved his stock of goods to what has since been known as Whitmanville.

The first death that occurred in the Township was that of David, son of William Wright, in the spring of 1829.

The Township was organized in 1829, and at that time comprised what are now Wayne, La Grange and the north half of Jefferson.

The first election was held at the house of Isaac Shurte, on the 5th of April, 1830 and was the only election, of which there is any record, held in that year. Thomas McKenney was elected Moderator, and Martin C. Whitman, Clerk of the election. At this election eighteen votes were cast, and Joseph S. Barnard was elected Supervisor; Martin C. Whitman, Clerk, and Eli P. Bonnell, Collector. It was also voted to hold the next at a school house, on Townsend's prairie, if one should be built at that time, but for some cause the place was not changed until 1836.

On the 10th of April, in the same year, the Township was divided into two school districts.

In 1831 Eli P. Bonnell settled on La Grange prairie, and commenced the manufacture of pottery ware, of the various patterns in use among pioneers, which he continued for a number of years.

In 1829 Job Davis built a saw mill where Whitmanville now stands, and in 1831 sold out to Martin C. Whitman, who, in 1832, commenced to build a grist mill, which was not completed until the next year.

In August, 1834, Whitman laid out the village of Whitmanville, comprising eighty lots and four blocks. In September, 1836, he laid out an addition of five hundred and four lots, and in April, 1836, E. H. Spaulding laid out another addition of two hundred and one lots under the name of La Grange.

Whitman sold out to Goddard and Wells, who carried on business for a short time and were succeeded by E. H. Spaulding, who replaced the grist mill with a much larger one and greatly extended the business. He became embarrassed, after running three or four years, when the property passed into the hands of some Boston parties who held mortgages on it.

In 1835 there were four dry goods stores in the place, all doing a flourishing business.

Isaac Cross and Harvey Bigelow commenced the manufacture of furniture here in 1836, which was continued by Mr. Bigelow until his removal to Dowagiac in 1850.

Perry, Root & Co. purchased the mill property of the Boston parties. Under their administration the buildings were burned and the water power remained out of use until purchased by the Van Ripers in 1855, who rebuilt the grist mill, put up a woolen factory and a foundry and machine shop.

About the year 1844 Wilson and Edgcomb built a distillery and carried on a large store, their chief qualification would seem, from the reports handed down, to have been to contract debts with everybody, a greater part of which they were never able to liquidate.

Among the early anticipations of the proprietors of this place was that of securing the County seat. The water-power, combined with the pleasant location, gave them hopes that they could secure the prize, but like many anticipations of man, it came to naught; but for a number of years it was a strong mercantile competitor with Cassopolis, and carried away a good share of the trade.

It now has a population of about one hundred and fifty, a grist mill, a woolen factory, a foundry and machine shop, a saw mill and carding machine, a basket factory, one grocery store, cooper shop, and blacksmith shop. The grist mill is one of the best in the country. The woolen manufactory employs, when running, from fifteen to twenty hands, and represents a capital of from $20,000 to $25,000. There is also a Methodist Society here, who have a fine house of worship, built about eighteen years ago.

In 1830 Henry Jones and Hardy Langston built what has ever since been known as the "Jones' Mill." Mr. Langston sold his interest a few years after building, to Mr. Jones, who, in about 1836, added carding machinery, which was run until the Van Ripers started at Whitmanville, who bought it. There is now at the place a saw mill and furniture manufactory.

The village of Mechanicsburg was laid out by John Pettigrew, March 17th, 1837, comprising sixteen lots. Of this embryo city there is little to be said. It never made any great pretensions, consequently had not far to fall.

In 1830 William Renniston built a building and put in two carding machines, on the Dowagiac Creek, and in a year or two afterward, put up a grist mill near what has since been known as the thriving village of Dowagiac. Soon after completing the grist mill, he sold out to Mr. Spaulding, by which name it was known until it came into the possession of the present proprietor, Mr. Colby.

The above mentioned are all the villages, past and present, within the Township limits, excepting Dowagiac and Cassopolis, which will be treated of in separate chapters. The following is a table of the principal officers that have been elected since the organization of the Township:

DATE.	SUPERVISORS.	TREASURERS.	TOWN CLERKS.
1831	James Kavanaugh.	Eli P. Bonnell.	Samuel Wilson.
1832	James Kavanaugh.	Eli P. Bonnell.	James H. C. Smith.
1833	James Kavanaugh.	Eli P. Bonnell.	M. J. McKenney.
1834	Jesse Palmer.	J. B. Wade.	William Arrison.
1835	John Flewelling.	Thomas W. Sherman.	William Arrison.
1836	Jesse G. Beeson.	*	William Arrison.
1837	John Flewelling.	*	William Arrison.
1838	John Flewelling.	*	William Arrison.
1839	*	*	Benjamin Gould
1840	*	*	T. Barnum.
1841	*	*	Benjamin Gould.
1842	Elias B. Sherman.	*	*
1843	Eli P. Bonnell.	*	*
1844	Eli P. Bonnell.	*	*
1845	Eli P. Bonneli.	*	*
1846	Eli P. Bonnell.	Levi Tietsort.	David Histed.
1847	George B. Turner.	Elias Simpson.	Daniel S. Jones.
1848	Henry Tietsort, Jr.	Elias Simpson.	Daniel S. Jones.
1849	Henry Tietsort, Jr.	Elias Simpson.	Daniel S. Jones.
1850	Simeon E. Dow.	Elias Simpson.	Daniel S. Jones.
1851	Henry Tietsort, Jr.	Elias Simpson.	D. S. Kingsbury.
1852	Henry Tietsort, Jr.	Elias Simpson.	Daniel S. Jones.
1853	Daniel S. Jones.	Elias Simpson.	F. A. Graves.
1854	Daniel S. Jones.	Elias Simpson.	Charles G. Banks.
1855	C. B. Tietsort.	Edward Graham.	Charles G. Banks.

*No record of who was elected.

—13

DATE.	SUPERVISORS.	TREASURERS.	TOWN CLERKS.
1856	Henry Walton.	Elias Simpson.	Charles G. Banks.
1857	William G. Wiley.	Elias Simpson.	Charles G. Banks.
1858	Daniel S. Jones.	S. S. Chapman.	Charles G. Banks.
1859	Daniel S. Jones.	S. S. Chapman.	Charles G. Banks.
1860	Daniel S. Jones.	S. S. Chapman.	Charles G. Banks.
1861	William R. Fletcher.	A. Tietsort.	Charles G. Banks.
1862	Daniel S. Jones.	Edward Graham.	Charles G. Banks.
1863	Daniel S. Jones.	A. Tietsort.	Charles G. Banks.
1864	Daniel S. Jones.	A. Tietsort.	Charles G. Banks.
1865	Daniel S. Jones.	Byron Bradley.	Lowell H. Glover.
1866	Daniel S. Jones.	Joseph Graham.	Lowell H. Glover.
1867	William T. Tinney.	Joseph Graham.	Lowell H. Glover.
1868	Daniel S. Jones.	Joseph Graham.	Lowell H. Glover.
1869	L. H. Glover.	Josiah Hathaway.	Eber Reynolds.
1870	Abram Fiero.	Isaac Wells.	E. C. Deyo.
1871	Daniel S. Jones.	Isaac Wells.	Eber Reynolds.
1872	Daniel S. Jones.	Isaac Wells.	Eber Reynolds.
1873	Daniel S. Jones.	Isaac Wells.	Eber Reynolds.
1874	Robert Wiley.	Isaac Wells.	Henry J. Webb.
1875	Robert Wiley.	A. Tietsort.	Charles G. Banks.

POKAGON.

This Township was named after the old Chief Pokagon, who, previous to the settlement by the whites, made his home on the west side of the prairie that still bears his name.

Here occured the first settlement in the County, in the season of 1825, by Uzziel Putnam, Sr., Squire Thompson and Baldwin Jenkins.

From its favored location and fertility of soil, this Township has been recognized from the beginning as one of the best. In the early settlements of the different localities, this one, having the start, was furnished a ready home market for all of its surplus productions, and after the others began to be competitors in the market, by its nearness to the St. Joseph river, it had a great advantage over the remaining portions of the County.

Of the earliest settlers only the first—Mr. Putnam—remains, who resides on the land he first located, and, with his wife, is passing his declining years in ease and comfort; both have long since passed the period usually allotted to man.

In 1826 Ira Putnam and family, Lewis Edwards and some others settled in the Township.

In 1827 William Garwood, Israel Markam and sons came in. Mr. Markam was a blacksmith by trade and the first one that carried on a shop in the County. It is related that on one occasion a man came from Beardsley's prairie with a plowshare to be sharpened, and when it was done was charged thirty-seven and a half cents, which he objected to as being too much, but Mr. Markam told him that he was obliged to have money to buy seed wheat and had to charge high on that account..

In 1828 Alexander Rogers and his five sons, Samuel, Alexander, John, Thomas and William, with William, Thomas and Andrew L. Burk made settlements.

From this time forward the increase of settlers was very rapid and in 1830 the prairie contained a greater population than it does at the present time.

The first entries of land were made in 1829 by Squire Thompson, on sections twenty, twenty-one and twenty-eight; Samuel Markam, on twenty-eight and twenty-nine; Israel Markam, Sr., Israel Markam, Jr. and Baldwin Jenkins, on twenty-nine; Alexander Rogers, on thirty and thirty-one; Lewis Edwards, Joseph Gardner and Jesse Toney, on thirty-one; Putnam and Clyborne, A. C. Clyborne, I. W. Duckett, Edwards and Gardner and Gardner and Duckett, on thirty-two, and N. Haines, on section thirty-three.

In 1830 entries were made in various parts of the Township by John Witter, H. and I. Dewey, James

A. Wood, B. Jenkins, Willam and Thomas Burk, McGwin and Curran, Lane Markam, Alexander Rogers, U. Putnam, Elizabeth Lowe and J. McPherson.

In 1831 the following persons made entries: Joseph Stretch, Alexander Rogers, William Taylor, H. Dewey, Samuel Morton and Joseph Garwood.

In 1832 entries were made by H. Salladay, A. W. McCullum, Thomas Burk, L. Markam, R. and J. C. Fairries, Jesse Sink, J. Ribble, J. G. Beeson, E. B. Sherman, J. Garwood, John Clifton, G. Van Vlear, Thomas Simpson, Jesse Garwood, T. Clyborne, D. Sink and J. B. Herbert.

The Hon. U. Putnam, Jr. was the first white child born not only in the Township but in the County.

The first school was taught by Miss Jane Brown and the next by Dr. Bragdon.

The first tan yard was built and run by David Sink, and was the first in the County, but of the exact date of its commencement I have been unable to learn.

In common with the four original Townships of the County, Pokagon was organized by the Territorial Legislature, on the 5th of November, 1829, and an election appointed at the house of Squire Thompson, but as all of the early records of the Township have been lost or mislaid, I have not been able to learn whether the intention of the Legislature was carried out or not, and the County records do not show that there was any representative from this Township in 1830 or in fact from any Township.

In August, 1836, the village plat of Sumnerville

was placed upon record, but the date of its being laid out is not given. The proprietors were J. H. Hatch and Isaac Sumner. About the year 1835 Sumner built a saw mill at this place, and in 1837 he he built a grist mill. About the same time Alexander Davis, the first merchant, commenced to sell goods. In 1848 Russel Cook and John R. Conine opened a store in the building now occupied by Mr. Goldie. Peabody Cook kept the first hotel, commencing in the year 1835.

The village now has one general store, one hotel, two blacksmith shops, one wagon maker, one photographer, one grist mill with three run of stone, one woolen factory and one water power saw mill. There are also two churches—the Freewill Baptist and Methodist.

The village of Shakespeare was laid out on sections eight, nine and seventeen, on the 17th of June, 1836, by J. Brown and E. B. Sherman, and comprised eighty-seven blocks. This can be truly classed as one of the paper towns of Michigan—laid out with numerous squares for public purposes; a contemplated canal reaching from one point of the Dowagiac river (as it is here called) to another, with a number of reserved lots on the water front for manufacturing purposes, and it is said that some of the plats that were sent to distant points for the purpose of selling lots represented vessels lying at the wharf. A large spring, which was named after the celebrated Chief Topennebee, was represented as being strong and high enough to furnish an ample supply of water for about two-thirds of the town. The spring is all that remains to mark the location of this once-promising place. It is to be said to Mr. Sherman's credit that soon after the laying out he became disgusted with the whole affair and disposed of his interest in the plat. Numerous lots were sold to parties in every direction, and as speculation was rife in everything that pertained to real estate, perhaps it might as well have been here as anywhere else.

The Village of Pokagon, on the line of the Michigan Central Railroad, was laid out January 15th, 1858, by William Baldwin. The first merchant here was Joel Andrews, and soon after Hoke & Stansel, both opening in the year 1858. In 1856 the present gristmill was built by the Kelley brothers. In the year the village was laid out Garret Stansel built the hotel building which is still used for that purpose.

The village now contains two dry goods stores, one drug store, two shoe shops, two blacksmith shops, one harness shop, one cooper shop, one wagon maker, one meat market, two physicians, three grain and stock dealers, one steam saw mill, a Masonic Lodge, a Grange of the Patrons of Husbandry and an order called the Free Laborers' Council, which was organized in the fall of 1875, and the only one we have found in the County, its object is to protect labor against the oppression of monopolies.

The Methodist Society of this Township own, in addition to their fine church at Sumnerville, and parsonage at Pokagon, the camp-meeting site, known as the "Crystal Spring Camp Ground," and at this place is located the State Fish Hatchery. The spring is situated about twenty-five rods south of the Dowagiac Creek, at the head of a ravine covered with a natural growth of timber. This ravine has been dammed to give sufficient depth of water and also to have the better control of the water for the purposes for which they may wish to use it. The volume discharged by the spring is estimated to be six hundred barrels per hour. The State has erected a building twenty by sixty feet, supplied with appliances for hatching a million of fish at a time. The hatching house is separated into two divisions—one being used for an office, the other a hatching room. A large pipe, running the whole length of the building, supplies the water for hatching, to which pipes, sixteen in number, are attached; the supply of water is regulated by faucets and turned on as the needs of the fish demand. The eggs are placed upon seives fourteen by eighteen inches square for hatching. When two months old the fish are ready for planting in the waters of the State. The principal varieties propagated are the California salmon trout and white fish.

The following are the principal Township officers elected since the organization of the Township:

DATE.	SUPERVISORS.	TREASUREES.	TOWN CLERKS.
1831	Squire Thompson.	*	*
1832	John Clark.	*	Joseph Gardner.
1833	Samuel Marrs.	*	Joseph Gardner.
1834	Lewis Edwards.	*	Joseph Gardner.
1835	Lewis Edwards.	*	Joesph Gardner.
1836	Lewis Edwards.	Mitchell Robinson.	Eli W. Veach.
1837	Henry Howser.	Mitchell Robinson.	Eli W. Veach.
1838	Henry Howser.	William L. Clyborne.	Eli W. Veach.

*No record of who was elected.

DATE.	SUPERVISORS.	TREASURERS.	TOWN CLERKS.
1839		Zimri Garwood.	Eli W. Veach.
1840		Squire Thompson.	Eli W. Veach.
1841		Squire Thompson.	Eli W. Veach.
1842	Squire Thompson.	William L. Clyborne.	Mitchell Robinson.
1843	Squire Thompson.	Moses W. Simpson.	William L. Clyborne
1844	William Burk.	Moses W. Simpson.	William L. Clyborne
1845	Henry Howser.	Moses W. Simpson.	William L. Clyborne
1846	Henry Howser.	Moses W. Simpson.	William L. Clyborne
1847	William L. Clyborne.	John Collins.	David Long.
1848	M. Robinson.	John Collins.	Charles G. Moore.
1849	William L. Clyborne.	John Collins.	Lewis Edwards.
1850	William L. Clyborne.	Franklin Brownell.	Lewis Edwards.
1851	M. T. Garvey.	Robinson J. Dickson.	Clark F. Johnson.
1852	M. T. Garvey.	Amos D. McCool.	Clark F. Johnson.
1853	Frank Brownell.	Robinson J. Dickson.	Ira Starkweather.
1854	M. Robinson.	William G. Straw.	Samuel R. Wheeler.
1855	Lewis Clyborne.	John Collins.	Ira Starkweather.
1856	M. T. Garvey.	John Bates.	Rollin C. Dennison.
1857	William L. Clyborne.	John Collins.	Joseph E. Garwood.
1858	M. T. Garvey.	Gideon Gibbs.	Strawther Bowling.
1859	D. H. Wagner.	John Bates.	Theodore Stebbins.
1860	M. Robinson.	Archibald Robertson.	Strawther Bowling.
1861	M. T. Garvey.	Archibald Robertson.	Philo D. Beckwith.
1862	Alexander Robertson.	Mitchell Robinson.	George Miller.
1863	Alexander Robertson.	Gideon Gibbs.	Elias Pardee.
1864	Alexander Robertson.	Augustus Allen.	Strawther Bowling.
1865	Alexander Robertson.	Abner G. Townsend.	Strawther Bowling.
1866	Alexander Robertson.	Stephen W. Tinkham.	Strawther Bowling.
1867	Alexander Robertson.	Albert G. Ramsey.	Strawther Bowling.
1868	Alexander Robertson.	Elam Harter.	Strawther Bowling.
1869	Alexander Robertson.	Elam Harter.	Rollin C. Osborne.
1870	David W. Clemmer.	Daniel M. Heazlett.	R. W. Schermerhorn
1871	B. W. Schermerhorn.	Daniel M. Heazlett.	John Rix.
1872	B. W. Schermerhorn.	Samuel Miller.	Rollin C. Osborn.
1873	B. W. Schermerhorn.	Samuel Miller.	Rollin C. Osborn.
1874	B. W. Schermerhorn.	Moses V. Gray.	Rollin C. Osborn.
1875	B. W. Schermerhorn.	Moses V. Gray.	Edwin W. Beckwith

PORTER.

This township was named in honor of John B. Porter, who was the Governor of the Territory at at the time of its organization.

It contains about fifty-four square miles and is usually designated as North and South Porter. On account of the original survey and platting, which denominated it as towns seven and eight south, making two Townships, the calling of it North and South Porter became necessary.

The first settler in this Township was John Baldwin, for whom Baldwin's Prairie was named, who commenced on the farm now owned by George Meacham, Esq., in the season of 1828.

In 1829 William Tibbetts and Daniel Shellhammer settled in South Porter, and in 1831 John White settled in North Porter, and, so far as as I have been able to learn, he was the first settler in this part of the Township.

In 1829 entries of land were made in South Porter by A. Davidson, A. Richhart and N. G. O'Dell, on section one; E. Beardsley, on seven; N. C. Tibbitts, Chester Sage and John Baldwin, on eight; George P. Shultz, O'Dell and Brooks, on section thirteen. In 1830 G. P. Shultz, George Jones, C. Calkins, Jacob Charles, Jarius Hitchcox, John Barm, N. G. O'Dell, Jr., F. Tobey, James O'Dell, Benjamin Carr, J. Virgil and Aaron Brooks made entries.

In North Porter the first entry of land was made by James Montgomery on the 1st of November, 1829, on section thirty-one. In 1830 an entry was made by A. Ferry, on section thirty-six. In 1831 Jacob Charles, D. Barnham, F. Smith, V. Shultz and John White made entries. In 1832 and '33 entries were made by Jacob, Lewis and Samuel Rinehart, Sarah Jones, William Hebron, J. P. Finney, Peter Cook, F. Driskel, John Bair, John East, N. Williams, H. H. Fowler, S. Davidson, Joseph Moor and S. Weed.

The Township was organized by an act of the Territorial Legislature, approved the 29th day of March, 1833, and an election was appointed at the house of Othni Beardsley. This election was held on the fourth Monday in April—following the act of organization—at the place appointed. Caleb Calkins was chosen Moderator and Jarius Hitchcox, Clerk of the election. The following were the officers chosen for that year: Othni Beardsley, Supervisor; Charles Calkins, Clerk; Thomas Pratt,

Jacob Pells and Nathan G. O'Dell, Assessors; David Shaffer, Jacob Charles and Thomas Burgett, Commissioners of Highways; Elam Beardsley, Collector; John Lough, O. Beardsley and Thomas J. Pratt, Commissioners of Schools; Jacob Charles, Levi Lough and Jarius Hitchcox, School Inspectors, and Jacob Virgil, Overseer of the Poor.

In 1831 Lewis, Samuel and Jacob Rinehart commenced to build a saw mill on the outlet of Shavehead lake, which was completed in the spring of 1832, and in the next year they sold in Chicago one hundred and ten thousand feet of lumber, for which they received seven dollars and fifty cents per thousand delivered at the St. Joseph river.

Williamsville was laid out by Josiah Williams, in March, 1848. He was also interested in the first store at this place.

It now contains a population of about three hundred, one general store, one blacksmith shop, one cabinet and paint shop, two physicians, one grist mill and one saw mill.

The First Baptist Church of North Porter was organized February 8th, 1857, with twelve members, and William Hebron, O. N. Long, G. W. Minor, James Motley and Aaron Shellhammer, were elected trustees. It has at present fifty-one members and a house of worship valued at two thousand dollars.

The Methodist Episcopal Church of North Porter was organized in 1846 with fourteen members, and in 1858 they built a church building at a cost of eight hundred dollars. At the present time it has thirty members.

There is also another Methodist Church building, erected in 1873, at a cost of five thousand dollars, and dedicated in December of the same year, but the denomination have no regular society at this place.

The village of Union is of comparatively modern origin, having been commenced about the year 1860, and is an enterprising go-ahead place, and doing as much business as any place of its size in the County. It now contains one general store, one builder, undertaker and painter, with the usual number of shops, mechanics, etc., and one physician.

In February, 1857, The Reverend Jacob Price organized a Baptist Society at this place with six members. It now has a membership of fifty-five, a brick house of worship erected in 1872, valued at $5,000, and they now employ a regular clergyman.

The Methodist Episcopal Society have a house of worship that was erected in 1858, and rebuilt and enlarged in 1874, but when the Society was organized, or the present number of members, I could not learn.

The Freewill Baptists also have a Society here, and occupy the Methodist Church a portion of the time.

A military road, constructed by the general Government from Detroit to Chicago, ran through this and all the southern tier of Townships, and the tide of emigration, setting westward following this road, furnished a home market for all their surplus produce; and many of the original pioneers that are now well-to-do in their declining years, were indebted to this source for the payment on their entries.

On the 30th of April, 1824, Congress passed an act authorizing the President to cause to be surveyed certain canals and roads of importance in a military point of view, and it is generally supposed that this important avenue came under this head. On the 2d of March, 1827, an act of Congress was approved appropriating twenty thousand dollars for the purpose of opening and constructing a military road from Detroit to Chicago, and the work was commenced in the same year. The road was cut out one hundred feet wide, and a space in the middle eighteen feet wide was grubbed clean and graded. The work was continued until the year 1836, when the bridge across the St. Joseph River at Bertrand was completed, and as a Government work it ceased. The records of this road in an early day were enclosed in a tin box and forwarded from Washington to Detroit, but were lost on the way and have never been found, consequently its exact location or bearings are not accurately known.

The following are the principal officers that have been elected since the organization of the township:

DATE.	SUPERVISORS.	TREASURERS,	TOWN CLERKS.
1833	Othin Beardsley.	E. Beardsley.	C. Calkins.
1834	Caleb Calkins.	A. B. Davis.	A. B. Davis.
1835	Caleb Calkins.	Joel Baldwin.	A. B. Davis.
1836	George Meacham.	Elihn Davis.	A. Dibble.
1837	Caleb Calkins.	L. Keeler.	A. Dibble.
1838	George Meacham.	R. K. Charles.	Seth Weed.
1839		O. Story.	Seth Weed.
1840		Moses Joy.	O. M. Long.
1841		R. K. Charles.	A. Dibble.
1842	Milo Powell.	O. Story.	Seth Weed.
1843	William R. Merritt.	Lewis Rinehart.	H. Shelden.
1844	Oscar N. Long.	J. Hartman.	A. Kennicott.
1845	Oscar N. Long.	L. Rinehart.	A. Kennicott.
1846	Rufus K. Charles.	J. Hartman.	S. Taylor.
1847	Rufus K. Charles.	J. Hartman.	A. Kennicott.
1848	John N. Jones.	George Hebron.	J H. Hartman.

DATE.	SUPERVISORS.	TREASURERS.	TOWN CLERKS.
1849	Jana Hitchcox.	J. Hartman.	S. Taylor.
1850	O. N. Long.	J. Hartman.	S. Taylor.
1851	O. N Long.	A. H. Long.	Milo Powell.
1852	Rufus K. Charles.	A. H. Long.	Milo Powell.
1853	Rutus K. Charles.	J. H. Hartman.	A. H. Long.
1854	Rufus K. Charles.	J. H. Hartman.	A. H. Long.
1855	Rufus K. Charles.	J. Motley.	F. Teesdale.
1856	Milo Powell.	J. Motley.	F. Teesdale.
1857	A. H. Long.	H. J. Dauchy.	G. Hebron.
1858	A. H. Long.	J. Hartman.	W. S. Stearns.
1859	A. H. Long.	G. W. Miner.	L. Beebe.
1860	Lucius Keeler.	J. Hartman.	L. Beebe.
1861	Lucius Keeler.	A. H. Long.	W. S. Stearns.
1862	Lucius Keeler.	O. Briggs.	W. S. Stearns.
1863	Lucius Keeler.	O. Briggs.	W. S. Stearns.
1864	J. H. Hitchcox.	O. Briggs.	W. S. Stearns.
1865	Thomas O'Dell.	William Rinehart.	G. Hebron.
1866	Thomas O'Dell.	J. Motley.	C. C. Parker.
1867	Lucius Keeler.	M. McHuron.	H. H. Bowen.
1868	Thomas O'Dell.	M. McHuron.	H. H. Bowen.
1869	Thomas O'Dell.	H. Meacham.	A. R. Thompson.
1870	Hiram Meacham.	H. Beardsley.	H. H. Bowen.
1871	Hiram Meacham.	H. D. Long.	H. H. Bowen.
1872	Hiram Meacham.	H. D. Long.	E. Motley.
1873	Hiram Meacham.	M. Nutting.	E. Motley.
1874	Hiram Meacham.	H. Beardsley.	M. McHuron.
1875	Nathan Skinner.	H. Beardsley.	M. McHuron.

CALVIN.

This Township was named for Calvin Britain, who, at the time of its organization in 1835, was a member of the Territorial Legislature.

This Township has many natural advantages, among which are one of the most fertile soils that the country affords, adapted to the culture of all the cereals of this latitude and the various fruits. In its earlier settlement the land was entered largely by speculators who held it for high prices, and thereby retarded settlement in a great degree for a number of years.

The first entries of land were made in 1829 by Nathan Young, on section five, and John Reid, on five and six.

In 1830 entries were made by John Reid and Levi F. Arnold, on six; Giles Norton, on seven; George Jones, on eight, and D. McIntosh, Jr., on section nineteen.

In 1831 George Nicholson, D. Bunham, F. Smith, Jacob Charles, Andrew Grubb, M. Zane, William

F. Noel, David Shaffer, John Ireland and Peter Shaffer made entries.

In 1832 H. H. Fowler, Joel East, H. Richardson, Thomas Bulla, T. Smith and Peter Shaffer made entries in various parts of the Township.

The first settlement in this Township was made in the year 1832, by Peter Shaffer, the widow White and her five sons, Andrew Grubb, John Reid and three sons, Nathan Thorp, and in 1833 William East and his sons, James, John, and Joel, Nathan Williams, and John Zeek made settlements and commenced improvements.

In 1835–6 the Osborne settlement was made, and the first nursery in the County started by them, for the sale of fruit trees.

The earlier settlers were nearly all Quakers or Friends, who came from the South, leaving that locality on account of slavery. In 1837 they organized a Church, and now have an unpretending house of worship. Samuel Bonine was the first minister and Joel East the next.

The Township was organized by an act of the Territorial Legislature, approved March 17th, 1835, and an election appointed at the house of John Reid, Sr. At this election Pleasant Grubb was chosen Supervisor and William T. Reid Clerk.

About the year 1834 or '35, Pleasant Grubb built a grist mill on the outlet of Diamond Lake, where Brownsville now stands, but he soon after sold out to the Brown brothers, from whom Brownsville takes its name. This village has never been platted, or if so, it has not been placed upon the record, consequently the exact data of its origin is hard to determine. It now contains a population of about one hundred and fifty, a grist mill, two general stores, and numerous mechanics, shops, etc.

The first school-house was built near the farm of Peter Shaffer, but in what year or who taught the first school, I have not been able to learn.

The first birth was that of Elnora Jane, daughter of Leonard Keene, in May, 1832.

The colored population of this Township number about one thousand, and the first permanent settlement by them was made in 1845, by John Stewart and Lawson Howell. The next one to locate was Ezekiel C. Anderson, who settled on the west side of Porter Township. Mr. Anderson served in the Indian wars under General Jackson, and was at the battle of the Horse Shoe, as well as several others. He was enrolled under the name of Ezekiel Cole, his full name being Ezekiel Cole Anderson.

The African Methodist Episcopal Church, of Calvin, known as the Mount Zion Church, was organized January 8th, 1853, with Hardy Wade, Joseph Allen, Richard Wood, William Scott, Benjamin Hawley, Lawson Harvey, and Lemuel Archer, as Trustees.

The Chain Lake Baptist Church (colored) was organized December 31st, 1854, and Green Allen, Moses Sanders, and Elisha Byrd were elected Trustees. Both of these Societies have houses of worship.

In 1865 the Hoosier Woolen Mill was erected by Samuel C. Van Mater and Isaac and Vincent Wright, at a cost of about fifteen thousand dollars, and for a number of years was run to its full capacity, but owing to the depression in woolens for the past year or two, it has remained out of use.

On the 24th of April, 1844, a most destructive hail storm passed over the south part of the Township, destroying nearly everything in its path, killing sheep, hogs, and birds, and injuring timber, buildings, etc. One remarkable feature was, that near Mr. Osborn's was a place where the blue cranes congregated to rear their young, and hundreds of these large birds were killed by the hail, which in some instances were as large as apples, and of all shapes.

There are now in the Township three post-offices, viz: Brownsville, Calvin, and Day. The following are the principal officers that have been elected since the organization of the Township:

DATE.	SUPERVISORS.	TREASURERS.	TOWN CLERKS.
1835	Pleasant Grubb.	William T. Reed.	William T. Reed.
1836	Pleasant Grubb.	Andrew White.	J. V. Whinery.
1837	William T. Reed.	Andrew Grubb.	J. V. Whinery.
1838	William T. Reed.	Thomas O'Dell.	William Brown.
1839		Alexander White.	William Brown.
1840		Charles Dennison.	J. V. Whinery.
1841		Charles Dennison.	J. V. Whinery.
1842	John V. Whinney.	L. D. Norton.	William Brown.
1843	John V. Whinney.	L. D. Norton.	A. Northrup.
1844	Peter Shaffer.	L. D. Norton.	William Brown.
1845	Elijah Osborn.	L. D. Norton.	J. C. Blair.
1846	Jesse Hutchinson.	Findley Chess.	S. T. Read.
1847	Jesse Hutchinson.	Findley Chess.	Henry Shaffer.
1848	Sylvador T. Read.	Findley Chess.	A. E. Peck.
1849	Johnson Patrick.	William H. Jones.	A. E. Peck.
1850	Leander Osborn.	Jefferson Osborn.	A. E. Peck.
1851	Jefferson Osborn.	Jesse Hutchinson.	A. E. Peck.
1852	Jefferson Osborn.	Jesse Hutchinson.	A. E. Peck.
1853	Jefferson Osborn.	Jesse Hutchinson.	A. E. Peck.
1854	Jefferson Osborn.	B. F. Harrison.	A. E. Peck.
1855	Daniel W. Gray.	B. F. Harrison.	B. A. Tharp.
1856	Johnson Patrick.	Levi J. Reynolds.	B. A. Tharp.
1857	Elijah Osborn.	Levi J. Reynolds.	B. A. Tharp.

DATE.	SUPERVISORS.	TREASURERS.	TOWN CLERKS.
1858	B. A. Tharp.	Levi J. Reynolds.	James Oren.
1859	B. A. Tharp.	Moses Brown.	James Oren.
1860	James Oren.	Moses Brown.	Lewis Cowgill.
1861	James Oren.	William Clark.	Lewis Cowgill.
1862	B. A. Tharp.	William Clark.	John Lee.
1863	B. A. Tharp.	J. F. Lemon.	J. N. Osborn.
1864	B. A. Tharp.	Thomas J. Osborn.	J. N. Osborn.
1865	B. A. Tharp.	Thomas J. Osborn.	John Lee.
1866	B. A. Tharp.	S. S. Davis.	James Rivers.
1867	Levi J. Reynolds.	S. S. Davis.	James Rivers.
1868	Levi J. Reynolds.	S. S. Davis.	James Rivers.
1869	Levi J. Reynolds.	James Rivers.	*James Rivers.
1870	Levi J. Reynolds.	James H. Gregg.	Leroy Osborn.
1871	B. A. Tharp.	James H. Gregg.	S. K. G. Wight.
1872	B. A. Tharp.	James H. Gregg.	†A. K. Wright.
1873	Leroy Osborn.	James H. Gregg.	James Rivers.
1874	Leroy Osborn.	James H. Gregg.	James Rivers.
1875	Leroy Osborn.	John Allen.	James Rivers.

Appointed to fill vancancy. *P. Gregg. †James Rivers.

JEFFERSON.

This Township derived its name from a town of the same name in Logan County, Ohio, which was probably named after the statesman Thomas Jefferson.

The first settlement was made in the fall of 1832 by Moses Reams, Nathan Norton, Abner Tharp, William Reams and Levi Norton, all from the above named town in Logan County, Ohio.

In 1833 and '34 the following persons made settlements: Aaron Reams, Samuel Collier, Pleasant Norton. Isaac Williams, William, Maxwell and Noah Zane, Peter and Richmond Marmon, Jonathan Collier, Silas Reams and John Miller. These were nearly all the voters at the first election.

The first entries of land were made in 1830 by Stephen Marmon, Aaron Brown, Peter Marmon and

D. T. Nicholson, on section one; Nathan Norton and Maxwell and William Zane, on twelve.

In 1831 entries were made by Barnhart and Smith, on section one; R. Harmon, on two; John Petticrew and John Petticrew, Jr., on section six.

In 1832 Adam Miller, David Carmichael, John P. Miller and the four Painters made entries.

In 1833 R. Painter, E. Thomas, A. Loux, John Stephenson, John P. Miller and John Vaughn made entries.

Adam Miller, of the Baptist persuasion, was the first minister to preach in this Township.

Minna V. Hunter, afterwards Sheriff of the County, taught the first school.

The Township was organized by an act of the Territorial Legislature, approved March 29th, 1833, and an election ortlered to be held at the house ot Moses Reams. Robert Painter was the first Supervisor; William Lane, Township Clerk; Levi D. Norton, Constable, and Enoch Lundy Assessor.

In 1833 or '34, Shaffer and Beardsley built a saw mill on the site that has since been known as Redfield's mills, which, in 1837, was purchased by George Redfield, who rebuilt the mill in 1850.

In 1862 it was burned by accident and rebuilt in connection with a flouring mill in the years 1863 and 1864. There are now, besides the mills, a post-office, one general store, and the usual complement of mechanics, shops, etc.

In 1835 Robert Painter built a grist mill a short distance below where the Redfield mill now stands, and about the same time the Petticrew mill was built in the northwestern part of the Township.

The First Baptist Church of Jefferson was organized December 7th, 1843, when the following men were elected trustees: Joseph Smith, Pleasant Norton, D. T. Nicholson, William Zane and Isaac Hull. When organized, and for a number of years after, it was the most prosperous religious society in the Township, and built a substantial brick house of worship which still remains, but the membership of the society has fallen off until but a remnant is left.

The Christian Church was organized in 1855 or 1856, under the leadership of a minister by the name of Kenneston, who got up a great revival and received many converts. Under his influence a house of worship was built and is about all that remains of this once numerous society.

The Disciple Society was organized and a church built in the fall of 1854. At one time the membership reached the number of eighty, under the leadership of David Miller, who was the minister who organized the society. The church building at the the present time is valued at one thousand dollars. The society is very small and there are no regular meetings held at the church.

About the year 1858 the Town Hall was built on the southwest corner of section fifteen, and in 1871 it was moved on to the line of the Chicago and Lake Huron Railroad, thoroughly repaired, painted and underpinned, and at present is valued at seven hundred dollars. It was the first building expressly for Township purposes built in the County.

In about the year 1842 this Township was infested by a gang of counterfeiters, by the name of Button, who lived on the farm now owned by John P. Miller. The extent of their operations is not positively known, but that they followed their nefarious avocations over southwestern Michigan and northern Indiana is generally believed. There were four brothers connected in the business and it is said that they kept a horse hitched constantly at the front door to assist them in a flight when necessary. To Colonel Glenn, then Sheriff of this County, belongs the credit of breaking up the gang or at least driving them from this locality. When he went with a posse of men to arrest them one jumped on the horse at the door and made good his escape, and while the officers were in pursuit of him the others left in another direction, since which nothing is positively known, but a rumor was afterwards circulated that they all brought up in the penitentiary. But a short time ago a die for making bogus Mexican dollars was found by Mr. Rhinehart, near their former place of operations, that was undoubtedly used by them.

The Chicago and Lake Huron Railroad runs through the Township from north to south, but has no stopping place within its limits.

The Air Line Railroad passes through the northern portion of the Township and has one station —that of Dailey—where large quantites of wheat and other farm produce are shipped. It also has a store, a few mechanics, etc.

The following are the principal officers that have

been elected since the organization of the township:

DATE.	SUPERVISORS.	TREASURERS.	TOWN CLERKS.
1833	Robert Painter.	*	William Zane.
1834	Pleasant Norton.	Levi Norton.	William Zane.
1835	Pleasant Norton.	Levi Norton.	D. T. Nicholson.
1836	Pleasant Norton.	David Reams.	William Zane.
1837	Pleasant Norton.	David Reams.	William Zane.
1838	Pleasant Norton.	David Carmichael.	William Zane.
1839		David Carmichael.	William Zane.
1840		Lorenzo Painter.	William Bosley.
1841		William B. Reams.	Marcus Sherrell.
1842	Joseph Smith.	Pleasant Norton.	William Bosley.
1843	Marcus Peck.	Pleasant Norton.	Marcus Peck.
1844	Joseph Smith.	Pleasant Norton.	Marcus Sherrell.
1845	Joseph Smith.	Pleasant Norton.	Marcus Sherrell.
1846	Barton B. Duning.	P. F. Carmichael.	Robert Crawford.
1847	Joseph Smith.	Henry Carmichael.	S. L. Higinbothan.
1848	Pleasant Norton.	Henry Carmichael.	Charles Amy.
1849	Pleasant Norton.	Samuel Patrick.	Charles Amy.
1850	Pleasant Norton.	Henry Carmichael.	Charles Amy.
1851	N. Aldrich.	Henry Carmichael.	A. C. Carmichael.
1852	Pleasant Norton.	Henry Carmichael.	A. C. Carmichael.
1853	Henry W. Smith.	L. Goodrich.	A. C. Carmichael.
1854	Nathaniel Monroe.	L. Goodrick.	N. C. Beach.
1855	J. N. Marshall.	L. Goodrich.	A. C. Carmichael.
1856	J. N. Marshall.	L. Goodrich.	George Tichnor.
1857	Marcus Peck.	G. W. Westfall.	George Tichnor.
1858	Marcus Peck.	S. E. Davis.	Charles Sherrill.
1859	Joseph Hess.	Henry Carmichael.	H. C. Holden.
1860	Joseph Hess.	Henry Carmichael.	J. C. Carmichael
1861	Hiram R. Schutt.	Corkin Hays.	J. C. Carmichael.
1862	Marcus Marsh.	A. W. Zane.	J. C. Carmichael.
1863	Marcus Marsh.	N. Hedger.	J. C. Carmichael.
1864	C. S. Swan.	H. C. Shurter.	J. C. Carmichael.
1865	G. W. Westfall.	Samuel Hess.	Nathan Marr.
1866	G. W. Westfall.	H. R. Scutt.	C. L. Neff.
1867	Andrew Wood.	H. R. Scutt.	C. L. Neff.
1868	Marcus Marsh.	A. Tietsort.	C. L. Neff.
1869	S. C. Tharp.	A. Tietsort.	S. W. Breece.
1870	John S. Jacks.	A. Tietsort.	N. B. Farnsworth.
1871	John S. Jacks.	P. F. Carmichael.	S. W. Breece.
1872	John S. Jacks.	P. F. Carmichael.	S. W. Breece.
1873	S. W. Breece.	N. B. Farnsworth.	Nelson Hedger
1874	Andrew Wood.	N. B. Farnsworth.	Nelson Hedger.
1875	Andrew Wood.	S. Breece.	Nelson Hedger.

*No record of who was elected.

HOWARD.

This Township derives its name from a very romantic source. At the time of its organization, March 7th, 1834, this County, in common with Berrien, was represented in the Territorial Legislature, then held at Detroit, by one Green of Niles, and while attending this term of the Legislature he became very much interested in a young lady, then a resident of the City of the Straits, by the name of Howard, and when it came to naming the township he named it in honor of his sweetheart. But, like many of the daughters of Eve, she proved fickle to the honorable gentleman and the match was broken up, but the Township still bears her name.

The first entries of land were made in 1829 by William Garwood, on sections five and six; Jou Ray, on six; John Ritter on seven, and Thomas Philips and Samuel Witter, on section seventeen.

In 1830 entries were made by I. W. Duckett, on section five; John Kinsey, B. Jenkins and William Garwood, on six; Solomon Landis, John Hersey,

William Morris, Jacob Kinsey and Joseph Harter, on eight; R. C. Meek, Joseph Harter, William Kirk and John Pool, Jr., on seventeen; Eli Ford, on nineteen; Chester Loomis on twenty, and Orrin Green, on section twenty-nine.

In 1831 George McCoy, John Pattengill, A. Chapman, Daniel Fisher, Sarah Stoner, Peter Barnhart, John Clark and William Garwood made entries.

In 1832 entries were made by I. W. Duckett, C. Albright, Solomon Blymer, John Coulter, John McDaniel, George Fosdick, Jonas Ribble, Catherine Stewart, William Young, Jonathan Hussey, and Ezra Williams.

What is usually termed "opening soil" largely predominates in this Township, with a small portion of Pokagon Prairie on the north and a section of heavy timber in the northwest corner.

The first settlement was made on the prairie portion of the township probably previous to 1830. In 1832 "Yankee street" was settled, and in the same year George Fosdick started a blacksmith shop on the north bank of Barron Lake—then called Lake Alone—where on the 27th of August, 1835, he laid out a village under the name of Howardsville, which was composed of sixty-four lots. Mr. Fosdick, in addition to general blacksmithing, carried on the manufactory of plows, and made a specialty of jail locks, and of the latter he furnished nearly all the the prisons in Southwestern Michigan and Northern Indiana. Of this pioneer village there is now nothing to mark the spot where it once existed.

The only religious society in the township is that

of the Methodist Episcopal, organized about the year 1838, and in 1860 they erected a house of worship which is known as the Coulter Methodist Church, and now has about forty members, and a Sabbath School.

The Air Line Railroad runs through this Township east and west and has a way station at Barron Lake for the accommodation of passengers.

There is a hotel on the east side of Barron Lake for the accommodation of pleasure parties, of which there are many during the summer season from the neighboring towns and villages.

The following are the principal Township officers elected since the organization of the Township:

DATE.	SUPERVISORS.	TREASURERS.	TOWN CLERKS.
1834	Samuel Marrs.	*	Peter Fraser.
1835	George Fosdick.	*	Peter Fraser.
1836	Henry Heath.	Joseph H. Abbott.	Peter Fraser.
1837	Henry Heath.	S. Dumbolton.	Z. Smith.
1838	Thomas Glenn.	Joseph H. Abbott.	J. W. Abbott.
1839		James Coulter.	Zenas Smith.
1840		James Coulter.	A. S. Cook.
1841		James Coulter.	A. S. Cook.
1842	Ezekiel C. Smith.	James Coulter.	David M. Howell.
1843	Ezekiel C. Smith.	William H. Doane.	Richard T. Heath.
1844	James Shaw.	H. D. Gallup.	Richard T. Heath.
1845	Oscar Jones.	H. D. Gallup.	Richard T. Heath.
1846	James Shaw.	H. D. Gallup.	Richard T. Heath.
1847	J. N. Chipman.	H. D. Gallup.	Richard T. Heath.
1848	J. N. Chipman.	H. D. Gallup.	Robert N. Peebles.
1849	Oscar Jones.	H. D. Gallup.	John M. Peebles.
1850	Elam Harter.	H. D. Gallup.	Thomas H. Huston.
1851	Oscar Jones.	H. D. Gallup.	John L. Schell.
1852	E. C. Smith.	H. D. Gallup.	John L. Schell.
1853	E. C. Smith.	H. D. Gallup.	John L. Schell.
1854	Elam Harter.	H. D. Gallup.	John L. Schell.
1855	E. C. Smith.	H. D. Gallup.	Thomas H. Huston.
1856	E. C. Smith.	Perry P. Perkins.	Thomas H. Huston.
1857	Benjamin Cooper, Jr.	Perry P. Perkins.	Thomas H. Huston.
1858	Benjamin Cooper, Jr.	Perry P. Perkins.	Thomas H. Huston.
1859	William Curtis.	James G. Willard.	Thomas H. Huston.
1860	E. C. Smith.	James G. Willard.	James A. Collins.

*No record of who was elected.

DATE	SUPERVISORS.	TREASURERS.	TOWN CLERKS.
1861	William H. Doane.	Alexander Cooper.	James A. Collins.
1862	William H. Doane.	Alexander Cooper.	James A. Collins.
1863	William H. Doane.	T. C. Raridon.	James A. Collins.
1864	William H. Doane.	T. C. Raridan.	James A. Collins.
1865	William H. Doane.	Samuel Ullrey.	James A. Collins.
1866	William H. Doane.	Samuel Ullrey.	Perry P. Perkins.
1867	William H. Doane.	John Dwan.	Perry P. Perkins.
1868	William H. Doane.	John Dwan.	Perry P. Perkins.
1869	William H. Doane.	E. Blanchard.	Jacob Keller.
1870	William H. Doane.	E. Blanchard.	J. G. Van Evera.
1871	H. S. Hadsell.	Walter W. Harder.	J. G. Van Evera.
1872	H. S. Hadsell.	Walter W. Harder.	J. G. Van Evera.
1873	H. S. Hadsell.	D. P. Garberich.	John Bedford, Jr.
1874	H. S. Hadsell.	Walter H. Harder.	John Bedford, Jr.
1875	Benjamin Vary.	Elbridge T. Reed.	John Bedford, Jr.

MASON.

This Township was named in honor of Stephens T. Mason, who, at the time of its organization, was acting Governor of the Territory.

The first entry of land was made by Elam Beardsley, on section twelve, January 4th, 1830.

In 1831 C. Fanning, William Jordon and Othni Beardsley made entries, on sections 4, 11 and 21.

In 1832 Samuel Laferty, Samuel Simonton, Ezra Beardsley, O. F. Kingsley, James Griffith, R. Cathcart and Betsey Curtis made entries.

A. Dibble, S. C. Garder, S. Adams, N. D. Snow, O. Grant, Simeon O'Dell, T. J. Curtis, John Richards, A. R. Kingsley, B. Eddy, J. Allen, M. Holmes and J. Curtis made entries in different parts of the Township—in 1833.

The exact time of the first settlement I have not

been able to learn, but it probably occurred in the season of 1833 or 1834. In 1835 the following persons were here: Moses Bird, Willis Jordon, John O'Dell, Simeon O'Dell, John Richards, Thomas J. Curtis, Jacob Ross, John Miller, F. Walker Miller, J. Curtis, Sr., Saxton P. Kingsley, John Worst, Levi Grant, John Garmon, Abram Miller, Jacob B. Pells, Henry Arnold, George Arnold, E. Roberts, Benjamin Hull, Benjamin O'Dell, Orris O'Dell, James McNeil and a Mr. Halse. These, with the exception of two, were all located on the Chicago road.

The first election was held on the 5th of April, 1836. At this meeting Jonathan Curtis was chosen Moderator, and Saxton P. Kingsley, Clerk, when the following officers were elected: Moses Stafford, Supervisor; Saxton P. Kingsley, Clerk; Reuben Allen, John Worst and Jacob Haight, Assessors; John Worst, Collector; Levi Grant and Jacob Ross, Directors of the Poor; James McNeil, John Garmon and John Richards, Commissioners of Highways; John Worst and John Miller, Constables; Orlean Grant, Frederick W. Miller and Edward Howe, School Commissioners.

The first church society, so far as I could learn, was that of the Free Will Baptist, who have a house of worship and a numerous congregation in the northern part of the Township.

The United Brethren have a prosperous society in the eastern portion of the Township, and in 1875 erected a house of worship at a cost of about two thousand five hundred dollars.

The Evangelical Soeiety have a membership of

about twenty and a house of worship located on the Chicago road, erected in 1874.

The village of Kessington was laid out April 12th, 1872, by Moses McKissick, but of the extent or population I can not speak from personal observation.

The soil of this Township is divided into two varieties, that of the south is what is usually termed openings, is very level and pleasant to cnltivate, and produces remunerative crops; while a good portion of the north part is a heavy timbered soil and somewhat broken but very productive.

The Chicago road passes through nearly on the dividing line between the two varieties of soil.

Fruit growing has received considerable attention from the farmers of this Township and it probably ranks first in this production.

The following table will show who have been elected to the principal offices since its organization:

DATE.	SUPERVISORS.	TREASURERS.	TOWN CLERKS.
1836	Moses Stafford.	John Worst.	S. P. Kingsley.
1837	Moses Stafford.	Orlin Grant.	J. McNeil.
1838		C. C. Landon.	J. McNeil.
1839		C. C. Landon.	Henry Follett.
1840		Henry Follett.	A. A. Goddard.
1841	S. P. Kingsley.	Henry Follett.	Henry Follett.
1842	John S. Bement.	John Miller.	Henry Follett.
1843	John S. Bement.	John Miller.	W. W. Bird.
1844	John S. Bement.	John Miller.	W. W. Bird.
1845	George Arnold.	John Miller.	W. W. Bird.
1846	Ezra C. Hatch.	John Miller.	P Sutton.
1847	Ezra C. Hatch.	John Miller.	P. Sutton.
1848	Ezra C. Hatch.	John Miller.	William Allen.
1849	John S. Bement.	John Miller.	P. Sutton.
1850	John S. Bement.	William B. McNeil.	P. Sutton.
1851	John S. Bement.	William B. McNeil.	P. Sutton.
1852	George Arnold.	William B. McNeil.	John S. Bement.
1853	Ezra C. Hatch.	John Miller.	John S. Bement.
1854	Ezra C. Hatch.	John Miller.	John S. Bement.
1855	George Arnold.	John Miller.	John S. Bement.
1856	George Arnold.	John Miller.	John S. Bement.

DATE.	SUPERVISORS.	TREASURERS.	TOWN CLERKS.
1857	E. W. Reynolds.	James C. Meacham.	William D. Coe.
1858	E. W. Reynolds.	Joseph H. Burns.	William D. Coe.
1859	E. W. Reynolds.	O. W. Hatch.	H. C. McNeil.
1860	E. W. Reynolds.	S. B. Glines.	Anson L. Dunn.
1861	Henry Thompson.	Henry Olds.	Stephen Colby.
1862	Henry Thompson.	J. A. McNeil.	H. C. McNeil.
1863	Henry Thompson.	J. A. McNeil.	H. C. McNeil.
1864	George Arnold.	J. A. McNeil.	H. C. McNeil.
1865	W. H. Stevens.	J. A. McNeil.	William D. Coe.
1866	J. H. Graham.	J. A. McNeil.	George B. Harker.
1867	J. H. Graham.	H. C. McNeil.	George B. Harker.
1868	William Allen.	H. F. Garmon.	George B. Harker.
1869	J. H. Graham.	H. F. Garmon.	H. C. McNeil.
1870	Lewis H. Miller.	H. F. Garmon.	H. C. McNeil.
1871	Henry Thompson.	H. F. Garmon.	H. C. McNeil.
1872	Henry Thompson.	H. F. Garmon.	H. C. McNeil.
1873	J. H. Graham.	H. F. Garmon.	H. C. McNeil.
1874	J. H. Graham.	A. Dickerhoof.	H. C. McNeil.
1875	J. H. Graham.	A. Dickerhoof.	H. C. McNeil.

ONTWA.

This Township was called after an Indian girl of that name, who, for a number of years, was in the employ of Thomas H. Edwards.

The first settlement was made by Ezra Beardsley and family in the season of 1829, and in the following year George and Sylvester Meacham, George Crawford and Chester Sage came in.

The first entries of land were made in 1829 by Ezra Beardsley, on sections five, six and seven; John Hunt, on six and eight; John Silsbe, on six; Wilson Blackmer and Catherine Schartz, on eight; Sterling Adams, on twelve; George and Sylvester Meacham, on seventeen and eighteen; George Boon, on seventeen; Jacob Smith, F. Garser and G. O'Dell, on section eighteen.

In 1830 entries were made by H. Beardsley, on section one; H. H. Fowler, on two; L. Johnson, on four; John Garwood, on four, five and seven; Rogers and Chapin, on four; Henry Whiting, on five; John Silsbe, on six; Edwards, Enos and Kimball, on seven; James Gelispie, on six; Wilson Blackmer, on eight; H. Beardsley, on twelve; Joseph Pool and Dempster Beatty, on seventeen; Adam Miller, George Crawford and Philip Shintaffer, on eighteen, and N. C. Tibbitts, Jacob Smith and Jacob Grimlich, on section twenty.

Entries were made in 1831 by J. E. Scwartz, Wilson Blackmer, J. E. Hunt, R. W. Acres, J. V. Natfian, Benjamin Gates, S. Adams, C. Kennedy and J. Crimlich.

In 1832 entries were made by Andrew Spear, P. B. Dunning, Andrew Jackson, E. Beardsley, J. A. Adams and George Stevens.

In 1833 entries were made by Calvin Bishop, B. Mead, John McIntosh, N. D. Snow, George Redfield, H. Judson and A. H. Redfield.

The Township was organized in the spring of 1829, and comprised at that time nearly the half of Cass County.

The first election was held at the house of Ezra Beardsley in the spring of 1830. At this meeting John Silsbe was chosen Moderator, and the following persons were elected to the different offices: Ezra Beardsley, Supervisor; Thomas H. Edwards, Clerk; Sylvester Meacham, Othni Beardsley and John Bogart, Commissioners of Highways; John Baldwin, Othni Beardsley and George Meacham, Assessors; Jacob Smith and George Boon, Overseers of the Poor; George Meacham, Constable and Collector;

Willam Bogart, Overseer of Highways; Ezra Beardsley and John Baldwin, Pound-masters; John Silsbe, John Bogart and John Baldwin, School Trustees.

The first road was laid out on the 24th of June, 1830, and run from the Chicago road to Niles.

In the winter of 1828 and 1829 Thomas H. Edwards and Sylvester Meacham were married to a daughter and step-daughter of Ezra Beardsley and were the first to be married in the Township.

The first birth was that of Charles, son of Sylvester Meacham, and the next was that of John S. Jacks, which occurred in August, 1831.

In 1828 Thomas H. Edwards, for whom Edwardsburg was named, commenced to sell goods and was the first merchant in the County. He continued in business until he sold out to Jacob and Abiel Silver in the fall of 1831. He also had a peddling wagon that was run over the County selling dry goods and groceries, which was driven by Joseph L. Jacks.

Edwardsburg was laid out by Alexander H. Edwards, August 12th, 1831, comprising thirty-one blocks. In 1834 Abiel Silver made an addition and in 1836 Silver and Sherwood still another. At this village occurred many of the most important events in connection with the early settlement of the County. Here the observation was taken which established a base for the survey of Southwestern Michigan. Here it was that the first court was held, when it required a travel of over two hundred miles to secure men enough to act as jurymen; and the first Board of Supervisors was convened at this place. The first store was kept in a small log shanty on Lake Street. Ezra Beardsley kept the first hotel on the bank of the lake, near where the residence of Dr. Sweetland now stands.

With the advent of the Silvers, who bought Edwards' stock of goods and interest in town lots and the Beardsley homestead, everything was pushed forward that would tend toward making this an important commercial center, and from this time until 1848 the growth was steady and substantial. At that date it had three churches, a brick school house and a population of about three hundred.

But with the iron, rail which reached Niles in this year, and about the same time Elkhart, a change for the worse came over the place, merchants began to pack up and leave, trade diminished in all its branches and dullness brooded over everything. This state of affairs continued until 1871, when the scream of the steam whistle announced the approach of the iron horse, giving a new impetus to business which is increasing from year to year.

It now contains a population of four hundred and fifteen, three dry goods stores, two drug and grocery stores and one hardware store, three wagon, three blacksmith and three shoe shops, two millinery and four dress-making establishments, two hotels, two preachers, six physicians, one lawyer, three school teachers, ten carpenters and joiners, two cabinet shops, one meat market, one harness shop, four masons, one planing mill and three lumber yards. There are also three churches—the Baptist, Methodist and Congregational, and each have a parsonage. The Patrons of Husbandry have a Grange, the Odd Fellows and Masons, a lodge each. The Baptist Society at this place was organized May 14th, 1835, and Myron Strong, Luther Chapin and Barak Mead were elected Trustees. At the organization there were but four members. In 1838, under the leadership of elder Price, the society became very prosperous and for a number of years it was the most flourishing society of this denomination in Southwestern Michigan. It has at the present time but eighteen active members, a brick house of worship, valued at two thousand dollars, and a parsonage worth twelve hundred dollars.

The Methodist Episcopal Church was organized February 13th, 1837, and Hiram Rogers, Clifford Shanahan, Leonard Hain, Henry A. Chapin and Asa M. Smith were elected Trustees. It now has a membership of between thitry and forty, a brick church, valued at fifteen hundred dollars, and a parsonage, worth two thousand dollars: there is also a Sabbath school having about seventy scholars with twelve officers and teachers in connection with the church.

The Congregational Church has a brick house of worship, valued at two thousand five hundred dollars, a parsonage, worth one thousand dollars, and a membership of between sixty and seventy: they also have a Sabbath school of about fifty scholars in regular attendance throughout the year. The date of the organization of this church I could not learn.

December 3, 1874, M. Milton Edminston commenced the publication of a newspaper called the *Index*. The first issue was printed at Mishawaka, Indiana, before the arrival of the press and office material. It acquired a circulation of about four hundred copies, but was suspended September 25, 1875; the proprietor absconding with the portable effects.

William A. Shaw started the *Argus* October 3, 1875. It is neutral in politics and has a circulation of three hundred and fifty copies.

Adamsport was laid out by Sterling Adams in September, 1832, and the village of Christianna, on the opposite side of the creek, was laid out by Moses Sage in 1834. Both now are known by the name of Adamsville. The first grist mill was built here by Sage and Snow in 1834, and has remained in the hands of the Sages ever since. Sage and Snow were also the first merchants. One Halsted built the first hotel about the year 1835 and the same building still furnishes a home for the weary traveler.

Sterling Adams was the first Postmaster at this place.

There is now a population of one hundred and twenty-six, one general store, one flouring mill with four run of stone, one saw mill and heading factory, one wagon, one blacksmith and one cooper shop.

Both these villages were largely indebted to the Chicago road, which passed through them, for their early prosperity.

The following officers have been elected since

the organization of the Township to the present time:

DATE.	SUPERVISORS.	TREASURERS.	TOWN CLERKS.
1831	Ezra Beardsley.	George Meacham.	T. A. H. Edwards.
1832	Dempster Beatty.	Eber Root.	T. A. H. Edwards.
1833	Dempster Beatty.	Eber Root.	T. A. H. Edwards.
1834	Dempster Beatty.	Ariel Robertson.	Luther Chapin.
1835	George Meacham.	J. L. Jacks.	B. F. Silver.
1836	Joel Brown.	Silas Baldwin.	B. F. Silver.
1837	Joel Brown.	W. H. Vandeventer.	H. H. Coolidge.
1838	Joel Brown.	J. L. Jacks.	H. H. Coolidge.
1839		J. L. Jacks.	H. H. Coolidge.
1840		J. L. Jacks.	H. Eastman.
1841		H. A. Chapin.	George Sherwood.
1842	William Bacon.	Edwin Clark.	Myron Strong.
1843	Myron Strong.	E. Taylor.	T. T. Glenn.
1844	James W. Griffin.	Abiel Silver.	Harvey Olds.
1845	George Redfield.	Abiel Silver.	Harvey Olds.
1846	Myron Strong.	N. Aldrich.	B. D. Sherwood.
1847	Cyrus Bacon.	J. S. Brady.	B. D. Sherwood.
1848	Cyrus Bacon.	S. Van Antwerp.	E. M. Curtis.
1849	J. L. Jacks.	D. S. Kenson.	B. D. Sherwood.
1850	James W. Griffin.	William R. Sheldon.	B. D. Sherwood.
1851	N. Aldrich.	Kellogg Allen.	H. Van Atter.
1852	Cyrus Bacon.	John S. Brown.	E. Shaw.
1853	Charles Haney.	J. Silver.	S. F. Ward.
1854	Charles Haney.	J. Silver.	Isaac Brown.
1855	A. Longstreet.	Kellogg Allen.	O. M. Dunning.
1856	Charles Haney.	David Bement.	J. Silver.
1857	Aaron Lisk.	F. Wilkinson.	J. Silver.
1858	Charles Haney.	A. B. Palmer.	M. H. Lee.
1859	Charles Haney.	S. Van Antwerp.	M. H. Lee.
1860	Charles Haney.	M. B. Robbins.	L. H. Glover.
1861	Moses H. Lee.	M. B. Robbins.	C. Kennedy.
1862	Charles Haney.	John S. Jacks.	S. H. Lee.
1863	Charles Haney.	John S. Jacks.	S. H. Lee.
1864	Charles Haney.	A. S. Cook.	S. H. Lee.
1865	George F. Silver.	A. S. Cook.	George F. Silver.
1866	Charles Haney.	N. S. Brady.	George F. Silver.
1867	Charles Haney.	N. S. Brady.	J. C. Schoch.
1868	J. B. Thomas.	O. H. Sanford.	J. C. Schoch.
1869	J. B. Thomas.	George Rogers.	J. C. Schoch.
1870	J. B. Thomas.	George Rogers.	J. C. Schoch.
1871	J. B. Thomas.	George Rogers.	William K. Hopkins.
1872	J. B. Thomas.	George Rogers.	William K. Hopkins.
1873	Moses H. Lee.	J. W. Argo.	Stephen Bacon.
1874	Moses H. Lee.	J. A. Howard.	J. A. Luckenbach.
1875	Moses H. Lee.	H. H. Bidwell.	G. F. Bugbee.

MILTON.

This Township was named by Peter Truitt for a township of the same name in the State of Delaware, which was the previous home of a large number of the first settlers.

The first entries of land were made in 1829 by Oliver Drew, on section one and two; John Hudson, on eleven; Annon Smith, on thirteen and fourteen; D. Harkenrider, on fourteen; J. Hathway and John Medville, on section twenty-four.

In 1830 Hiram Rogers, Luther Chapin and Calvin Taylor made entries on section one; B. F. Larned, on six and seven; J. F. Lord, on eleven; John Hudson, on twelve and thirteen; G. O'Dell, P. Shintaffer and Adam Miller, on thirteen, and Thomas Sullivan, on section twenty-four.

In 1831 D. Brown, O. Drew, Isaac Butler, Frederick Smith, H. Drew, Smith and Burnham and Peter Truitt made entries in different parts of the Township, and in 1832 and '33 entries were made by J. H. Smith, S. Toney, P. Truitt, C. Smith, H. O.

Heath, C. K. Green, N. Bacon, B. B. Kercheral, E. Shanahan, H. Truesdail, Otis James, Adam Ringle, Silas Baldwin and A. M. Smith.

The Township was organized in 1838, previous to which it formed a part of Ontwa. The first Treasurer was William Manning and the first Clerk, H. H. Hulin.

The Milton Methodist Episcopal Church was organized July 1st, 1839, when James Lowry, Thomas Powell and Nathaniel O. Bowman were elected Trustees, and in August, 1841, it was reorganized under the name of Smith's Chapel and the following persons were elected Trustees: Spencer Williams, Jesse Smith, John H. Smith, Thomas Powell, George Smith, M. Beauchamp and Matthew Griffith. There is now a membership of between thirty and forty, and they have a house of worship, valued at about seven hundred and fifty dollars.

The Township is devoted strictly to agriculture and has neither village or postoffice within its limits.

The following are the officers that have been elected since the organization of the Township:

DATE.	SUPERVISORS.	TREASURERS.	TOWN CLERKS.
1838	*	William Manning.	H. H. Hulin.
1839		William Manning.	H. H. Hulin.
1840		James Aldrich.	James Taylor.
1841		Peter Truitt.	H. Aldrich.
1842	G. Howland.	Thomas Powell.	H. Aldrich.
1843	Job O'Dell.	Thomas Powell.	H. Aldrich.
1844	James Taylor.	Thomas Powell.	Job O'Dell.
1845	Charles P. Drew.	George Smith.	H. Aldrich.
1846	James Taylor.	Wesley Smith.	Job O'Dell.
1847	Henry Aldrich.	John Ullery.	Asa M. Smith.
1848	Henry Aldrich.	John Ullery.	Asa M. Smith.
1849	Henry Aldrich.	James B. Smith.	Wm. H. Olmstead.
1850	James Taylor.	James B. Smith.	M. C. Beauchamp.
1851	Henry Aldrich.	James B. Smith.	M. C. Beauchamp.

*No record of who was elected.

DATE.	SUPERVISORS.	TREASURERS.	TOWN CLERKS.
1852	N. O. Bowman.	John Ullery.	M. C. Beauchamp.
1853	Urial Enos.	Samuel Ullery.	M. C. Beauchamp.
1854	Urial Enos.	George Smith.	M. C. Beauchamp.
1855	Henry Aldrich.	George Smith.	M. C. Beauchamp.
1856	N. O. Bowman.	George Smith.	M. C. Beauchamp.
1857	Henry Aldrich.	George Smith.	W. H. Olmstead.
1858	R. V. Hicks.	George Smith.	William H. Powell.
1859	Henry Aldrich.	George Smith.	William H. Powell.
1860	Isaac Babcock.	George Smith.	William H. Powell.
1861	Henry Aldrich.	George Smith.	William H. Powell.
1862	Urial Enos.	N. B. Dennis.	William H. Powell.
1863	Urial Enos.	N. B. Dennis.	William H. Powell.
1864	Urial Enos.	N. B. Dennis.	W. H. Olmstead.
1865	William H. Olmstead.	James B. Smith.	J. C. Genung.
1866	William H. Olmstead.	James B. Smith.	J. C. Genung.
1867	William H. Olmstead.	James B. Smith.	William H. Powell.
1868	William H. Olmstead.	Asa Jones.	M. V. B. Dunning.
1869	William H. Olmstead.	John Barber.	M. V. B. Dunning.
1870	William H. Olmstead.	John Barber.	M. V. B. Dunning.
1871	William H. Olmstead.	John Barber.	M. V. B. Dunning.
1872	William H. Olmstead.	John Barber.	M. V. B. Dunning.
1873	R. V. Hicks.	John Barber.	C. M. Dennis.
1874	R. V. Hicks.	Charles F. Rosewarn.	C. M. Dennis.
1875	R. V. Hicks.	Charles F. Rosewarn.	C. M. Dennis.

CASSOPOLIS.

Sometime in 1830 the County seat of Cass County was located at Geneva, on the bank of Diamond Lake, by Martin C. Whitman, Hart L. Stewart and Col. Sibley, Commissioners appointed by Governor Porter.

This location gave much dissatisfaction to all speculatively inclined settlers who had secured claims which they deemed adapted for the site of the seat of Justice — and there do not appear to have been any other kind of locations taken up. The Commissioners were openly accused of corruption and the Proprietors of niggardliness. A similar state of feeling existed in Branch and St. Joseph, concerning the location of their County seats.

During this excitement and before any public buildings, save a log shanty to serve as court room and jail, had been provided, E. B. Sherman, a young lawyer and surveyor, believing that a change could and would be effected, cast about over the eligible sites still unoccupied (and they were not few) for a speculative investment.

In his peregrinations he one day came to the southeast quarter of section twenty-six in La Grange. This impressed him favorably and he repaired to the cabin of Abram Tietsort, Jr., on the bank of Stone Lake, to rest and think the matter over.

While deliberating and waiting for supper (every house was a hotel in those days and every stranger welcome) three men, brothers, by the name of Jewell, came down and engaged in conversation with Mr. Tietsort. From their talk he learned that they had been looking land and had decided to enter the eighty he had in view. Mr. Sherman kept his own counsel, and, as soon as he could do so without awakening suspicion, took his leave and started on foot for Edwardsburg.

A few days previous to this he had met at the Land Office, at Pigeon Prairie, a young legal immigrant by the name of Alexander H. Redfield, who was in search of a place to set his stakes and "grow up with the country." On the representations of Mr. Sherman he had gone on to Edwardsburg, and as this enterprise seemed large enough for a partnership he (Sherman) naturally sought to offer his new friend the first chance.

He arrived at Edwardsburg just at nightfall, readily found Mr. Redfield and unfolded his scheme. His friend eagerly fell in with the proposition, but unfortunately he was possessed of only forty dollars, Mr. Sherman could show but fifty and the land would cost one hundred; he, however, had a friend at Pigeon, who, if flush, he thought, would loan him the remaining ten dollars, and armed with a requisition upon this party, McGaffey by name, Mr. Sherman set out through the cold rain and dismal darkness in this race for a County seat.

At "Meachams" his bedraggled limbs refused further duty, but he fortunately procured the loan of a horse and pushed on into Porter. Here he stopped in a deserted cabin and, stretching his weary frame on the puncheon floor, waited for daylight.

At the first streak of dawn he was up and on his way and in the early morning rode into Pigeon, found McGaffey, negotiated the loan, made his purchase and had ridden several miles on the back track before he met the three Jewells who had gone straight across the country.

The new proprietors lost no time in pushing their enterprise. A remonstrance against the action of the Commission was prepared and the signatures of all, not interested in the success of Geneva, readily obtained; and on March 4, 1831, we find an act of the Legislative Council authorizing the appointment of a new Commission to relocate the "seats of Justice" of Cass, St. Joseph and Branch Counties, approved by the Governor.

Now came the tug of war. Eligible sites were found, by their owners, upon nearly every settler's land and all sorts of inducements prepared to bait the new Commission.

Sherman and Redfield, who had associated with

them the three land owners whose boundaries cornered with theirs, Abram Tietsort, Jr., Ephraim McLeary and Colonel Johnson, seem to have gone at the matter with so much more system and liberality than their neighbors that, upon the final arrival of the Arbitrators, their claims and those of Geneva were the only ones considered.

They prepared a plat of a village to be called Cassapolis, containing one hundred and sixty acres of land, and each of the four proprietors signed an agreement to donate to the County one-half of his portion of the same, providing the County seat should be located thereon.

Learning in advance the names of the new Commissioners they cunningly named three of the principal streets in their honor, viz: O'Keefe, Rowland and Disbrow.

These, and perhaps other inducements, then and now unknown, prevailed; the Commission reported favorably upon the change and, as soon as their fees and expenses were paid by the proprietors, a proclamation was issued by the Governor fixing the seat of Justice for Cass County at Cassapolis.

The exact date of the proclamation is not known, but it was probably in November, 1831, as the village plat was recorded on the 19th of that month, which would not be likely to have been done until the receipt of the news that a final order had been reached.

Repeated attempts were afterward made by Whitmanville, Geneva and other ambitious villages to re-open the question, but they who had secured the prize proved themselves capable of retaining it until the amount invested in public buildings precluded all further discussion of removal.

At the time the plat was recorded there was not a building of any description within its limits and, with the exception of Mr. Tietsort and Hiram Jewell, it had no neighbors within a mile and a half or two miles of its public square.

Ira B. Henderson, who built a double log cabin and opened therein a hotel, was the first to take advantage of the opportunity afforded by the new village to indulge in the excitements and turmoil of metropolitan life. John Parker came next and erected an aristocratic hewn log house on lot number three, block one south, range one east.

In the spring of 1832 Jacob Silver, of the firm of H. & B. F. Silver & Co., of Edwardsburg, and Robert Painter, came in and commenced selling goods; the former in part of Henderson's tavern and the latter in a small building at the southeast corner of the public square.

During this year Sherman and Redfield erected a large frame dwelling on the northeast side of the square; the Silvers put up what has since been known as "old red store" and Eber Root built a frame building on the site of the present Cassopolis House. These were the first permanent structures in the village.

On August 7th occurred the first death—that of J. R. Coats who was dashed against a tree by a runaway horse and instantly killed. He was buried from Henderson's tavern.

The first birth took place before the village was laid out, viz: that of Julia Ann Tietsort, on July 3, 1830.

The first court was held in the fall of 1832 by Judges Sibley and Woodbridge, under an oak tree, just south of the public square. Messrs. Redfield and Sherman were the only lawyers in attendance and no records of the business can now be found. The second term was held in Painter's store and those succeeding in the tavern building, until 1835.

The first wedding occurred on January 1st, 1833, in the loft over the new store. The high contracting parties were E. B. Sherman, Esq., and Sarah, only daughter of Jacob Silver. Bishop Chase performed the ceremony and afterward conducted the first religious services ever held in the village.

April 19th, 1833, by an act of the Territorial Council, the Cass County Academy was duly incorporated with a limited capital of twenty thousand dollars. B. Jenkins, William Burk, I. Shurte, Jacob Silver, M. B. Shields, Abiel Silver, A. H. Redfield, Dempster Beatty and E. B. Sherman were named as Trustees. This school was to have been located at Cassapolis, but there is no record that a definite site was ever secured or any portion of the capital paid in.

In the same month, a division of the lots of the plat was made by the proprietors, and the portion set out to the County formally accepted by the Board of Supervisors, who appointed A. H. Redfield their agent to sell a sufficient number, at prices varying from ten to forty dollars each, to build a jail

—the terms of payment being one-fourth down and the remaining three-fourths in six, twelve and eighteen months from the day of sale. The lots were first offered at public auction on the 4th of July and afterward at private sale.

The contract for erecting and furnishing the jail was awarded to Eber Root (the details of the building and terms of contract have been already stated on page 118 of this work). Owing to the sickness of the contractor, the building was not finished until nearly mid-winter and rogues were obliged to put up with the private hospitality of the Sheriff and his Deputies. It was located on lot number five, in block one south, range two west, where it still remains a relic of pioneer justice.

In the fall of this year (1833) the Silvers put up a large distillery in the hollow, on State Street, west of the public square. The frame was so heavy that it required the united efforts of nearly the whole male population for a circuit of ten miles to raise it. Eber Root was the contractor but, he being sick at the time, Amos Huff, of Volinia, took charge of the raising, which lasted three days. The distillery was a first-class one for those days and, by furnishing a home market for grain, materially aided the growth and prosperity of the new village. It was run by the Silvers about three years, then sold to John M. Barber who in turn transferred it to Asa Kingsbury in 1837.

A postoffice was located here in this year and was kept by A. H. Redfield in the Silvers' store.

The first school teacher was a widow Beach who

taught in a log house situated on the lot now owned and occupied by Joel Cowgill. The next was a man named Harrison. Abram Tietsort, Jr., was the first mechanic who worked in a shop. He manufactured furniture, coffins and such other cabinet-ware as the times demanded, in a log building north-east of his residence.

The village was now fairly launched on its career and soon attracted a sufficient population of traders, artisans, etc. to enable it to take a fair rank among similar frontier centres. It drew trade from La Porte Prairie on the southwest; Mottville on the southeast; Little Prairie Ronde on the northeast, and to the limit of settlements on the northwest. Goods were sold at large profits and the spring stock was usually entirely gone before the fall goods were received. Every one who attempted so to do made money, and the prospective promise of Cassapolis was as bright and hopeful as that of any town in the new Northwest.

January 24th, 1832, Eber Root and Allen Munroe received licenses as tavern-keepers from the Township Board, as, in the language of the license, "The Board considered taverns a necessity and the applicants of good moral character and of sufficient ability to keep a tavern."

The second death in the village—that of Mrs. Eber Root—occurred in this year.

In October a contract was let to Joseph Harper for building and furnishing a Court House, on lot number four, block two north, range one west, as described on page 122.

The County increased so rapidly in population and consequent litigation, that within five years its legal needs had quite outgrown the limited space afforded by this building, and in February, 1839, the Board of Commissioners decided upon the erection of a new edifice of sufficient capacity to accommodate the blind Goddess, her ministers and suppliants.

David Hopkins, Henry Jones, and James W. Griffin, County Commissioners, entered into a contract on the 7th of February, of the same year, with Jacob Silver, Alexander H. Redfield, Joseph Harper, Asa Kingsbury, and Darius Shaw, for the construction of the present Court House.

The contract called for a frame building forty-six feet wide, fifty-four feet long, and twenty-four feet between the sill and plate, with a fire-proof vault in the basement story for the use of the County Officers, on which building the contractors were to expend six thousand dollars in material and labor. In consideration thereof the Commissioners deeded to the Company "all the interest the County had in all lots, etc., (reserving therefrom the lots the present Court House and jail now stand on) in said village," and agreed to pay them, in addition to this, two thousand dollars, in two annual payments of one thousand each.

The building was enclosed and used in 1841, but was not formally accepted by the Board until March 9th, 1842.

In the Presidential campaign of 1840 the whole country run mad over "log cabins," "gold spoons," "coon skins," "British gold," and other equally meaningless party catch words. Real issues and political principles were entirely lost sight of, and partisan frenzy was rampant. Cassapolis shared the prevailing mania with her neighbors, and the most intense political excitement, and the most enthusiastic mass meetings in her history, occurred during that canvass. One advantage to the village accrued from this agitation. Joseph Harper won from Jacob Silver lot number eight, in block one north, range two east, on the result of the election in Pennsylvania, and, two years afterward, donated it to the District for school purposes.

A school house was erected upon this lot in the spring of 1843, which was the first frame building used exclusively for school purposes, and a very creditable structure for that day—previous to this time the children had been taught in log cabins, and, for a year or two, in the old Court House. This answered the purpose for which it was designed until 1857, when the Union School House, now in use, was built by Daniel S. Jones, at a cost of one thousand four hundred and ninety dollars.

In 1874 a building on the corner of Rowland and York streets was rented for a primary department. The school now occupies five rooms and employs the same number of teachers. The whole number of scholars enrolled in the District is two hundred and fifty-one.

In 1842-7 occurred the "general training" and "Kentucky Raid," previously described in these pages.

In 1848 black bears were strangely and suddenly numerous in this vicinity. Some twenty were killed in the neighborhood of the village, and one was shot within the grave-yard inclosure.

About this time the completion of the Michigan Central Railroad through the north part of the County, and that of the Lake Shore & Michigan Southern just beyond the southern boundary, put a stop to the further development of the village. Many of the more enterprising business and professional men moved to the railroad and aided largely in establishing the village of Dowagiac.

For about twenty years Cassapolis remained almost at a stand still, drawing its support from an agricultural trade of limited area, and the interest on its capital previously acquired.

In 1851 the present jail was built by Joseph Griffith, and in 1860, the Board of Supervisors, alarmed by the evidence of the insecurity of the public records, shown at the time of the burning of the old Cassapolis House, authorized the construction of a fire proof building for County offices, which was put up the same year by Major Smith.

In 1863 the village was incorporated by the Board of Supervisors, under the general State Law.

The first election was held November 9th, of that year, and the following list of officers chosen:

Joseph Smith—President.

Trustees—H. Walton, Peter Sturr, Barak Mead, C. W. Clisbee, A. Garwood, and C. G. Banks.

C. H. Kingsbury—Treasurer.

Joseph Harper—Clerk.

J. H. Powers and J. Tietsort—Assessors.

D. Histed, S. T. Read, and I. Brown—Street Commissioners.

W. K. Palmer—Marshal.

J. Graham, L. R. Read, Murray Baldwin, H. Shaffer, and Arthur Smith—Fire Wardens.

During the winter of 1874–5 a special charter was procured from the Legislature, under which the Corporation is now governed.

In 1868 the slumbering village was aroused by an early prospect of railway facilities, and has maintained a healthy growth in population and business expansion ever since.

The first iron was laid to the corporate limits by the Michigan Air Line Railway Company, November 28th, 1870, and through to Niles, January, 2d, 1871.

The first regular passenger trains commenced running on this road January 16th, 1871.

The Peninsular was not far behind. Iron was laid to the village February 9th, 1871, and regular trains, east, were started June 26th, of the same year.

Both roads have changed hands since their construction, the Air Line having been leased to the Michigan Central for ninety-nine years, and the Peninsular consolidated into the Chicago & Lake Huron Railroad.

The first religious services ever held here were conducted by Bishop Chase, of the Northwestern Episcopalian Diocese, in the winter of 1832–33, in the loft over the Silvers' new store. He was soon followed by Methodist "Circuit Riders," who, with the energy and devotion which at that time characterized their sect, were zealously pushing their way along the frontier and into the wilderness, sowing the seeds of eternal life.

A noble race of God-fearing and God-serving men were these Pioneer Itinerants. Believing themselves called to the work, they abandoned home, friends, and the ease and comforts of civilization, and, without hope of earthly reward or honor, taking their lives in their hands, they went forth in obedience to their Master's injunction, "Go ye into all the world and preach the Gospel to every creature." Did space permit, hundreds of instances of their courage and self-sacrifice might be given, but tradition has, perhaps, familiarized most of our readers with their unrecorded heroism.

They have passed away with the state of Society which called for their labors and abnegation, and their places are occupied by those who preach, according to the statement of one of their leading divines, "The Christianity required by the times."

The first definite result of their toil in this vicinity was the establishment of the Edwardsburg Circuit, in 1838, and the organization of the first Church Society in Cassapolis. No records can be found anterior to 1859, and it is impossible to give the names of the officers and membership of the Society at its inception.

Their meetings were held in the School and Court House, which they shared with the Congregationalists, Baptists and others until the completion of their various houses of worship.

In 1846 Jacob Silver and Joshua Lofland, the former an Episcopalian, the latter a Methodist, erected a Church edifice on Rowland Street for the joint use of their own denominations and, when not occupied by either of them, it was open to all for religious worship.

Mr. Silver, a short time after its completion, became a convert to the doctrines of Swedenborg, and a strong but unsuccessful effort was made to organize a Society of that sect.

In 1854 a sale was made of the building to the "United Brethren;" William Shanafelt becoming responsible to Mr. Silver for his share, and a mortgage being taken for the remainder by Mr. Lofland. No payments having been made on the mortgage and the Society exhibiting no prospect of financial success, in January, 1855, upon a proposition by Lofland to Shanafelt, the building was turned over to the Methodists as a free gift by them. The last named denomination held and occupied it until 1874 when it was moved away to make room for a better and more commodious edifice.

The new Church was built that year at a cost of about six thousand dollars, and dedicated November 22nd.

In 1861 the Society purchased a house and lot on the corner of O'Keefe and York Streets which they still hold as a parsonage.

The present Church numbers forty-eight members and the total value of its property is about eight thousand dollars. A Sunday School, composed of a superintendent, eleven teachers and about ninety scholars, is connected with it.

The following is a list of clergymen who have ministered to them since 1838—those joined in couples having served together under the circuit system: Knox and Williams, Knox and Harrison, Jones and Van Order, Meek and Tooker, Colins and Worthington, Kellogg and Eldred, Cook and Granger, Shaw and Erkenbrack, John Erkenbrack, Horace Hall, J. W, Robinson, T. H. Bignal, V. G. Boynton, Isaac Abbott, P. H. Johnson, E. L. Kellogg, G. W. Hoag, Isaac Bennett, Edgar Beard, A. G. Graham, J. Fowler, James Webster, J. P. Force, William Coplin, and J. W. H. Carlisle.

March 19th, 1842, agreeable to previous notice, a meeting of those friendly to the organization of a Presbyterian Church was held in the Court House.

The Rev. Noah M. Wells presided and delivered an address, at the conclusion of which it was "Resolved, That we proceed to organize in Cassapolis a Church, on what is termed the 'accommodation plan,' to be known as the First Presbyterian Church."

The following persons, presenting regular letters of dismissal from other Churches in good standing, were duly organized into a Church, viz: Samuel F. Anderson, Mahala Anderson, Carlos W. Baldwin, Amelia Fuller, Margaret Sears, Eliza Ann Beckwith, Hervey Bigelow, Wells Crumb, Lucy Ann Crumb and Susannah Hopkins.

After the organization the following persons were admitted upon profession of their faith, viz: Joseph

Harper, Caroline Harper, William F. Huyck and Lewis C. Curtis. Hervey Bigelow and Samuel F. Anderson were then duly elected deacons and the meeting adjourned.

On the following day Phebe Wheeler, Harriet Smith, Miss L. A. Hurlbut, Amos Fuller, Mathias Weaver and Catharine Weaver were received by letter, and William Sears, William Mansfield and Margaret A. Mansfield, on profession of faith.

November 6th, of the same year, the Church employed the Rev. A. S. Kedzie (now of Dowagiac) to labor with them for six months.

July 9th, 1843, the Rev. Alfred Bryant was engaged to minister to their spiritual wants a portion of his time.

February 3rd, 1844, Joseph Harper was chosen clerk of the Church and Society and served until June 7th, 1851 (in person or by proxy) when the present clerk, E. B. Warner, was elected.

In 1845 they commenced the erection of a house of worship, but got no farther than its enclosure that year, from lack of funds. In 1846 a Fourth of July dinner was had in the building, for the benefit of the building fund, and with this, increased subscription and the sales of pews from a schedule, they were enabled to complete and dedicate the edifice in November of that year.

June 13th, 1855, they purchased the house and lot on the corner of O'Keefe and State Street which still serves as a parsonage. The present value of their Church property is about three thousand five hundred dollars.

In 1872 the Church adopted the plan of rotary Elderships. The present Elders are S. F. Anderson, S. B. Hadden, Dr. Alonzo Garwood, George Mansfield and E. B. Warner.

The total membership since the commencement of the Church organization is two hundred and eight-four, the present list containing sixty-five names of resident members. There are one hundred and one scholars and eight teachers, exclusive of the superintendent, in the Sunday School at the present time.

There have been employed since 1842 the following clergymen, viz: A. S. Kedzie, Alfred Bryant, M. Harrison, James McLauren, M. Bacon, Thomas Jones, George C. Overhiser, Eli W. Taylor, George H. Miles, E. B. Sherwood, A. H. Gaston, Theodore B. Hascall and O. H. Barnard.

A Baptist Society was organized March 8th, 1862, by the Rev. Jacob Price, with an original membership of thirteen.

In 1868 they commenced the erection of a Church building on the east side of the public square which was dedicated March 16th, 1869. Its cost, exclusive of the lot on which it stands, was about four thousand five hundred dollars. They have as yet no parsonage. The present number of members is thirty-five.

Jacob Price, B. P. Russell and T. S. Wooden have served as pastors in charge of this Church. Mr. Wooden's engagement terminated in the spring of 1875, since which time the Rev. O. N. Fletcher has acted as supply, a portion of the time. E. H. Brooks, of the Newton Theological Seminary, has recently accepted a call and will commence his labors next June, Providence permitting.

The first Secret Society, of which there is any record, was a Lodge of the "Ancient and Honorable Order of the Eclampsus Vitus," which was instituted in the spring of 1846, with Dr. E. J. Bonine, Laban Harter, J. P. Osborn and Dr. L. Osborn as charter members.

The Order was in broadest burlesque of legitimate secret organizations and was afterward merged in the "Sons of Malta," which died from exposure (by Frank Leslie) in the next decade.

The candidates for admission were bound fast, blindfolded and dragged into the hall by halters. They were placed in the most ludicrous positions and required to pledge themselves to performances and courses of conduct which, by a cunningly devised *double entendre* in the wording of the pledges, were either impossible or eminently ridiculous.

A peculiarity of human nature, which renders the victim of a "sell" restless and unhappy until he has inveigled others into the same meshes, insured the rapid growth and financial prosperity of this monstrous hoax. Numerous neophites were found to assuage the grief and soothe the wounded pride of the earlier victims.

A grand ball was given by the Lodge in the winter of 1846–7, at the Union Hotel, at which over two hundred badges of the "Ancient and Honorable Order" were displayed, and that, too, by men who stood among the highest in popular esteem and respectability.

The (dis) Order collapsed in 1847, partly from lack of raw material and partly from a growing satiety amounting to disgust on the part of the better portion of the members, but it was successfully resurrected in 1860, under the alias of "The Brothers of Charity."

The second edition, although enlarged and improved, was of "few days and full of trouble" to all except the charter (?) members.

On the 16th day of January, 1847, a Dispensation was granted by Andrew J. Clark, Grand Master, to A. H. Redfield, George Sherwood, George B. Turner, Henry R. Close, and W. G. Beckwith, authorizing the institution of Cass County Lodge, No. 21, I. O. of O. F.

Pursuant to this the first Lodge was instituted in the ball-room of the Cassapolis Hotel, on February 18th following. The first officers were:

A. H. Redfield, N. G.

George B. Turner, V. G.

George Sherwood, Secretary.

Henry R. Close, Permanent Secretary.

W. G. Beckwith, Treasurer.

Two years afterward the Lodge purchased the south sixty feet of lot number one, block one north, range one east, of David Histed, and remodeled the second story of the building thereon for their use. In 1854 they allowed it to be sold to Henry Tietsort at Sheriff's sale, but in 1865 Mr. T. gave them a perpetual lease of the Lodge room and approaches.

At this time the Lodge numbers thirty-nine members, and is in a sound financial condition. The present officers are:

E. G. Black, N. G.
H. L. Barney, V. G.
Isaac Brown, Secretary.
C. E. Voorhis, Permanent Secretary.
John Hess, Treasurer.

The regular meetings are held on Saturday evening of each week.

May 11th, 1874, Cass Encampment, No. 74, I. O. of O. F., was organized by Fayette S. Day, G. P., with seven members. The first officers were:

R. H. Wiley, C. P.
H. H. Bidwell, H. P.
J. W. Argo, S. W.
H. Dasher, J. W.
A. P. Gaston, Scribe.
H. Tietsort, Treasurer.

The present officers are:

H. H. Bidwell, C. P.
J. W. Argo, H. P.
H. Dasher, S. W.
Charles Morgan, Scribe.
H. Teitsort, Treasurer.

Its membership is twenty-one, and regular meetings are held on the second and fourth Tuesdays of each month.

In 1848 a Division of the Sons of Temperance was organized which flourished for two or three years, but, as all records and papers were returned at its disbandment, I have been unable to obtain statistics of the extent or permanency of its work.

A Union of the Daughters' of Temperance was run in connection with the Division.

The first meeting of resident Free and Accepted Masons was held in the Union Hotel, June 12th, 1852. A petition for a dispensation to form a Lodge at this place was prepared and a preliminary organization effected.

The first officers were James M. Spencer, W. M.; Asa Kingsbury, S. W., and E. B. Sherman, J. W. The Lodge was named Backus, in honor of Grand Master Backus.

The first meeting under a dispensation was held in the Odd Fellows' Hall, July 9th, 1852, which hall they occupied until, in April, 1860, they moved into Kingsbury's Hall, where they remained until January 1st, 1876. Their present Lodge room is in Chapman's building, in the center of the brick block on the public square.

They own no real estate. The value of their regalia and appurtenances is about two hundred and fifty dollars.

Regular meetings are held on the Friday evening on or before the full of the moon of each month.

The number of members now in good standing is seventy-five. The present officers are:

Joel Cowgill, W. M.
James H. Farnum, S. W.
S. S. Chapman, J. W.
I. V. Sherman, Treasurer.
William Jones, Secretary.

W. H. Mansfield, S. D.
H. Messenger, J. D.
Robert George, Tiler.

Kingsbury Chapter, No. 78, Royal Arch Masons, was organized March 10th, 1871, and named in honor of Asa Kingsbury. The first officers were:

Isaac A. Shingledecker, H. P.
Asa Kingsbury, K.
Charles W. Clisbee, S.
James H. Farnum, C. of H.
Henry Tietsort, P. S.
George T. Shaffer, R. A. C.
Samuel Stephenson, M. 3d V.
Jonas Mechling, M. of 2d V.
Amos Smith, M. 1st V. and Secretary.
William Condon, Treasurer.
L. D. Thompkins, Guard.

The present officers are:
James H. Farnum, H. P.
Asa Kingsbury, K.
Levi J. Reynolds, S.
William J. Kelsey, C. of H.
George T. Shaffer, P. S.
Samuel Stephenson, R. A. C.
William E. Bogue, M. 3d V.
A. J. Tallerday, M. 2d V.
Henry C. Westfall, M. 1st V.
William Condon, Treasurer.
Joel Cowgill, Secretary.
L. D. Thompkins, Guard.

The present membership is twenty-four. Regular

convocations are held on the Tuesday on or after the full of the moon, in each month, at one o'clock P. M., in Masonic Hall.

A Lodge of the Independent Order of Good Templars was instituted about the year 1852 and existed several years, but no records of its transactions or history are now available. It was terminated by the absconding of its Treasurer with the Society funds.

August 15th, 1865, a second Lodge of the same Order was organized which lasted until 1869.

September 20th, 1870, a meeting was held in the dental office of James M. Shepard to take the preliminary steps in organizing a public Reading Room. Subsequent meetings were held in C. W. Clisbee's office and the Presbyterian Church, and October 14th a permanent organization was effected at the latter place, under the name of the Cassopolis Reading Room and Library Association.

Rooms were procured over Peck & Maginnis' store, periodicals and newspapers subscribed for, and the nucleus of a Library formed by private contributions and purchase.

The Society was incorporated February 11th, 1871, under an act of the Legislature, by W. W. Peck, William P. Bennett, Charles S. Wheaton, John F. Stevens, A. Garwood, A. B. Morley, A. Maginnis, H. Norton, O. Rudd, M. L. Howell, J. Tietsort, James M. Shepard, L. H. Glover and J. B. Boyd.

An Open Reading Room was maintained through the summer and fall of 1871.

March 1st, 1871, the Society secured a large hall over McIlvain's store, fitted it up with stage, scenery and seats, and have occupied it ever since.

The principal revenues of the Association have been derived from public entertainments, which are deservedly well patronized, and the regular dues of its members—no donations of money have ever been solicited or loans negotiated.

At present the Library contains over five hundred volumes carefully selected and well preserved.

The first newspaper in Cassapolis was the *Cass County Advocate*, which was started March 11th, 1845, by E. A. Graves. It was Democratic in politics. In October, 1846, it was sold to Abram Townsend, but did not prove a financial success and, in 1850, it fell into the hands of Ezekiel Smith who removed it to Dowagiac in 1851.

In 1846 one O. V. H. McKinney published a small paper called the *Literary News*. It was a scurrilous sheet devoted to petty gossip and slanderous personalities and proved to be short lived and unremunerative.

The *National Democrat* was established March 17th, 1850, by a Stock Company, with George B. Turner, editor, and H. C. Shurter, publisher. It was sold to G. S. Bouton in 1854, who transferred it to W. W. Van Antwerp, September 5th, 1854. Daniel Blackman edited it several years for Mr. Van Antwerp. In 1858 it was resold to the original Stock Company, who employed Blackman to edit and H. B. Shurter to publish it.

It was next sold by the Sheriff in 1861 to Messrs.

Norton, Howell and Smith, who transferred it to L. D. Smith, under whose management it was issued during the first two years of the war, but in March, 1863, it again fell into the hands of the stockholders, and was edited by Major Smith and published by C. C. Allison, until May 5th, when it was purchased by the latter gentleman, who has retained it ever since.

In politics it has always been all that its name imples. Its present circulation is seven hundred and twenty copies.

The CASSOPOLIS VIGILANT was started on the 16th day of May, 1872, by D. B. Harrington and M. H. Barber, On the 28th of February, 1873, it was sold to C. L. Morton and W. H. Mansfield, and in July, of the same year, Mr. Mansfield bought Morton's interest and has continued the publication ever since. The paper was enlarged from twenty-eight to thirty-two columns by Morton & Mansfield. It has always been Republican in politics, and has a circulation of seven hundred and sixty-eight copies.

The mechanical work of this book was executed at this office, and of its character I leave the reader to judge.

Asa Kingsbury opened a banking office in June, 1855, and in May, 1871, organized the First National Bank, with a capital stock of fifty thousand dollars.

The connecting vowel used in compounding the name of the village has been changed, by general consent, from *a* to *o* and the uniform spelling at present is Cassopolis. This change is of comparatively recent date—the *National Democrat* making the substitution in 1865—and is without appreciable reason, excepting, perhaps, a fancied improvement in euphonism.

There are, within the present corporate limits, about one thousand inhabitants, twenty-two business houses, handling the variety of goods, implements, etc., usually to be found in country villages, two printing offices, one planing mill, one foundry and machine shop, one wooden bowl factory, two hotels, three meat markets, and one livery stable.

The professions are represented by two clergymen, eight practicing lawyers, six physicians, and three dentists.

The amount invested in merchandise is eighty-three thousand seven hundred and fifty dollars, and the annual sales aggregate two hundred and ten thousand dollars.

Cassopolis is noted as a radical temperance town, and, during the life of the Prohibitory Law, it was one of the very few places in the State where the open sale of intoxicating liquors was persistently prevented.

Since the foregoing was in print, I have learned that a Universalist minister, by the name of George R. Brown, came to Cassapolis in the winter of 1835–6, and remained about a year, when he abandoned the charge for want of support. He would, therefore, rank as the first settled clergyman.

DOWAGIAC.

Dowagiac, located in the corners of Pokagon, Silver Creek, Wayne, and La Grange Townships, upon a small but industrious stream, from which it derives its name, is essentially a village of to-day.

Born of the Michigan Central Railroad, and nourished by an enterprising agricultural district, rarely surpassed for fertility or improvement, its growth and prosperity have been rapid and substantial.

It has had no pioneering experience to record, and no serious reverses or stand-stills. Its history is seen in its buildings and manufactories, its thronged streets, bustling traders, and busy artisans; its ample school and Church facilities, and the enterprise, public spirit, and that general young Americanism of its people, which has set the wise heads of its drowsy neighbors to nodding in prophesy of financial disasters not yet realized.

In short it is a wide-awake, go-ahead, make or break, Western burg; an honor to the County and an example deserving imitation by its elder sisters.

In 1847 Nicholas Cheeseborough, of the celebrated Morgan abduction case notoriety, was employed by the Michigan Central Railroad Company to procure the right of way from Kalamazoo to Niles.

As soon as the location of the depot sites was determined at headquarters, he associated with himself Jacob Beeson, of Niles, and together they purchased (in Mr. Beeson's name) the northeastern eighty acres in Pokagon Township and soon after had it platted in village lots.

They dealt liberally with the Railroad Company, donating a right of way through their purchase, with spacious depot grounds, a portion of which was set aside as a public park.

Soon after this Patrick Hamilton and D. McOmber, who owned the adjacent land in Silver Creek and Wayne, made additions to the plat from their farms.

The first goods kept for sale were supplies for the railroad employees, furnished by the contractors, E. H. Fettiplace and A. Kendall. A. C. Balch next brought in a small stock of groceries, for the same market, but the first assortment of general merchandise was that of E. S. & Joel H. Smith, of Cassapolis.

This firm erected a small frame building on Front street, in February, 1847, which, with the goods and business interest, was put in charge of M. T. Garvey, who may justly claim to be the pioneer trader of Dowagiac.

Joel H. Smith took up his residence here in the following November, and his brother, Ezekiel, came a year or two later. Their first building soon proving too small for the business, they put up a larger one on the adjoining lot. Isaac S. Bull bought the abandoned shell and converted it into a tavern, under the name of the Railroad House.

The first postmaster was A. C. Balch, who served but a short time, and was succeeded by M. T. Garvey. The latter was also the first resident Justice of the Peace.

The first birth in the new village was that of a son to the Civil Engineer of the Railroad Division, a Polish exile, Huliniski by name.

The proprietors of the town gave to this baby boy a village lot, the first they deeded to any person.

The first daughter born was the present Mrs. Greenleaf, *nee* Ware, who still resides here.

The first funeral was the burial of Bogue Williams, who was buried near the present site of the Union School building.

As was stated at the commencement of this chapter, Dowagiac had little or no pioneer history. From its very inception it was apparent to all that it was destined to become an important commercial point at no distant day, and business men and artisans hastened to secure suitable locations to take advantage of its assured prosperity.

Perhaps as concise a detailed description of the village in 1850 as can be given, is found in the following extracts from an historical discourse delivered by the Rev. A. S. Kedzie, at the quarter centennial anniversary of the organization of the Congregational Church, July 9th, 1875:

"How much of a village was visible to the naked eye twenty-five years ago? Beginning with the central germ of the village, there was the depot, the old passenger house, recently removed, half of it was used as a residence. Near it was the freight house, since improved. Where is the "Mineral Spring House" was a two story hotel, kept by A. J. Wares and called the "Dowagiac House." In the rear of it was a blacksmith shop kept by Parker Holmes and standing near where Mrs. Stebbins resides. On the corner where is J. T. Foster's shoe store, was the "Railroad House" kept by Isaac S. Bull; first built for a store by Joel H. Smith, who soon after built bigger on the next lot. Gilman C. Jones in company with Lybrook & Lofland who came here from Cassopolis, built and occupied a brick store on Front street near Cooper & Mosher's. This first brick building has since been burned down. The second brick building is where Marshal Henderson lives. G. W. Clark kept store on Front street. Mr. N. Bock kept hotel at his present stand. West of him on the same side of the street were seven houses, reaching up to where Horace Jones lives. Horace Mott, well-digger, had a shanty where T. T. Stebbins lives. Strawther Bowling had a shoe shop on Front street. There were two houses north of Mr. Bock's hotel. One of the earliest built houses was what was called the "Cataract House." It stood on the lots where Mr. Stoff lives—is yet standing, though divided into house and barn. It was built as a boarding house for railroad hands. In it the Postoffice was first kept and in it was the first (regular) preaching. The School house built in 1850, stood where now is the Methodist Church. It was since removed, and now stands on the lot this side of Mr. Harwood's, occupied by Mr. Parker.

* * * * * * *

The business done here in those early days may be summed up in this:—After the depot was located at this point, Ezekiel S. and Joel H. Smith, who traded at Cassopolis, established a branch store here, under the charge of Joel H. Smith. . This was the first store opened here for general trade; though Fettiplace & Kendal, builders of the Freight House, had goods in the house now occupied by Mrs. Brazier, kept chiefly for the accommodation of their hands. G. C. Jones, Lybrook & Lofland, merchants; G. W. Clark, merchant; Wells H. Atwood, merchant, being successor of Joel H. Smith; Balch & Fettiplace, grocers; Nicholas Bock, A. J. Wares and I. S. Bull kept taverns; John Rogers, Parker Holmes and Daniel Poor did the blacksmithing; Milton Hull sawed lumber; Erastus H. Spaulding run the upper one of Mr. Colby's mills, and, with Frank Spaulding, kept store near where now is the manufactory of H. Bigelow & Sons; S. Bowling had a shoe shop near where the National Bank now stands; Israel Becraft, Marvin Pond, John Parker and H. C. Hurlbeck were carpenters; Samuel Sheriden and Nicholas Johnson made shoes; Arad Balch, and after him M. T. Garvey, kept the Postoffice; Drs. Barnum, Raymond and Brayton looked after the sick in those sickly times; David Gibbs was teamster; Gideon Arnold, laborer; Mr. Kendal kept a boarding house; Charles

Wood, and after him William Bannard, were railroad agents."

In 1852 a virulent form of typhoid fever raged as an epidemic, carrying off one-thirteenth of the total population. At one time there were not well ones enough to care for the sick, or even to prepare their food, and it was necessary to send to adjacent towns for aid. Many patients were removed from the village for nursing and care, while others were too sick to be removed, or had no place within reach to which they could go. Of the thirteen first attacked, all died save two—Henry Michael and Julia Bull. Out of nearly every house some died and one entire family, (Mr. Cone's) consisting of four persons, was swept away.

This gave the locality an undesirable reputation for unhealthiness, but did not seriously check its advancement.

In 1855–6, thanks to an active agitation of the subject by Mrs. Lippincott, (Grace Greenwood), many shade trees were set out on the Park and along the principal streets, which, to-day, form the chief attractive feature in the village landscape.

In 1856 a large frame school house was built, but it was destroyed by fire in 1858 and replaced by the present brick Union School building in 1861. In 1864 a fine Ward School was added and, at present, the estimated value of school buildings, apparatus and fixtures is thirty thousand dollars. The number of scholars enrolled is five hundred and twenty, with an average attendance of four hundred and thirty.

The village was incorporated by an act of the Board of Supervisors, February 3rd, 1858.

At the first election, held at the house of Nicholas Bock, Justus Gage was chosen President; H. Bigelow, Azro Jones, J. H. Smith, D. Larzelere, A. Townsend and I. Brownell, Trustees; R. C. Dennison and E. Jewell, Assessors; H. C. Lybrook, Treasurer, D. H. Wagner; Clerk, John Letts; Street Commissioners, F. G. Larzelere, J. A. Lee, and C. B. Foster; Poundmaster, M. Amidon.

During this winter there was an epidemic of scarlet fever which proved very fatal. The same disease exhibited itself with similar results in 1870. At each of these times some thirty children died from the malady.

In January, 1863, and again in January, 1864, destructive fires swept through the business blocks on Front and Commercial streets, leaving vacancies which were speedily filled with substantial brick buildings.

Riverside Cemetery, beautifully located on a rise of ground south of the corporation, was laid out in 1872, and contains twenty-two acres. It is being rapidly improved and embellished, and compares favorably with the burial places of other corresponding villages. Its present value is about two thousand six hundred dollars.

In July, 1848, the Rev. Jacob Price preached the first sermon ever delivered in Dowagiac, in the Michigan Central Railroad freight house, which was then inclosed but unfinished. The services were held in the forenoon, and a goodly congregation, in point of numbers, assembled from the village and surrounding country.

The next religious services were conducted by the Rev. Richard C. Meek, a Methodist Circuit Rider, who preached at stated intervals in the ball-room of the Railroad House.

In the summer of 1848 a Methodist Society was organized at this place. They afterward held their meetings in common with other denominations, in the School House. The records of their early struggles are not to be found.

In 1859 they erected and dedicated their present Church building, and soon after purchased a parsonage.

The value of their property is about six thousand dollars. The present membership is one hundred and three. A Sabbath School is connected with the charge, but I have been unable to obtain its statistics.

July 9th, 1850, a Congregational Society was organized, at the residence of Patrick Hamilton, by Rev. S. S. Brown, an agent of the Connecticut Domestic Missionary Society, with twelve members.

Milton Hull and Edward Cowles were the first Deacons ordained in the Church. They worshiped in the School House and Baptist Church, until, in 1855, they commenced the erection of a Church edifice, which was dedicated in the spring of 1856. Since its organization there have been admitted to membership some two hundred and fifty persons. The present roll numbers sixty resident members. A flourishing Sabbath School, having a membership of over two hundred, is connected with the Church.

The following is a list of clergymen who have ministered to this congregation since their organization: S. S. Brown, Thomas Jones, L. F. Waldo, N. H. Barnes, T. C. Hill, T. W. Jones, H. Cherry, E. H. Rice, D. W. Comstock, E. F. Strickland, H. H. Morgan, and A. S. Kedzie.

Deacon Hull is the sole resident survivor of the original membership.

A Baptist Society was organized by the Rev. S. H. D. Vaughn in the summer of 1851. They immediately set about building a house of worship, which was completed and dedicated in the following year. At present they have no settled pastor, and I have been unable to find any records of their past transactions. They have a resident membership of about forty.

The Universalist Church Society was organized by Rev. D. P. Livermore, December 18th, 1858.

On January 5th, 1859, an election of Trustees was held, at which the following members were chosen:

D. M. Heazlitt, G. S. Wilbur, Justus Gage, J. H. Smith, John Gage, and G. C. Jones. These in turn selected as officers, D. M. Heazlitt, Chairman; Justus Gage, Clerk, and G. C. Jones, Treasurer.

Five days afterward it was resolved "to raise three thousand dollars by subscription for the purpose of building a house of worship," which was done, and the building completed the same year. The present value of the Church property is five thousand dollars.

In connection with the Church is a prosperous

Sabbath School, having seventy-five scholars in attendance. P. D. Beckwith has occupied the Superintendent's chair for ten successive years.

The following is a list of ministers employed since the organization: A. G. Hibbard, J. Straub, A. W. Bruce, Asa Countryman, H. Hersey, G. W. Harmon, J. S. Fall, and H. Slade.

Revs. Hargrave, Chaplin, Gage, and others have served as supplies during temporary vacancies. Justus Gage acted as Clerk until his death, in 1875.

The first secret society of which there is any record, was the Dowagiac Lodge, No. 57, I. O. of O. F., which was instituted September 12th, 1851, by G. B. Turner, Deputy Grand Master, assisted by H. Tietsort, A Wood, D. A. Clews, and S. V. Tietsort, of Cass County Lodge, No. 21. The charter members were J. W. Maitland, W. G. Wiley, E. Ballengee, D. H. Wagner, E. A. Allen, C. A. Mills, K. B. Miller, and M. L. Pond. The first officers were:

J. W. Maitland, N. G.
W. G. Wiley, V. G.
K. B. Miller, Secretary.
E. Ballengee, Treasurer.
D. H. Wagner, Warden.
M. L. Pond, Conductor.

The present officers are:
Thomas Henwood, N. G.
G. W. Denyes, V. G.
G. B. Crawford, Secretary.
R. Watson, Treasurer.
T. J. Rice, Permanent Secretary.

The present number of members is sixty. The Lodge owns the hall which it occupies, which, with the regalia, etc., is valued at one thousand five hundred dollars.

Olive Wreath Encampment, No. 50, was instituted April 13th, 1871, by D. G. Palmer, G. P., and F. S. Day, G. S., assisted by J. H. Hollenbeck, J. McKinney, and others, of Monitor Encampment, of Lawton. The charter members were H. Michael, B. E. Coon, R. H. Wiley, J. H. Cullom, N. B. Crawford, W. O. Van Hise, and W. H. Debolt. The first officers were:

H. Michael, C. P.
R. H. Wiley, H. P.
N. B. Crawford, S. W.
J. H. Cullom, Scribe.
W. O. Van Hise, Treasurer.
B. E. Coon, J. W.
W. H. Debolt, J. S.

The present officers are:

C. H. Brownell, C. P.
T. J. Rice, H. P.
A. E. Bacon, S. W.
H. Michael, Scribe.
R. Watson, Treasurer.
H. W. Snider, J. W.
W. W. Bates, J. S.

The present membership is twenty-two. The meetings are held in the Subordinate Lodge room.

Dowagiac Lodge, No. 10, F. and A. M., was organized January 11th, 1855, with the following officers:

A. M. Worden, M.
George Shrackenhast, S. W.
E. H. Foster, J. W.
D. H. Wagner, Secretary.
S. M. Spencer, Treasurer.
—— Dickson, S. D.
P. B. Holmes, J. D.
No Tiler elected.

The number of members at the time of organization cannot be ascertained. The officers for 1875 were:

A. H. Mason, M.
D. McOmber, S. W.
Thomas Keatley, J. W.
S. C. Doolittle, S. D.
M. S. Snyder, J. D.
Enos Chappell, Secretary.
C. B. Northrup, Tiler.

The present membership is between eighty and ninety. They rent a lodge room.

Key Stone Chapter, No. 36, R. A. M., was organized, under a Dispensation, November 12th, 1864, with

I. A. Shingledecker, H. P.
James M. Spencer, K.
Hubbell Warner, Scribe.
A. N. Alward, C. H.
Henry Tietsort, P. S.
William Houser, R. A C.
Joel Andrews, M. 3rd V.
D. C. Marsh, M. 2nd V.
H. C. Parker, M. 1st V.
A. N. Alward, Sentinel.

The first regular meeting, under a charter, was in February, 1865. The present officers are:

D. W. Clemmer, H. P.

Arthur Smith, K.

Thomas Rix, Scribe.

A. H. Mason, Treasurer.

Charles Starrett, C. H.

O. M. Sherwood, P. S.

T. J. Edwards, R. A. C.

C. L. Sherwood, M. 3rd V.

E. O. Adams, M. 2nd V.

D. Henderson, M. 1st V.

L. S. Henderson, Sentinel.

The present membership is fifty-six and, in common with the Peninsular Lodge, they own property to the amount of four thousand dollars.

Peninsular Lodge, No. 214, F. and A. M., was organized November 19th, 1866, with ten charter members. The first officers were:

Arthur Smith, M.

E. O. Adams, S. W.

Thomas Shidler, J. W.

Ambrose Thomas, Treasurer.

Charles Fletcher, Secretary.

D. W. Clemmer, S. D.

C. R. Miller, J. D.

A. H. Reed, Tiler.

The present officers are:

O. M. Sherwood, M.

T. J. Edwards, S. W.

S. H. Lee, J. W.

D. W. Clemmer, Treasurer.

B. L. Dewey, Secretary.

John Crawford, S. D.

E. Gale, J. D.

L. S. Henderson, Tiler.

With a membership of sixty-eight.

Dowagiac Council, No. 28, was organized January 17th, 1870, with

Rev. J. Boyinton, T. I. G. M.

E. T. Avery, Deputy T. I. G. M.

D. W. Clemmer, P. C. O. W.

R. C. Osborn, Treasurer.

C. L. Sherwood, Recorder.

George Miller, C. O. G.

Charles Starrett, C. O. W.

A. H. Reed, Sentinel.

They now have twenty-nine members.

The Ladies' Library Association was organized in April, 1872. It is a chartered corporation of about two hundred members, has a well furnished room, which is open one day in each week. The library contains about six hundred volumes, valued at two thousand dollars. The books are freely used by the members, but a rental of ten cents per week is charged to outsiders. The membership fee is one dollar, and annual tax the same.

The officers are appointed by a Board of Directors, who, in turn, are elected by the Association for three years. The present officers are:

Mrs. Willis Farr, President.

Mrs. F. J. Atwell, Vice President.

Mrs. C. J. Greenleaf, Secretary.

Mrs. C. L. Sherwood, Treasurer.

Some of the leading business enterprises of Dowagiac are deserving of more than a passing mention. Conspicuous among these is the Stove and Seed Drill Manufactory of P. D. Beckwith.

In 1854 Mr. Beckwith bought out a small machine shop and furnace of one Davis, which he enlarged into a general jobbing shop and operated it so successfully that, four years afterward, he was able to build a new one, on the bank of the creek. Here he commenced the manufacture of the "Roller Drill."

To John S. Gage, of Wayne, belongs the credit of the invention of this very popular agricultural implement. It was suggested to him by hearing an Englishman explain the process, in use in some parts of England, of dibbling in wheat by hand, which method largely increased the yield.

Mr. Gage, readily comprehending the advantage of this manner of planting, set his wits to work to devise a machine that should accomplish the same thing. The result is the Roller Drill "consisting of a series of V shaped rollers, that make a furrow in which the wheat is planted, followed by a series of followers that cover the grain."

Mr. Beckwith has materially improved it in many parts until it is as nearly perfect as any machinery now used on the farm. One hundred have been manufactured annually for a number of years and may be found in every wheat growing State in the Union.

It is the only drill of like character manufactured in the United States and, strange to say, the patent upon which it is based has never been infringed.

In 1867 the present commodious establishment was completed, and Mr. Beckwith added to his business the manufacture of heavy iron heating stoves of his own invention which are growing in popularity and rapidly coming into general use.

The Basket Factory of Jones, Gibbs & Co. is a mammoth institution of its kind, employing from thirty to forty hands. They make use of forty-seven separate patents in the manufacture of stave baskets.

Colby's Mills ship over twenty thousand barrels of flour annually to non-wheat growing regions, and, with several other business features of the village, might be profitably described at length did space permit.

The Shoe Drill Works occupy the shop on the creek formerly owned by Mr. Beckwith. The works are superintended by Mr. Tuttle, the patentee of this popular drill. The firm of Warner & Tuttle also manufacture Cullom's plaster sower and do a general jobbing business.

In 1856 H. B. Denman opened the first banking office in the village, and in 1865 organized the present First National Bank, with a capital stock of fifty thousand dollars. He remained until 1869, when a controlling interest in the last named institution was purchased by the Lyle Brothers and others, who are its present managers.

C. T. Lee commenced to do a brokerage business in 1867, and in November, 1875, opened an exchange bank, in one of the most elegant banking rooms to be found in the State.

Below will be found a partial statement of the mercantile business for last year. Some lines are omitted at the request of parties interested, and some from the lack of trustworthy statistics:

	AMT. INVESTED.	AMT. OF SALES.
Dry Goods and Clothing,	$75,000	$203,000
Hardware,	27,000	66,000
Drugs,	11,000	24,000
Groceries,	22,800	107,000
Boots and Shoes,	16,000	52,000
Furniture,	19,500	28,500
Photograph Gallery,	1,500	3,000
Colby's Mills,	50,000	175,000
Basket Factory,	45,000	———
Planing Mills,	13,000	15,000
Saw-Mill and Handle Factory,	7,000	4,800
Marble Yard,	3,500	15,000
Livery Stables,	6,000	———
Stove and Drill Works,	———	———
Drill and Plaster Sower Works,	———	———

AGRICULTURAL SOCIETY.

This Society was organized in 1850 or 1851, the exact date of which I have been unable to determine as the records of its early doings are not to be found. The second annual meeting, according to the *National Democrat*, was held in Cassopolis, March 1st, 1852. At this meeting Justus Gage was elected President; Joseph Smith, Treasurer; G. B. Turner, Secretary, and D. M. Howell, Corresponding Secretary.

For a number of years they held fairs on Samuel Graham's land, and in 1857 bought of Andrew Woods ten acres of land for a fair ground where the Air Line depot now stands. With the advent of the Peninsular Railroad, which ran through the grounds, a sale became necessary, the purchaser being S. T. Read. A new ground was bought of C. H. Kingsbury, since known as the Chicago property, but they had hardly got settled in their new quarters when the Air Line Railroad came through necessitating another change, and in May, 1871, they bought the present tract of twenty acres of land for three thousand dollars, of Samuel Graham.

The changes have been a sad detriment to the financial condition of the Society, as they were each time made at a loss, and a consequent depression that almost invariably follows anything that gets on the downward grade, however meritorious it may be of itself or important to the general welfare of the public. The grounds and buildings are valued at four thousand dollars. The present officers are: J. Boyd Thomas, President; Hiram Hadsell, Treasurer, and Charles L. Morton, Secretary, with a director from each Township in the County.

CASS COUNTY IN THE WAR.

The first company raised for the suppression of the rebellion was organized on the 18th day of May, 1861, at Dowagiac, and was the twenty-seventh company organized in the State. It was composed of one hundred men, with the following officers: D. McOmber, Captain; William R. S. Townsend, First Lieutenant; N. H. De Foe, Second Lieutenant: and Luman Roberts, Orderly Sergeant. They remained in Barracks at Dowagiac six weeks, and were assigned to the Fourth Regiment of Infantry, then organizing at Adrain, but soon after were changed to the Sixth Regiment, and ordered to report at Kalamazoo; and immediately afterward the privates were ordered to disband and the officers be sent to a military school at Detroit.

Both these orders the company protested against, and sent R. C. Dennison and Lieutenant Townsend to Governor Blair to get him to recind them, which was of no avail.

At the start the company was enlisted for three months, but when informed that no more men were wanted for that length of time, every man put his name down for three years.

When the Governor refused to grant their petition, they in turn refused to comply with his requirements, and were disbanded, with the understanding that they should come together at the call of their officers.

About the middle of June, the officers made an arrangement for the acceptance of the company into the Douglas Brigade, then forming at Chicago, when they were called together, and by a unanimous vote resolved to go. Upon an application to the Governor they were refused transportation, but the citizens clubbed together and furnished teams and wagons by which the boys were carried to Berrien Springs, from whence they were transported in boats.

On their arrival at Chicago, they found neither regiment or brigade, but a full line of officers that were working to get a regiment accepted, who informed them that they could stay at the public expense or go home, subject to call, and it being near haying and harvesting, after remaining three days, they returned home.

Immediately after the first Bull Run defeat, the Douglas Brigade was accepted, and the company called together and mustered into the United States service at Dowagiac on the 26th of July, by Captain Webb, United States mustering officer, as Company E of the Forty-second Regiment of Illinois Volunteers, and went to Chicago the same evening, where they remained ten weeks, during which time McOmber, through the intrigue of Townsend, was superseded by D. W. Norton, of Chicago, as Captain.

From Chicago the Company went to St. Louis and joined Fremont's army, and took part in his Springfield campaign.

In the spring of 1862, they took part in the capture of Island Number Ten. From thence they went to Corinth and Covington, under Grant, and participated in the battle of Chickamauga, where they lost a number of their men. They also participated in the siege of Chattanooga, Lookout Mountain, Mission Ridge, and from thence to Knoxville, under Sherman, where they re-enlisted as veterans.

In 1864 they went through to Atlanta with Sherman, and returned to Nashville under Thomas, and participated in the battle of that place.

In 1865 they went to Texas and remained until disbanded.

Among those that arose from the ranks to that of commissioned officers were: E. Hurson, to First Lieutentant; William Clark, to the same rank; Leonard Norton, to that of Captain; William H. Colburn, to the same; and Charles Munger, to that of First Lieutenant.

I have followed this Company somewhat in detail through its various campaigns, to give some general idea of the part they took in the war, and as the experiences of the others were much the same, and the limited space I have to devote to the subject, is the only apology for not treating them all in full.

The next Company was that of D, in the Michigan Sixth, organized at Dowagiac, with Charles E. Clark as Captain; Frederick Clark and James Ellis, First and Second Lieutenants, and William H. Gage, Orderly Sergeant. Of these Captain Clark arose to the position of Colonel; Ellis to Captain, and Gage to Lieutenant. Frederick Clark was killed on the Mississippi River at Port Hudson, and W. W. McIlvain was promoted from the position of Corporal to the rank of First Lieutenant. At the time of organization the officers of the regiment were sent to Detroit to a military school where they remained under instruction six weeks.

In August, 1861, the regiment was sent to Baltimore and remained six months guarding the city; from thence they went to Virginia where they remained but a short time, and then were sent to Ship Island, in the Gulf of Mexico, where they were drilled thirty days. Their first active service was in taking the forts at the mouth of the Mississippi River, and to this regiment belongs the credit of escorting the National colors into New Orleans. From this point they went to Baton Rouge, from thence to Vicksburg and re-enlisted as veterans at Port Hudson. They remained in the South during the entire war and were sent back to Kalamazoo to disband.

The third was Company A, of the Michigan Twelfth, organized at Niles, with Joseph Harper as Captain; William Van Riper and M. M. McClellen, First and Second Lieutenants, in the spring of 1862.

Their first move was to Pittsburg Landing, from thence to Boliver, Tenn., where they were employed in guarding the railroad for some time, then they were sent to Vicksburg, after its surrender, and from thence to Arkansas, where they stayed through the remainder of the war. Among those that arose from the ranks to that of commissioned officers from this County, were William Stevens and Robert Fox.

Company M, of Michigan First Cavalry, organized at Detroit, by Colonel Broadhead, went from this County with R. C. Dennison, Captain; Charles Sprague and William M. Heazlitt, First and Second Lieutenants, and D. W. Clemmer, Orderly Sergeant. William M. Heazlitt was promoted to the position of Major, as was also D. W. Clemmer; S. G. Morse to that of Second Lieutenant, and was killed at the second Bull Run; R. N. Van Atter to Second Lieutenant; Albert Vincent to the same rank, and died in prison at Andersonville; P. T. Bently to the same rank, and was killed at Thoroughfare Gap; James McElheney to the same rank, and was killed at Gettysburg; John H. Simmons to the rank of First Lieutenant, and the following to that of Second Lieutenants: L. C. Roberts, L. D. T. Poor, H. B. Babcock and C. B. Bateman. The regiment served nearly through the entire war in Virginia, and at the close was sent to Texas.

Company A, of the Ninth Michigan, which was organized at Dowagiac in Septemper, 1862, with Joel H. Smith as Captain; George Shaffer, First and Reuben Larzelere, Second Lieutenants, and I. Z.

Edwards, Orderly Sergeant. Their first war experience was at Gravel Pit, on the Ohio River, where the regiment was stationed to protect the country from Morgan's raids, which, at that time, were becoming too numerous for the comfort of the inhabitants.

From here they went to Covington Ky., where they were brigaded with Indiana and Wisconsin troops, and immediately marched into the interior, arriving at Lexington in the latter part of the year. In January, 1863, they were ordered to Nashville, Tennessee, where they were re-armed with Enfield rifles. The regiment remained in Tennessee until Sherman's celebrated "march to the sea," in which they participated. George Shaffer was promoted from a Lieutenant to that of Colonel, and I. Z. Edwards, H. J. Ohls, William Kirkwood and William Slipper, to that of Second Lieutenant.

About one-half of Company M, of the Fourth Michigan Cavalry, was raised in this County, under Captain Plimpton, of Niles, and Lieutenant Beals, of Dowagiac. The laurels this regiment won, in the capture of Jeff. Davis, will be remembered as long as the memory of the rebellion lasts, and to the credit of Cass County, it is to be said, that some of her men participated in the actual capture.

Company L of the Ninth Michigan Cavalry, organized at Coldwater, was made up largely of Cass County men, under Captain George Miller, Lieutenants E. M. Watson and I. B. Riford, and William Butler, Orderly Sergeant. Watson arose to the rank of Captain, and was killed at Resacka, Henry

L. Barney from First Duty Sergeant to that of Lieutenant of Company C of the One Hundred and Seventeenth Regiment U. S. C. T., and commanded Company K from its organization, in September, 1864, until the 1st of January, 1865, when he was placed on the staff of General Weitzel, of the Twenty-fifth Army Corps, where he remained until the 8th of July, when he resigned and came home.

Besides the companies mentioned, which were raised wholly or in part in this County, many men enlisted in companies out of the County and State. Among them were many in the Third Michigan Cavalry, in which Moral Wills arose to the rank of Lieutenant.

Company I, of U. S. Sharpshooters, had about twenty-five men from this County, from which W. H. George was promoted to the rank of Major and C. W. Thorp to a Lieutenancy.

Samuel Ingling received a silver medal as the best marksman in the Regiment, and a gold medal for the best string shooting in the Bridage. The silver medal was struck by a buckshot, while in his fob pocket, and saved his life.

These comprise all the regular companies organized in the County, but, as before stated, many men enlisted outside the limits, of which there is no available record, and, consequently, no credit can be given to the County. In order to get the information as correct as possible I made application to the Adjutant General's office, at Detroit, for the required data, but was informed that their books did not show the part each county performed in this important contest, and the sole reliance was on such information as could be gained from the participants. If any have been overlooked, or not given proper credit, it is from a want of proper information and not intentional.

It is estimated upon good authority, that this County furnished at least five hundred men, and had they all been enlisted at home, and a proper credit given, no draft to fill vacancies would have been necessary.

PIONEER BIOGRAPHY.

UZZIEL PUTNAM, Sr.

Uzziel Putnam, Sr., the first white settler of Cass County, was born in Wardsborough, Vermont, March 17th, 1793, when three years old his parents moved to Oneida County, New York, and again in five years afterward moved to New Salem, Massachusetts, where they remained until 1806, when they removed back to Jefferson County, New York.

In the fall of 1811 they came to Detroit, where they remained during the winter of 1811 and 1812, in the spring going to what is now Sandusky City, Ohio. On the 19th of October, 1812, young Putnam entered the United States service as teamster, enlisting for three months, but continued in the service until after the defeat of General Winchester, when he was discharged and paid. He afterward received a land warrant in addition for his services.

In 1822 he was married to Anna Chapman, of Sandusky County, Ohio, and on the 7th day of May, 1825, started for Michigan in company with Abram Townsend and Israel Markam.

Putnam obtained his first information of the St. Joseph Country from an Indian trader, named Parker, who had been here previous, but having some trouble with the Indians, had to leave. They followed up the Sandusky River to the mouth of Nigger Creek, from thence they crossed over the country to the St. Mary's River, which, at this time, was very high from long continued rains making it impossible to proceed farther with the loaded team. A council was held and they determined to build a boat, which was done by the party with the assistance of an Indian, the material used was elm bark, when completed and launched on the river, it was loaded with all the luggage of the wagon, except what was absolutely necessary for the use of the family, and floated down the river to Fort Wayne, by Townsend and Markam, while Putnam and family came on with the team, arriving some time after the boatmen.

Owing to bad roads the oxen had become foot-sore and a rest was made necessary. While the other two took the boat and went down the Maumee to Toledo, and from thence home, Putnam went to work to earn another yoke of cattle, which he had accomplished on the 9th of August. Not hearing anything from his companions since their leaving he determined to push out alone, but had proceeded only about one mile when he was overtaken by Townsend. The two came on together to Covert's Creek, in the south part of this County, where they cut and put up thirty tons of hay. While Putnam returned to Fort Wayne for his family, Townsend came on to Pokagon and cut twenty tons more hay.

On the 25th of October Putnam and family had got back as far as Covert's Creek, where he camped all night, on getting up from breakfast next morning not an ox could be seen, and for five days he searched the woods but no trace of the straying cattle could be found. On the 2nd of November he started back having previously sent word to Kirk to come and get his family. When within twenty-five miles of Fort Wayne he found his cattle, and not liking to lose his time he bought another wagon and loaded it with sixteen bushels of corn, a barrel of flour, a large iron kettle, and when ready to start Judge Hanna induced him to take in addition about three hundred pounds of Indian goods to Coquillard, at South Bend. On getting back to Covert's Creek he found their hay all burned except one stack of about four tons. The next day he arrived at Kirk's, where his family were staying, and on the 22nd of November he moved on to his land in Pokagon, where he has resided ever since.

His first cabin was built of small poles and covered with bark, in which he lived until the following January, by which time he had completed a cabin of more comfortable dimensions. The first work on arriving was to fence in the hay to protect it from the stock, and the next to build the cabin referred too. Markam remained and assisted in the work about two weeks, when he left for Ypsilanti on a trapping tour. At this time there was no trail, nor anything to mark the way in that direction, but on consulting with an Indian as to the route he received a correct chart on a piece of elm bark, which he was enabled to follow through the trackless wilderness.

When Mr. Putnam left Kirk's for his new home he bought of John Lybrook a hog weighing one hundred and eleven pounds, which was the principal meat for the winter Hominy was the leading article of diet, a part of which was pounded in an iron mortar. During the first winter one of the oxen bought at Fort Wayne died, furnishing an ample supply of wolf bait, and thirteen of these animals were captured, by Putnam and Baldwin Jenkins.

In the spring work commenced in good earnest; about the middle of March a young man named Duckett arrived from Ohio and was employed to assist in opening up the new farm. On the 2nd day of April they commenced making rails, and in one month had forty acres of land fenced and the breaking plow started. On the 14th of May they commenced putting in the crop of corn by dropping in every third furrow. The plow share was sharpened on a small grind stone which had been brought along, as there was no blacksmith nearer than Fort Wayne, except at the Mission, and this institution turned rather a cold shoulder on all settlers coming in, the accommodations they received were not the most cordial, although Mr. Putnam bought of them, the first spring after coming in, two sides of bacon, at eight cents per pound, and four bushels of potatoes, one half of which were small for seed, from which he raised a good crop, and, as he jovially remarks, "We have had potatoes ever since." Their corn crop also proved a good one, yielding about forty bushels per acre.

Mr. Putnam and wife still reside on the old homestead, in the enjoyment of all their faculties, having long since passed the age allotted to man. Many incidents of an interesting character could be related, in connection with their early life, did space permit. Uzziel Putnam, Jr., the first white child born in the County, is their son, he has represented the County in the State Legislature, and filled many other responsible positions.

WILLIAM BALDWIN JENKINS.

William Baldwin Jenkins was born in Greene County, Pennsylvania, October 4th, 1783. In the year 1799 his father moved from Pennsylvania to the Cumberland Valley, Tennessee, settling on Stone River, near the present site of Murfreesboro. His mother died on the route and was buried at Crabapple Orchard, Kentucky.

Leaving his family, consisting of four sons, of whom Baldwin (the subject of this sketch) was the oldest, and one daughter, he returned to Pennsylvania on business, and remained all winter. During his absence his sons killed, and assisted in killing, fifty-two bears, in which the country greatly abounded.

From here the family again emigrated, in 1804, to Greene County, Ohio, settling where New Burlington now stands, the father dying there in 1808.

In 1812 Baldwin visited his birth place, in Pennsylvania, where he married Mary Hackney, and, returning to Ohio, cleared up a large farm in the heavy timber, and built a saw mill and flouring mill. Having heard from the Indian traders glowing accounts of the St. Joseph Valley, he determined to explore this region.

In the fall of 1823, in company with five others, he started on the trip. On their arrival at the trading post at Fort Wayne, his companions declined to go any farther into the unbroken wilderness. Taking a pack of provisions on his back, a blanket and shot-gun, (the latter for the purpose of kindling fires more than anything else) he started alone, taking the direction of the Wabash River, and, following it down to a trading post, where the present city of La Fayette stands.

Retracing his steps to a French trading post, on the present site of Logansport, he struck north toward the St. Joseph River, coming to it where South Bend now stands, and following down the south bank to Carey Mission, one mile west of the present city of Niles. After exploring the southeastern portion of Berrien and the western portion of Cass Counties, he returned up the St. Joseph River to the mouth of the Elkhart, then following the course of that stream some distance, he took a southeasterly direction to Fort Wayne, and from thence back home.

In the spring of 1825, in company with Benjamin Potter and wife, (the latter a niece of Mrs. Jenkins) he set out for the new country. After many drawbacks and hindrences, without track or bridge, they arrived near the site of the present city of Niles,

Mr. Potter settling one mile north on the road to Sumnerville.

Mr. Jenkins succeeded in putting in a small patch of corn, on what was then known as the old Indian fields, his only implement being a hoe. After getting in his corn, he, in company with a man named Coon, started down the St. Joseph River in a canoe to ascertain the navigability of the stream. Arriving at the mouth on the 3d of July, they celebrated the 4th by catching an abundance of fish. During the season he cultivated his patch of corn and cut a quantity of marsh hay, on the present site of Niles, near where the Central Railroad depot stands.

In the fall he returned to Ohio, rented his property, and on the first day of November, with his family, (wife and nine children) he started for the St. Joseph Valley. His equipment consisted of thirty-six head of cattle, including three yoke of working oxen, five fat hogs, a wagon, household goods, etc. On the 10th they arrived at Fort Wayne, where he laid in an extra supply of provisions, and pushed on, arriving at Wolf Lake on the 16th.

On the night of their arrival at this place, the snow fell to the depth of ten inches, in consequence of which, in the morning, Mrs. Jenkins got into the wagon to ride, for the first time since starting—she insisting upon walking that more of the necessary articles for their wilderness home might be transported.

Crossing the St. Joseph, where Elkhart now stands, they arrived at Squire Thompson's on the 18th, and on the next day reached Mr. Potter's;

and on the 22d day of November, arrived at their future home, in Pokagon, a short distance north of Sumnerville, going into an Indian wigwam, where they lived the first winter. This was the second white family within the present limits of Cass County, and had it not been for the Indian ponies destroying his corn, which obliged him to stop and harvest it, would have been the first—Mr. Putnam coming only two days before. At this time there were but nine white families (except the Mission) within the limits of Cass and Berrien Counties, two in the former and seven in the latter, comprising a population of about sixty persons. The nearest settlement was Fort Wayne, Indiana, distant one hundred miles.

The hay which Mr. Jenkins had made in the summer, was burned by the Indians while he was gone for his family, leaving nothing on which to winter his cattle, but meeting one of the Markam's, who wished to move out in the spring, he made an arrangement with him to take his work cattle back to Ohio and winter them, using them to come back with in the spring. For the remainder of his stock he succeeded in getting some hay of Mr. Putnam, and, by felling timber for them to browse on, the most of them lived through the winter, but were so thin in the spring that they could hardly stand alone.

The effect of poor keeping seriously retarded the spring's work, the cattle being in such weak condition that nothing could be done until grass came in sufficient quantity for them to live upon, and even then it was necessary for the settlers to double teams to do the work, consequently but half the amount of land could be brought under cultivation in the season that they would have been enabled to if their teams had been well fed.

During the first winter, Mr. Jenkins carried all the grain for their breadstuff on his back to the Mission, a distance of nine miles, and ground it on a hand mill, with the exception of what was pounded at home in a wooden mortar. Part of the time the snow was two feet deep, without a broken path, and required two days to make the trip.

After the first year they succeeded finely, the incoming immigration furnishing a ready home market for their surplus productions. Mr. Jenkins' house was a synonym for hospitality of almost worldwide reputation, nearly every settler coming in making it a temporary stopping place while looking at the country; and after the country became somewhat settled, their market being at the mouth of the river, and his house at the only bridge on the Dowagiac Creek, it became a general stopping place. Many times the barn-yard would be filled with wagons and the barn with teams, for which he would not receive any compensation except the gratitude of his guests, which, to a generous heart like his, was ample.

Mr. Jenkins was a man of uncommon intellectual power, though his abilities had never been cultivated by any systematic training. He had a most remarkable memory, and was perfectly at home on almost any local historical subject that could be mentioned. He kept a complete diary of events in his mind, and could at any time recall the state of the weather and the work which had occupied his time on the day of the month, five, ten, or twenty years previous. He could tell the name and age of every man, woman and child in the neighborhood. He was the first Justice of the Peace in Cass County and one of the first County Judges, appointed under the Territorial law. He was a member of the Convention that framed the first State Constitution. He owned large tracts of land in Cass and Berrien Counties, and, for a man of his generous disposition, accumulated and left to his children a goodly competence. He died at the house of his daughter (Mrs. Isaac Murphy) in Berrien Center, in 1847, respected and mourned by every one that knew him.

Of his family one son lives in Oregon; one son and two daughters in Berrien County, and his oldest son John lives in Jasper County, Indiana, to whom I am indebted for the foregoing sketch of his father and many other incidents in connection with the early history of the western part of Cass County.

SQUIRE THOMPSON.

Squire Thompson was the pioneer farmer of the St. Joseph Valley, a Virginian by birth, but for a number of years previous to coming to Michigan a resident of Ohio. He came to Michigan in 1823 and chose a location on the St. Joseph River, a short distance above Niles, and put out a crop of corn in the spring of that year.

While preparing to plant his crop he was visited by a number of Indians who were undoubtedly instigated by the people of the Mission, who were unfriendly toward any farther settlement by white people. The Indians tried to intimidate him by telling him that they did not wish him to plant corn, as their ponies would break over and destroy it, which would make trouble. Mr. Thompson, after some parley, in which the various treaties by which the Indians had ceded the lands was discussed, coolly told them that he "would raise corn or die." At this they gave a grunt and saying "much brave," paddled across the river in their canoes.

In the fall he returned to Ohio for his family and on his return found that his crop had been destroyed by some evil disposed Indians. Such a man, however, was not easily discouraged. He soon built a cabin for his family, consisting of a wife and two children, and brought food for the winter from Indiana. In the spring of 1826 he moved to this County, settling north of Sumnerville, where he lived until he moved to California, where he died in 1850, in the sixty-sixth year of his age.

JOHN LYBROOK.

John Lybrook was born in Giles County, Virginia, in October, 1798. In 1811 his parents moved to Preble County, Ohio, where John remained until 1823, when he came to Michigan, arriving in December. He came to assist Squire Thompson in moving, and, when first starting, only intended to go fifty or sixty miles, or until he was fairly on the way, but as circumstances seemed to demand his assistance the entire distance, he came along, and then assisted in putting up a house and getting things in shape for the winter, then fairly upon them.

At the time of starting he had but a single suit of clothes, and that of rather light material, as the season was not yet far enough advanced to require heavy clothing. Before his return to civilization his clothes had been torn, and patched, in every conceivable manner.

On the last day of December he started back to Ohio on foot, accompanied by a young man named Eaton. The first night they encamped near where Mishawaka now stands, the snow was falling very fast and continued until it was knee deep. On the next night they encamped on the Elkhart and on the next they fell in with some Indians with whom they traveled until reaching Blue River. In the meantime Eaton had frozen his feet so badly that he had to be left with the Indians, while Lybrook pushed on to Fort Wayne and procured assistance to go back after him. After enduring many hardships from hunger and exposere he reached home.

At this time wages were from five to seven dollars per month, but Mr. Lybrook being an expert hewer could by hard work earn fifty cents a day. Previous to his leaving with Thompson he had taken quite a heavy contract for getting out timber with the expectation of being gone but a few days and much to his surprise, after so long an absence, found that the job was still open.

In the fall of 1824 he came out with quite a stock of cattle, having made an arrangement with Thompson, the previous summer, to prepare feed for them.

In the spring of 1825 he planted eleven acres in corn on what was known as the Indian fields, below Niles. This land had to be grubbed and fenced, as the Indian system of improvement was very imperfect, they preferring to cultivate around grubs to digging them out and guarding the growing crops from stock, to making rails and fencing.

After the corn was planted he returned to Ohio with a yoke of oxen hitched to the back wheels of a lumber wagon, and among other things brought back was a barrel of wheat, which he sowed that fall and which was probably the first sown in Southwestern Michigan. The grain was harvested the next 4th of July and yielded between thirty-five and forty bushels per acre.

In passing through Fort Wayne Mr. Lybrook had noticed a pair of hand burr stones thrown one side, and after raising a crop it was found necessary to procure some way of grinding it. In December he went back and bought them for seven dollars. They were afterward owned by Squire Thompson and quite generally known and used throughout the country for many miles around.

In the spring of 1825 he bought a grindstone in Detroit for one dollar, which was shipped around the lakes, and the scarcity of this important article may be imagined when we are informed that men came a distance of forty miles to grind on this stone

His broad ax was also lent frequently to men twenty miles away and in one instance to a man on Pigeon Prairie where, it not being returned, he had to go after it himself.

In the spring of 1828 Mr. Lybrook moved on to his present farm, on La Grange Prairie, where he has resided ever since. He had the previous year, in looking over the country, selected this land and set some stakes to mark the location, but when coming on in the spring found it occupied by a man named Kavanaugh, who had already made some improvements, and it took one hundred dollars to liquidate his claim.

Mr. Lybrook has for many years been a hopeless cripple but otherwise is in the enjoyment of all his faculties.

GEORGE MEACHAM.

Hon. George Meacham, the subject of this sketch, was born in Oneida County, New York, in 1799. While quite young his parents moved to Jefferson County, where George remained until coming to Michigan.

In September, 1826, he embarked on a small schooner at Sackett's Harbor, bound for Rochester, where he arrived the next day, from thence taking a canal boat to Buffalo, where he took passage on the steamboat Superior, bound for Detroit, arriving on the 22d of that month.

On the 23d he left Detroit for Pontiac, on the stage, where he arrived next day in time for dinner, distance twenty-four miles. From Pontiac he went to Ann Arbor, where he remained until the 1st of April, 1828, when, in company with his brother, Sylvester Meacham, George Crawford, and Chester Sage, he started for the West.

Their outfit consisted of three yoke of cattle, a heavy lumber wagon, a supply of provisions, ammunition, a plow, and camp equipage. They arrived at Beardsley's Prairie on the 11th of the same month. The only inhabitant living in the south part of the County at that time was Ezra Beardsley, whose cabin was located on the south bank of Pleasant Lake, near where Dr. Sweetland now lives.

The location of a cabin was the first thing to be determined upon by the party, and as there was some difference of opinion, it was decided by throwing a chip in the air, with the well known exclamation of "wet or dry." Mr. M. remarks that this was his first as well as his last gambling.

Their cabin was known far and wide as "Bachelor's Hall," and was a general stopping place for explorers looking at the country. At such times a "field bed," or "shake-down," was made that would extend across the entire room in front of the fire.

On one of these occasions, when a considerable company were sleeping as described, a pig that had been given to Sylvester by Mr. Beardsley when only one day old, and had been brought up in the chimney corner—his pigship assuming a place in the hearth that had become hollowed out by sweeping—finding it rather cool toward morning, began to look around for more comfortable quarters, nosing his way under the blankets, he located himself between Mr. Sage's arm and body, expressing his satisfaction at the same time by a contented grunt, but he had hardly got settled when Mr. S. awoke, and, taking him by the leg, threw him against the wall accompanying the action with epithets that were more expressive than elegant, saying that it was "bad enough to lay on logs without sleeping with hogs."

After getting their cabin erected they commenced breaking up the prairie, which required an occasional visit to the blacksmith shop to get the share sharpened. The nearest shop at that time was Israel Markam's on Pokagon Prairie, a distance of ten miles, and the conveyance a man's shoulder.

It was the original design of the company to trade with the Indians — not supposing that the country would be settled in their day—and only to raise grain enough for their own use, and to keep a team, which they would need in the transportion of their goods, but, soon finding the country settling up rapidly, the Indian project was abandoned, the Meachams settling down to agriculture, and Crawford and Sage removing to Elkhart where they built a mill.

On the 6th of October George was married to Catherine Rhinehart and the following is an inventory of his outfit which Mr. Meacham takes great pride in detailing: "One cow that gave rather poor milk, (but not much of it), an iron bake kettle, one skillet, one coffee pot, six cups and saucers, two stools and a long bench, and bedsteads manufactured by myself. Our fire-place was quite an elaborate affair built of stone laid up in clay mortar with two blocks of wood for andirons, and a clap-board fire shovel. For light we had one six light window with seven by nine glass, the sash made by myself with an ax and jack knife. The floor of our house was made of split puncheon and the roof of clap-boards. In summer I went bare-foot and in winter wore moccasins and sometimes shoes or boots. My pants were faced behind and before with dressed deerskin to make them durable."

In 1836 Mr. Meacham moved from his first location to Baldwin's Prairie, where he has lived ever since. He was the first Sheriff of the County, which office he held about two years, and while acting in that capacity summoned the first grand and petit juries, a part of which were drawn from the village of St. Joseph, then within the bounds of the County. At that time, to be a qualified juror, a man must have paid a tax of at least fifty cents, and it took about all the qualified men in the County to fill the quota.

Mr. Meacham has served the people of the County twice in the Legislature and in numerous other responsible positions, he is universally esteemed for his many good qualities and Christian virtues wherever known.

ISAAC SHURTE.

Isaac Shurte was born near Pearson's Mills, New York, July 11th, 1798. When one year old his parents moved to Sussex County, New Jersey, where he lived until twenty-one years old, when he started for Ohio — going on foot to Pittsburg, a distance of between five and six hundred miles. At Pittsburg he bought a small skiff in which he rowed down the Ohio River to Cincinnatti—then a smart little town—from thence he went across the country to Butler County, where he remained until September, 1827, when he came to Michigan. He first settled at Niles, where he built a cabin, and remained two years, when he sold out for twenty dollars, and removed to La Grange, where he has resided ever since.

On the way out from Ohio his children were very sick, which, with broken wagons and muddy roads, made him feel at times almost homesick and discouraged, but with the courage that was characteristic of all pioneers he would push ahead. He brought with him, from Ohio, three yoke of cattle, one pair of horses, milch cows, hogs, &c. Of the stock brought along he lost heavily the first winter from a lack of feed.

The first winter he threshed wheat at the Mission, getting every ninth bushel as wages—at this rate he could earn one bushel a day. After earning the wheat he took it to Ford's mill to get it ground and then boated it over to the Mission and bolted it on a hand bolt belonging to that establishment.

Mr. Shurte bought the claim for his present homestead of a man named Loux, giving in exchange a horse, saddle and bridle. For two bushels of seed wheat, he traded to Israel Markam a cut of leather, (a strip wide enough for two soles across a side of leather,) and then went seven miles to borrow a harrow to put it in with. The grain was sown among weeds and grass, and, much to his surprise, made an excellent crop.

In 1830 he bought the first fanning mill used in the Township, which was manufactured by a man named Parker, then living near the present site of Cassopolis. Mr. Shurte says, "we lived the first two years after coming to La Grange on corn and buckwheat bread, excepting wheat bread for company and on rare occasions. The yarn for all our wear, both woolen and linen, was spun in the house, and for a number of years after coming to Michigan we did not have a cotton sheet in the house."

In 1832 he planted an orchard, the trees for which were procured from a New York man named Jones, he had but little faith and called them "Yankee trees," but after they came into bearing was so well pleased that he filled up all vacancies.

Mr. Shurte was a captain in the Black Hawk (Soc) war and several times was ordered out for service and expected to provide himself with three days' rations, when it was more provisions than they had in the house. He has always been noted for keeping good stock, especially horses, of which there are but few better in the country.

ORLEAN PUTNAM.

Orlean Putnam was born in the Town of Adams, Jefferson County, New York, on the 7th of May, 1809. While an infant his parents moved to Huron

County, Ohio, stopping at Detroit a month on the way.

On the 20th of June, 1813, he, his mother and eleven others were taken prisoners by the Tawas Indians, at the head of Colt Creek, in Huron County. Five of the prisoners were killed at the time of capture, and soon after two more, by knocking on the head with a pipe tomahawk, after which they were scalped and their brains knocked out against a tree. The Indians, sixteen in number, were under the leadership of a chief, named Pontiac, and at one time a tomahawk was raised over the boy's head, but before the blow fell the chief jumped in and prevented it, at the same time telling Putnam's mother to put the boy on his back and follow close in his footsteps, and he would protect them.

At the time of the capture they were about three miles from Maumee Bay, to which point the captives were rapidly marched, and the whole party embarked in canoes bound for a peninsula two or three miles distant. The peninsula was about three-fourths of a mile wide, across which the canoes were dragged—the captives being compelled to assist in the laborious task.

On the opposite side of the Peninsula the Indians had a large dug-out (canoe) filled with sand and sunk in the water. This was emptied and raised, and with the bark canoes, furnished a conveyance to Malden, whither the party proceeded. On the way they stopped one night at a place where the Indians held a "pow-wow." The captives were placed around a stake, and while the chief chanted and shook a rattle-box, the others danced around the prisoners.

On the arrival of the party at Malden, the prisoners were treated to a pan of bread and milk, and, after remaining a few hours, they were taken over to Brownstown, where Mrs. Putnam was given by Pontiac to a half-breed French trader, named Ironsides.

Young Putnam was taken to Detroit by the chief, and while there, was met by Judge May, who asked Pontiac what he was going to do with the little boy. "Raise him; make chief," was the reply. The Judge told him that it was a friend's boy, and that he must send him back to his mother, and, after reasoning with him for some time, and working on his feelings, he agreed to do it, which promise he fulfilled; but every time Pontiac got drunk, he would go and want the boy back. Finally Mrs. Ironsides bought and paid for him thirty bottles of whisky, which settled the matter.

The prisoners were kept about ten days, when they were treated for by a Government agent, named Captain Randall, and sent home in a schooner. Mr. Putnam was nicknamed Pontiac, by which he was known until grown up to manhood. For some time after his return from captivity he was the lion of the day, and received many pennies for singing and dancing in imitation of the Indians.

In 1825 Mr. Putnam came to Michigan, stopping the first winter with his brother, Uzziel, and working the next summer for William Kirk, near Niles. In the spring of 1827 he went to work for William

Brookfield, as back chainman of a surveying party, which was then running the land into Townships between the Indiana and base line. The next summer he assisted in sub-dividing the Townships into sections. While out the first year he was with the party when Young's Prairie was discovered, and was snowed in nearly two weeks while encamped on the bank of Diamond Lake, and thinks their party cut the first stick ever cut by white men in that vicinity.

In 1832 he was again employed in surveying in the Grand River region. While at the mouth of the river, a boat came in and brought the news of the Black Hawk war, and about the same time their pack ponies strayed away, but owing to the excitement caused by the report, no one was willing to go into the Indian country to look for them. Finally, as an inducement, the Surveyor offered one dollar per day extra for the service, when Putnam volunteered to go. He, in company with a man named Stocking, followed up the Kalamazoo River to the mouth of the Thornapple, where they found the ponies. They were assisted in catching them by some Pottawatomie Indians, who had a large village at this point, and at the time were much excited by the Black Hawk scare.

Mr. Putnam, after coming back from the surveying party, stood a draft for the Soc war, but got clear; but a man named Godfrey, who was drafted, wishing to procure a substitute, Putnam offered to go for the wages if he would furnish him a horse to ride. This G. readily agreed to do; but after the service was concluded, he kept the horse and collected the pay also.

On the 15th of April, 1834, he was married to Amelia Vanderhoof, with whom he still lives. They have reared quite a large family, who have mostly gone from home and are doing well by themselves.

IRA NASH.

The subject of this sketch was born in Danbury, Connecticut, August 12th, 1806. When three years old his parents moved to Chenango County, New York, where he lived until coming to Michigan in 1829 — arriving at Detroit on the 6th of December. He came in the employ of John Agard, who was seeking a suitable location for a store in the then far West. From Detroit they pushed out on foot, following an Indian trail via Ypsilanti, White Pigeon, (where he spent Christmas day,) Beardsley's Prairie to Niles, which at this time contained but two or three log cabins.

On the 8th day of March, 1830, they settled at Geneva—then the prospective County seat. Mr. Nash continued in the service of Agard until the 10th of January, 1833, when he went in business for himself. He bought his goods in Detroit, where he went on foot twice a year, preferring this mode of travel to that of going on horse-back. From Detroit the goods were shipped around the lake to the mouth of the St. Joseph River, and thence poled up on flat boats to Niles and then carted to Geneva.

In the winter of 1832 and '33 the river froze up very early and consequently the goods had to be teamed all the way from St. Joseph. At this time there was no road from Berrien to Royalton and when Nash came up with his teams the men were at work opening a road there and he was detained in assisting them several days. Among the commodities, was an anvil for John White, which had been bought in Detroit, this, when they were nearly at the top of a high hill, rolled off the sled and stopped only when it reached the bottom, causing a deal of trouble and delay in getting it back.

In the spring of 1830 Mr. Nash set out a small orchard at Geneva and made additions to it nearly every year while he stayed here, his first trees were procured from a small nursery near Baldwin's Prairie.

In the spring of 1831 he was elected clerk of Penn Township, which office he held eleven consecutive years, and in August, 1836, he was chosen Justice of the Peace, in which capacity he served eight years.

In 1844 he removed from Geneva to Charleston, on Little Prairie Ronde, where he sold goods until 1850, when he removed to Dowagiac, where he remained but one summer and then moved to Decatur, where he was in trade twenty years. While at Decatur he dealt largely in produce.

He was in the Black Hawk war and went as far west as the Kankakee River. When starting, they expected to meet the Indians before reaching Niles, but the farther west they got the farther off were the Indians.

Mr. Nash has always been known as an honest upright man, he now resides with his son-in-law, G. L. Linder, at Vandalia.

LEWIS EDWARDS.

Lewis Edwards was born in Burlington County, New Jersey, in May, 1799, where he lived until 1820, when he went to Warren County, Ohio. From Warren County he came to Michigan, in 1826. At the time of his coming there were no inhabitants between Fort Wayne and Bertrand. He brought with him a peacock (cast) plow, a set of iron harrow teeth, a one-horse plow, scythes, sickles, etc. The first harvest after coming he reaped wheat for the Mission, by which he earned three bushels. This he let to Mr. Putnam to sow on shares, and the yield was sixty bushels.

Mr. Edwards settled on the west side of Pokagon Prairie, the location being the one previously occupied by the old chief, whose name the Prairie and Township bears, for gardening purposes.

In the spring of 1830 Mr. Edwards brought from Ohio three hundred apple and one hundred pear trees, a quantity of currants, raspberries, etc. The apple orchard is still in a thrifty condition, but the pear trees were mostly killed by the hard winter of 1855–6.

When he came to Michigan he brought with him some improved Durham cattle, purchased of the Ohio Shakers, and has added to his herd from time to time since; and probably no man in the County has done more for the improvement of neat stock than Mr. Edwards.

He was one of the first jurors in the County, and as such attended the first court at Edwardsburg.

Mr. Edwards visited La Grange Prairie in the fall of 1827, then one vast flower bed, with not a person living on it. He, in common with all the earlier settlers, had his wheat killed by the June frost of 1835, and what was not killed was made "sick" by freezing.

He was one of the first Justices of the Peace in the County when they were appointed by the Governor, but as he remarks* "the best times we ever had were before we had any law." Mr. Edwards, now in the seventy-sixth year of his age, resides on the land he first occupied fifty years ago; he is an active, intelligent man, for his years, and respected by all who know him.

COLONEL JAMES NEWTON.

Colonel James Newton was born in England in 1777, and came to this country when a mere boy. He first resided near Morristown, New Jersey, and from thence moved to Pennsylvania, and from there to Ohio, in 1804. He came down the Ohio River on a flat boat, and was offered an acre of land where Cincinnati now stands for a day's work, but did not think it worth while to accept.

*What is meant by no law, was that, previous to the organization of the County in 1829, there were no resident officials in force, consequently the people were without practical law.

He settled on the head waters of the Miami, at a place called Seven Mile Creek, about forty miles north of Cincinnatti. He acquired the title of Colonel from commanding a regiment of militia in Ohio. He was also an Orderly Sergeant in active service during the war of 1812, serving under General Harrison. He had command of Fort Black, north of Greenville, for a time, and afterward of Fort Meigs, his term of service expiring a few days before the battle of Mackinac.

He was a member of the convention that framed the State Constitution, and also a member of the House of Representatives for this and Van Buren Counties in the winters of 1837–38 and 1838–39. He was commissioned as Judge by Governor Mason but never accepted the position.

His son, Hon. George Newton, was born in Preble County, Ohio, on the 10th day of August, 1810, and in company with his father came to Michigan in 1831. They started on the 6th day of April with three yoke of cattle and a wagon. The streams at the time of moving were all very high from the spring rains and nearly all of them had to be swam by the teams. A sucking colt would be taken into a boat and carried across while dam swam beside. On the third night out they encamped on the battle ground of Fort Recovery. They crossed the St. Joseph River by ferry at Sage's Mill, where Elkhart now stands, and followed up the course of the Christiana Creek to Young's Prairie, from thence to their future home it was an unbroken wilderness without track or blaze, but, taking the direction and with an ax to clear the way, they set out, and, after no little trouble, made the point which ever since has been called home. Their first habitation was a wigwam formerly occupied by the Chief Weesaw as winter quarters.

In the spring of 1832 corn, from some cause, would not grow, when George made a trip east of White Pigeon and bought one bushel for which he paid two dollars and fifty cents.

Mr. Newton has served in the Legislature one term, and was for a number of years Supervisor of the Township, all of which positions he has filled creditably to himself and constituents. For a number of years he has been nearly blind, but, by an operation performed last fall, he has partially recovered his sight.

JOSEPH L. JACKS.

Joseph L. Jacks was born in Erie County, Pennsylvania, on the 18th of May, 1804. When twenty-two years of age, he moved to Chautauqua County, New York, where he was married to Susannah Silsby, and immediately set out for Michigan, arriving at Edwardsburg on the 4th of July, 1829. When he came in, the people were celebrating the National birthday, which was probably the first time that a luxury of this kind was indulged in in the County.

Mr. Jacks was the first Clerk of the County, appointed by Governor Cass, on the 31st of July, 1830, and sworn into office by Baldwin Jenkins, then one of the Associate Judges, on the 4th day of September, in the same year. He was Clerk about two years, and was succeeded by M. C. Whitman.

He also held under Governor Cass a commission as Lieutenant of Militia, but never was attached to any organized company. In 1831, he was elected assessor of Ontwa Township, when it comprised nearly the South half of the County, and made the assessment in five days.

Mr. Jacks served five days in the Black Hawk war in 1832; he held the office of Corporal in his Company, and by reason of the office, received an extra half dollar as pay. He has followed the avocation of farmer, nearly through life, but recently he has retired from active labor, and now lives in Edwardsburg.

JACOB MORELAN.

Jacob Morelan was born in Virginia September 11th, 1797, his wife, Sarah Poe, was born in Greene County, Ohio, August 15th, 1805; they were married May 4th, 1826; came to Michigan in the fall of 1829, staying the first winter on the farm of Joseph Gardner, in Pokagon; removing to Volinia in the spring of 1830, settling on the south side of Little Prairie Ronde, where he lived until the time of his death, which occurred February 16th, 1854, at the age of fifty-seven. His vocation through life was that of a farmer. Mrs. Morelan is still living among her children in the immediate vicinity of the place of their first settlement, and relates many incidents of their early experiences. At one time a hawk came and alighted on a tree near by, when none of the men were at the house, Mrs. Morelan took down the rifle and shot it; at another time a wolf came and tried to get some pigs that were in a pen near the house, when she again tried her hand at shooting, but not with as good success as before, but succeeding in driving the wolf away. At one time when the mill was out of order she had to grind buckwheat on the coffee-mill for bread.

EDWARD SHANAHAN.

Edward Shanahan, the subject of this sketch, was born in Sussex County, Delaware, in the year 1806, where he lived until 1828, when he moved to Dover in the same State. In 1829 he was married to Rebecca Kimmey, with whom he still lives, and who has borne him fifteen children.

In 1832, to better his condition, he came to Michigan, moving the entire distance of eight hundred miles with a horse team. On the road as he neared Michigan, he met many people leaving the country who were frightened away by the Black Hawk war—not one of whom would stop long enough to tell what was the matter, but recited their tale of woe as they passed by.

Mr. Shanahan located on the northwest corner of Beardsley's Prairie, where he lived until 1855, when he removed to his present residence in Jefferson Township. He has always taken an active part in politics and represented the Southern District in the House of Representatives in the winter of 1860 and '61. His occupation through life has been that of a farmer, in which avocation he has been successful far above the average—accumulating between seven and eight hundred acres of valuable land. His brother, Judge Clifford Shanahan, came to Edwardsburg in 1834, and in 1844 was elected Judge of Probate, which office he filled until 1864.

DANIEL SHELLHAMMER.

Daniel Shellhammer was born in Germany, in the year 1785. He was a soldier in the war of 1812, for which he drew a pension at the time of his death, which occurred in June, 1873, at the advanced age of eighty-eight years. He came to Michigan in 1827, in company with John and Joseph Bair, and put up a cabin on the east side of Porter Township, near Mottville. In the fall he returned to Ohio, and in the spring of 1828 removed his family, consisting of his wife and eleven children, to Michigan. His team consisted of a yoke of cattle, hired for the trip, and a yoke of light three-year old steers, owned by himself.

John Shellhammer, his oldest son, was born in Schuylkill County, Pennsylvania, September 11th, 1811. In 1826 his parents moved to Crawford County, Ohio, where he remained until coming to Michigan, at the age of seventeen.

Mr. Shellhammer's recollections of early life and incidents are remarkably clear and correct. He relates that the first season they came in (1828), previous to harvest time, all their bread-stuff consisted of corn, that had been brought overland from

Detroit, and cost four dollars per bushel, and, after purchasing it, was carried on their backs to the east side of Pigeon Prairie, where a man named Hill had a cast iron mill, something after the pattern of a huge coffee mill, in which they ground their grist by hand and returned the same day, the distance being eight miles and back.

On one of these occasions, as they were returning, they were hailed at the bank of the river by a small French tailor, who wished them to stop and witness the marriage ceremony between himself and a lady weighing about two hundred and fifty pounds. The absurdity of the whole affair can be seen by imagining a bandy-legged Frenchman, weighing one hundred and twenty-five pounds being tied to a Yankee girl weighing double that of himself, and the ceremony witnessed by a man and boy that could scarcely understand a word of English. But after receiving a glass of good cheer for their trouble, they wended their way homeward.

The only persons living at that time on Pigeon Prairie were the above named Hill and a man named Savory, who was building a hewed log house on the south side of the Prairie. At the time that John Baldwin was so badly treated by the Indians, Mr. Shellhammer had a brother and sister in the house, and he was one of the first on the ground after the tragedy took place, of which he has a vivid recollection.

ELIAS B. SHERMAN.

Elias B. Sherman was born in Oneida County, New York, in 1803. When he was four years of age he removed with his father to Cayuga County, where his boyhood and youth were spent in labor and the acquirement of a good common school education.

In 1825 he migrated to Michigan, stopping first at Detroit, but soon after moved to Ann Arbor, where he studied law and was admitted to the bar in 1829.

In September of that year he came, via White Pigeon, to Beardsley's Prairie, and spent considerable time looking over Berrien, St. Joseph and Cass Counties, with a view to speculative investments and a permanent settlement. He first made a claim on the north side of Little Prairie Ronde, which he sold to Elijah Goble, in 1830, for sixty-five dollars. He next engaged in putting the City of Shakespeare on the market, but, becoming disgusted with the course of his associates, sold out his interest, taking in exchange some property in Lockport, St. Joseph County.

His next and most permanent venture was the establishment of the village of Cassopolis and securing the location of the seat of Justice therein. He was one of the original proprietors and has always since preserved a large proprietary interest in its welfare. January 1st, 1833, he was married to Sarah, only daughter of the late Jacob Silver, by Bishop Chase, a brother of Chief Justice Chase. This was the first wedding in Cassopolis.

Mr. Sherman was appointed Prosecuting Attorney by Governor Cass, November 7th, 1829, and served under this commission until 1836, when he was elected to the same position by the people. He was appointed District Surveyor July 31st, 1830, which office he held six years. March 4th, 1831, he was appointed Judge of Probate, and continned to act in that capacity until the Whig revolution of 1840.

Although now passed the allotted "three score years and ten," his memory of the pioneer days is remarkably clear and to it these pages are indebted for many incidents otherwise unpreserved.

HON. GEORGE REDFIELD.

Hon. George Redfield was born in the State of Connecticut on the 6th of October, 1796. While quite young his parents moved to Ontario County, New York, where he remained until 1822, when he went South for the purpose of teaching school. He remained in the South four years, teaching in the vicinity of Millegeville, Georgia, and while there he became acquainted with, and had for his pupils, those who were afterward some of the leading spirits of Georgia, among whom was State Treasurer Jones.

In 1868 Mr. Redfield visited the former scenes of his labors, in the South, to find desolation spread abroad on every hand—where luxury and ease had once been the rule, now was poverty in the extreme —but he was met with a cordial welcome wherever he went.

In June, 1831, Mr. Redfield, in company with

eleven other young men, came to Michigan. Prominent among the party were Sans McCamley, since one of the leading men of Battle Creek; Nathan Pierce, of Calhoun County, a thousand acre farmer; John Downer and Amassa Gillett, the former settling in Washtenaw County and the latter near the present site of Manchester. They were all adventurers seeking homes in what was then considered the wilderness of the far West. The trip out from Detroit was made on foot, the travelers carrying their provisions, camp utensils, clothes and a small tent on their backs, and camping out wherever night overtook them.

While the party were encamped one night, on the bank of the Kalamazoo River, at a point where a small stream put in, leaving just room enough for their tent, they were awakened by some very unpleasant sensations which proved to be caused by craw fish crawling between their blankets as they were moving from one stream to the other.

Mr. Redfield returned to New York, after coming as far west as White Pigeon, much pleased with the country, intending to return the next spring, but with the next spring came the memorable cholera season of 1832 and the trip was abandoned for a time.

In 1833, in company with his brother, Lewis H. Redfield, who still resides at Syracuse, New York, he made a trip through the West, and in the summer of 1834 George again came to Michigan and made a purchase of eight hundred acres of land where he now resides. During this summer he spent three months with his brother, Alexander H. Redfield, at Cassopolis.

On the 9th of Jnne, 1835, he was married to Julia A. Mason, of Palmyria, New York, and immediately moved to Michigan, living the first summer on the farm now owned by J. Boyd Thomas, moving on to his present home farm in the fall of the same year, where he has resided ever since.

In 1836 Mr. Redfield purchased of the General Government, three thousand acres of land in Calvin Township, one thousand acres in Jefferson, one thousand acres in Mason, beside numerous other tracts in various parts of the County, making in all between eight and ten thousand acres, of which he still retains two thousand, the remainder he has disposed of from time to time, selling nearly the entire amount to men of limited means, giving them a chance to improve and make their payments from the land. In a number of instances the payments have been deferred over twenty years, the land in the meantime increasing many times in value. Mr. Redfield's generosity has become almost proverbial, and for years it was a common quotation of the neighbors, "going down to Egypt for corn," when the colored people of Calvin would come to him for assistance, and I am creditably informed that they never went away empty handed.

He was elected to the House of Representatives, and served in the memorable one hundred day session of 1841. He was also elected Senator, and served in 1842 and '43, and Presidential Elector in 1844. In 1845 he was appointed State Treasurer by Governor

Barry, but positively declined a nomination for that office in 1846. In January, 1850, he was appointed Secretary of State, which office he filled during the session of the Legislature, resigning at its adjournment, and in the same year was elected to the convention that framed our present State Constitution, which ended his political career. His strong domestic attachments, combined with his many home duties, made it impossible to his mind to participate farther in political matters, although frequently solicited, and had he been ambitious in this particular, he might have accepted the highest office in the gift of the people of the State.

In 1837 Mr. Redfield bought the only water saw mill in Jefferson Township, and rebuilt it in 1850, and again after being burned in 1862 in connection with a flouring mill, which is still running.

His wife died in August, 1848, leaving him three children — two daughters and one son. He married again in September, 1854, Jane E. Hammond, daughter of Judge Hammond, of Essex County, New York, who died in November, 1865, leaving him three daughters and one son, all of whom are living with or near him.

In 1870 Mr. Redfield became partially blind from cataract of the eye, from which he has suffered ever since, not being able to read or write and only at the most favorable times is he able to see the dim outlines of large objects. Notwithstanding his misfortune he has had, in a great measure, the superintendence and care of his home farm and an oversight of his general business.

WILLIAM RENNISTON.

William Renniston was born in Mifflin, Pennsylvania, in the year 1796. When twenty-two years of age he moved to Indiana and settled near Richmond, where he lived until coming to Michigan in 1830. He first settled at what has since been known as the Spaulding mill property, near Dowagiac, where he erected a woolen mill, bringing the carding machines on wagons from Southern Indiana. In 1833 he built a grist mill at the same place, the irons for which were made at Cincinnati and wagoned across the country, a distance of over two hundred miles. The burrs were quarried and dressed near Elkhart, Indiana.

After running the grist mill for one year he sold the whole property to Holmes Spaulding, and bought the farm that he has resided on ever since. While a young man he learned the trade of clothier, which busines he followed while in Indiana and four years after coming to Michigan. Since selling his mill property his occupation has been that of a farmer, which he has followed for nearly forty years. Mr. Renniston is a close, economical man, having a penchant for saving and preserving every thing and allowing nothing to be destroyed or go to waste. His collection of old-time implements, harness, etc., to be seen in his barn, is well worth the attention of those interested in pioneer relics.

JOHN ALEXANDER.

John Alexander was born in North Carolinia

about the year 1779, and died in Cass County, Michigan, in 1849, at the age of seventy years In 1811 he emigrated to Wayne County, Indiana, where he remained until coming to Michigan in 1831, settling on the farm now owned by Robert Dool. His first house, or shanty, was a three-sided affair, covered with basswood bark, in which he lived several months, and its exact location was where the Chicago & Lake Huron Railroad now crosses the highway running north and south. In an early day he was a member of the New Light or Christian denomination, but after coming to Michigan joined the Christian Church, of which he was a consistent and devoted member. He was a very quiet, peaceable man, never sued but one man in his life and never was sued. He was very punctual in all his dealings and required the same of others, but more by the force of will than fear of law, his general character may, perhaps, be better illustrated by the following incident than anything that could be said at the present time:

One year grain of all kinds was very scarce and high, corn and oats bringing from seventy-five cents to one dollar per bushel readily. Mr. A. having a good supply of these products, put the price to settlers at fifty cents per bushel, and would sell to no others.

His son, Ephraim, resides in Redwing, Minnesota, John and Peter on Young's Prairie, the oldest daughter in Silver Creek, another in Douglas County, Oregon, another in Wexford County, this State, and still another in Penn Township.

ASA KINGSBURY.

Asa Kingsbury was born at Newton Heights, near Boston, Massachusetts, on the 28th of May, 1806. When a young man he learned the trade of carpenter, which he followed three or four years. In 1830 he came West and settled at Cleveland, Ohio, where he engaged in the manufacture of glue, which art he learned after leaving off the carpenter trade.

In 1833 a business man in Cleveland made a proposition to Mr. Kingsbury to go farther West and take a son of his who was a wild, reckless fellow, offering him whatever capital he would need in business. Mr. K., after considering the matter, concluded that as he had everything to gain and nothing to lose, he would accept. Loading about three thousand dollar's worth of general merchandise on the schooner New York, with his portege, he started up the lakes without any definite point in view.

While on the St. Clair River, their vessel was becalmed several days, during which time the young man under Mr. Kingsbury's charge, in company with several sailors, went over into Canada and stole a lot of chickens, for which they were arrested. Mr. K. went over and got him out of this scrape, but in a day or two he ran away and got on board of another vessel, after which he never heard of him.

Mr. Kingsbury continued on his way alone, stopping off at Green Bay, but, not finding it to suit him, kept on to St. Joseph. The rough weather prevented a landing for three weeks, during which time they were beating around the upper end of the lake. One day while the crew were below at dinner Mr. K. assisted the captain in managing the vessel; in making a change in the course the boom came around very suddenly, taking with it a fifteen dollar fur cap, and had he been three inches taller this sketch would not have been written.

Soon after his arrival at St. Joseph he struck out on foot to look up a location for trade, arriving at Berrien after night. The hotel where he stopped was all dark, and on going into the bar-room in the basement the first thing which attracted his attention was a dead man who had been killed on the river—he ran against the cadaver in the darkness.

The next day he went on to Bertrand, then in the heighth of its prosperity, where he secured a location, had his goods brought up the river, and went into business, dealing in real estate, burning brick &c. The burning of brick came near being a failure, the clay containing small particles of lime, which, on coming to the air, would slack and break the brick. To avoid a loss he put them into buildings, some of which are standing yet.

In 1835, finding that Bertrand was on the down grade, Mr. Kingsbury moved to Cassopolis, where he bought of John M. Barbour a store and distillery. This proved to be his final stake setting, and he has ever since been prominently identified with the business of the village.

In company with his brother Charles, who joined him in 1838, he dealt extensively in general merchandise and real estate for about twenty years, and upon their separation opened a private banking office which he managed successfully until it was merged into the First National Bank of which he is President.

MAJOR JOSEPH SMITH.

Major Joseph Smith was born in Bottetourt County, Virginia, on the 11th of April, 1809. When three years old his parents moved to Clark County, Ohio, where he remained until coming to Michigan in 1831, making a location at the ancient City of Glasgow (in Calvin), where he bought a mill property, and moved out in 1832, accompanied by his father and brother John. He ran the mill until 1835, when he sold out and bought one thousand acres of land in Jefferson Township, which he immediately commenced to improve.

His father and brother became disgusted with the country and went back to Ohio, after staying one year.

In 1847 Mr. Smith went into partnership with Joshua Lofland and Henley C. Lybrook in the sale of merchandise, which was continued about three years, since which time he has carried on business on his own account nearly all the time, removing to Cassopolis in 1855, where he has ever since resided, Mr. Smith has been known through all his life as a hard money Democrat and has always taken an active part in politics. He served in the Legislature in 1835 and again in 1836, and was a member of the convention that accepted the proposition of Congress by which Michigan was admitted into the Union. He was a Captain of Militia in Ohio, and appointed Major in Michigan, by which title he has been known ever since.

HENLEY C. LYBROOK.

Henley C. Lybrook was born in Giles County, Virginia, November 20th, 1802, where he resided until coming to Michigan in 1830, arriving at Pokagon Prairie on the 15th day of May. He taught school six months of the first year, working on a farm between school terms.

In the spring of 1831 he taught school at Geneva a short time and then went to work on a farm on La Grange Prairie, and the next winter taught school in Howard Township, near Joseph Harter's. In the spring of 1832 he again engaged in farming, but the Black Hawk war coming on he enlisted in Captain Shurte's company and was gone until June. Soon after returning from war Mr. Lybrook engaged as clerk with Robert Painter, in Cassopolis, and continued with him until closing up his business in the fall of the same year. Mr. Painter started to New York for a fall and winter stock of goods with one thousand dollars in money, which he carried in a pocket-book in his coat pocket. At Detroit he took deck passage on a steamboat in the evening and toward morning he fell asleep, awakening to find his pocket-book gone, when he returned home and Mr. Lybrook closed up his business and soon after went to work for Jacob Silver, in whose employ he continued several years. In 1834 he was appointed County Clerk, in which capacity he served until about 1840.

In 1842 he went into mercantile business on his own account, six months after taking in W. G. Beckwith as partner. He was afterward connected with B. F. Silver and Dow and then with Joshua Lofland. In 1850 they moved to Dowagiac and G. C. Jones was made a member of the firm.

REV. LUTHER HUMPHREY.

Rev. Luther Humphrey came to Beardsley's Prairie about the year 1830. He was sent out as a missionary by the Presbyterian Church of New England and labored over Cass and Berrien Counties. After remaining a number of years he went to Ohio, where he died but a short time since.

He was a man of many peculiarities, among which was the belief that every family should raise as nearly as possible all they consumed, and this principle he put in practice to the extent of seeming penuriousness. His prejudice against slavery was of the most ultra character, and he would neither eat nor wear anything made by slave labor, and to obviate the necessity of eating sugar from this source, he annually raised a quantity of corn from which he expressed the juice and boiled down to a molasses, which answered the purpose of sweetening. He was also a very strict temperance man and had no patience with those that tippled, although such was a very common practice at that time.

JAMES ALDRICH.

James Aldrich was born twelve miles from Providence, Rhode Island, in the year 1786, where he resided until a man grown, when he moved to Palmyria, New York, and then to Erie County, where he remained until 1829, when he removed to Chautauqua County. In 1834 he came west and settled at Niles, and in 1837 came into this County, buying the farm now owned by James Beauchamp, on Beardsley's Prairie, where he lived until the time of his death. In 1808 he was married to Hannah Comstock, by whom he had nine children, Doctor and Henry are the only sons remaining in the County.

PHILIP SHINTAFFER.

Philip Shintaffer and family, consisting of three sons and two sons-in-law, came to Beardsley's Prairie in 1831 and settled on the farms owned by Barber and Runkle.

They came from the Wabash country here, but probably they were natives of Virginia, and as rough specimens of humanity as could be found anywhere.

They kept a large number of horses and a huge wagon and sled, either of which they would take to the woods, and backing to a tree, no matter how large, and fall it across the axle, and then hitch team enough to it to draw it home. At one time the old man professed to get religion, and the numerous anecdotes of his religious experience, as related by the old settlers, are amusing but hardly appropriate to be recorded. The family remained here but a few years, when it became too thickly settled and they moved west.

ALEXANDER ROGERS.

Alexander Rogers was born in Rockbridge County, Virginia, in the year 1788. When twenty-two years old he moved to Preble County, Ohio, where he lived eighteen years, or until he came to Michigan in 1828. He stopped one year after coming where Sumnerville now stands and then moved on to the farm now owned and occupied by his sons, where he resided until the time of his death in 1867. His sons Samuel, Alexander, John, Thomas and William, all, with the exception of one, live in Pokagon Township, the other, Samuel, lives in Illinois.

SAMUEL C. OLMSTED.

Samuel C. Olmsted was born in Huntington, Hartford County, Connecticut, July 10th, 1801. In 1813 he removed to Cayuga County, New York, where he was married to Eunice M. Jackson, November 11th, 1823. In the latter part of the year 1829 he removed to Chautauqua County, where he made a purchase of land from the Holland Land Company, making a payment down and running in debt for the balance. His land was a tough, tenacious clay soil, covered with a heavy growth of beech, maple, ash, and hemlock timber, requiring a vast amount of labor to bring it under cultivation. Clearing land, making payments on the same, and supporting a family, he soon found to be up-hill business, and in 1836 determined to try his forture in the West. Selling out in New York, he removed to Michigan, arriving at Edwardsburg on May 20th of that year.

The first season he rented land on shares, but in 1837 he made a purchase of twenty-eight acres of land on section four, of Ontwa Township, and built a house on it, which he moved into in the fall when there were neither doors or windows to keep out the cold. He continued to add to his possessions until he owned two hundred acres of land, on which he still resides.

Of those that came with him to Michigan, but two are now living, viz., himself and his oldest son, J. C. Olmsted. His mother died in 1837, and was among the first to be buried in the Edwardsburg cemetery. His father, Deacon Sylvester Olmsted, died February 3d, 1861. His wife, Eunice, died September 22d, 1854.

Mr. O. is by profession a Congregationalist, and during the entire time of his residence in Michigan he has been a member of the First Congregational Church of Edwardsburg, of which he is also a Deacon.

SPENCER WILLIAMS.

Spencer Williams was born in Sussex County, Delaware, May 2nd, 1807, where he lived until man grown. In 1828 he made a trip to Ohio, but not liking the country returned home again. In June, 1831, he emigrated to Michigan, settling in Ontwa Township, where he rented a farm for two years, when he bought the place on section twelve, of Milton Township, where he has since resided. In 1833 he was married to Sarah Smith, with whom he has lived ever since. At the age of eighteen he joined the Methodist Episcopal Church and has continued in active membership to the present time. Soon after coming to Michigan, at the organization of the Society, at Smith's Chapel, he was elected one of the trustees, and has acted in that capacity ever since, with the exception of one year. When he was not worth over five hundred dollars he gave one hundred toward the erection of the Church, and fifty dollars more before it was completed.

In the fall of 1831 Mr. Williams made a trip to Chicago. At that time there were but sixteen one story houses in the place. Just previous to his going there there had been quite a freshet which had washed a number of graves open on the bank of the river and numerous corpses were distributed around creating a nauseating stench.

At the breaking out of the Black Hawk war in 1832, Mr. Williams started with the first express for Detroit but, overtaking the stage at White Pigeon, was relieved. The nest day on returning he volunteered for the war. On the way to Chicago he was put in baggage-master, in which capacity he acted until mustered out. While encamped he pastured his horses where the city of Chicago now stands, and many times, on going after them in the morning, would have to wade in water ankle deep. Mr. Williams is a man of no education whatever, but at the same time has managed a considerable business for himself as well as others, and is much respected by all that know him.

JOSEPH GOODSPEED.

Joseph Goodspeed was born in the town of Sandwich, Massachusetts, on the 1st day of April, 1797. In 1825 he was married to Miss Sarah B. Fish, who was born in Barnstable, Massachusetts. For three years after marrying they lived on the Island of Nantucket, and then moved to Cayuga County, New York, where they remained until coming to Michigan in 1836. On the road out one of their little boys fell out of the wagon and broke his arm. In the season of 1838, which was known as the "sickly season," their whole family was down, with the exception of William, then a small boy, and on him devolved the duties of cook, nurse and general chore boy.

Mr. Goodspeed served eleven consecutive years as Township Treasurer, of Volinia. His vocation through life was that of a farmer. He died on the 30th of April, 1850, at the age of fifty-three. Mrs. Goodspeed is still living at the old place, in the enjoyment of all her faculties, has a large circle of friends and is respected wherever known.

JOHN NIXON.

John Nixon was born in Randolph County, North Carolinia, in 1806, where he lived until coming to Michigan in August, 1830. In 1832 he was married to Esther, daughter of Henry Jones. When a young man he learned the trade of tanner and courier, which he followed two or three years previous to coming to Michigan. Ever since he has been a farmer.

At the time of his wedding lumber was so scarce that a door had to be taken down to splice out the table to make it long enough to seat all the company. The cranberries for sauce on the occasion were gathered by Mrs. Nixon, in a neighboring marsh. A quantity of dried blackberries were donated by some Indian squaws, who frequently came around and got an idea of what was going on. They have had a family of eleven children, nine of whom are still living.

STEPHEN BOGUE.

Stephen Bogue was born in Perquimans County, North Carolinia, October 17th, 1790. In 1811 he moved to Preble County, Ohio, where he cleared up and brought into cultivation a farm in the heavy timber, where he lived until coming to Michigan in 1831. Here he bought a farm on Young's Prairie, on which he lived until the time of his death, October 11th, 1868, a period of thirty-seven years. Mr. Bogue was a thorough Abolitionist, from nature and education. Born and brought up amidst slavery and its surrounding evil influences, he early imbibed the anti-slavery sentiment of the Friends' Society, of which he was a life-long, consistent and devoted member. He voted the Free Soil ticket when there was but three or four more men in Penn Township of the same political faith.

His house was a station on the Under Ground Railroad from the opening of that route through this County, and continued so as long as it was used. Many colored men are indebted to him for the food and assistance they received on the road from bondage to freedom. In the memorable Kentucky Raid of 1847, Mr. Bogue was among the men prosecuted and put to great expense, the trial being held at Detroit in order to take it as far as possible from the defendants.

EPHRAIM HUNTLEY.

Ephraim Huntley was born in Saratoga County, New York, September 10th, 1798. At the age of eighteen he removed to Erie County, where he remained until the fall of 1833, when he came to Michigan, settling in Howard Township, where he has since remained. In the same fall he went back on business and was shipwrecked on the steamer George Washington, then on her fourth trip across the Lake (Erie), at Long Point, Canada, the steamer going ashore and breaking in two. One passenger was drowned in attempting to swim ashore from the wreck.

Mr. Huntley has been almost a life-long Free Mason, very enthusiastic in his devotion to the Order, was one of the charter members of Niles Lodge, No. 4, in the State, and was only about fifty miles from where the Morgan excitement existed in New York.

REV. JOHN BYRNS.

The subject of this sketch was born in Ireland, in the year 1816. When six years old his parents emigrated to this country and settled in Syracuse, New York, where he remained until coming to Michigan in 1837, settling in Pokagon Township, where he has remained ever since. In 1840 he was converted and joined the M. E. Church, and shortly after was licensed to exhort, and in 1841 was licensed to preach, in which capacity he has remained ever since. He has never been a member of the annual conference, but has filled numerous circuits by appointment from the Presiding Elder. There is probably no man in Southwestern Michigan who has devoted himself more unselfishly to the work of the Church than has Mr. Byrns. When placed upon a a circuit it was usually one so poor that they could not afford to employ a regular minister, and as a matter of necessity, he would have to work on his farm during the week and preach on Sunday, frequently traveling from fifty to seventy-five miles on horseback each week, besides his regular work. When not employed on a circuit, he had numerous charges within ten or fifteen miles of home, which he attended regularly.

Mr. Byrns is a man of untarnished reputation, is

a supporter and leader in everything that tends to the moral as well as spiritual elevation of mankind. While many others around him, of less energy and perseverence, have grown rich, he has been content to live on a small piece of land, and devote his talents to the cause of religion, believing that in so doing he will finally reap the reward that comes from an unselfish devotion to the cause of his Creator.

HON. JESSE G. BEESON.

Jesse G. Beeson was born in Wayne County, Indiana, in the year 1807, where he lived until coming to Michigan in 1833, having been here in 1830 and made a location on the land now owned by Abram Fiero, where he first settled. In 1837 he made a change, selling out and buying the farm where he still resides. Mr. Beeson is of English descent, his great-grandfather and two brothers coming from England in an early day, one of them settling in Pennsylvania, Mr. B.'s ancestor settling in North Carolinia, and, so far as known, all of the name can be traced to these three brothers. They are a strong, robust, hardy family, combining a healthy body with strong intellect. The subject of this sketch is probably as well known as any man in Cass County, was a Clay Whig we might almost say by birth and education, a member of that party when not another man on McKenney's Prairie agreed with him in political faith. He has always been a leader in whatever measures have been before the public, has been Supervisor of the Township, and was State

Senator in 1853, besides holding numerous other responsible positions.

JOSHUA LEACH.

Joshua Leach was born in Vermont, in the year 1812. When six years old his parents moved to Erie County, Pennsylvania, where he remained until 1833, when he came to Michigan, settling on Young's Prairie, where he has remained ever since. He has always followed the occupation of farmer, and he paid for the first piece of land he ever owned by chopping and clearing. In 1850 he went to California, and when two hundred miles west of St. Joseph, Missouri, his team was stolen by the Indians, when he took a pack on his back and walked the remainder of the way. He went by way of Salt Lake (one hundred and fifty miles out of his way) where he traded a blanket for fourteen pounds of flour, and on this and some bacon which he purchased, he lived the rest of the way.

ELIJAH GOBLE.

Elijah Goble was born eight miles north of Cincinnati, in the year 1805. His parents were Holland Dutch, and moved from Morristown, New Jersey, to Ohio in 1801. In 1818 his parents again moved to Preble County, in the same State, and in 1820 they moved to Franklin County, Indiana, where Elijah remained until he came to Michigan in 1828. He first came on a tour of inspection, in company with Jonathan Gard and a man named Tony, and in the spring of 1829 returned and made a location on the northwest corner of Little Prairie Ronde. In September, 1834, he was married to Eliza Tittle, with whom he still lives. Mr. Goble kept hotel at Charleston for over twenty years, ten years of which it was a stage station, and his fund of pioneer information is almost sufficient for a book of itself.

GALLUP FAMILY.

O. D. S., John S., and D. Harmon Gallup came to Michigan and settled in Howard Township in the season of 1834, O. D. S., the older brother, coming in the spring and making a location and putting out a crop, the family moving in the fall.

They were born in Franklin County, Vermont, in the years of 1806, 1816, and 1819, respectively. Their parents were from England, and settled in Cincinnati in 1831, where the father and one sister died of cholera in 1832. The older brother was well educated, and went into trade in Vermont and then to Cincinnati, where he carried on merchandising until coming to Michigan. About the year 1839 he went to Naperville, Illinois, and in 1852 he went to California, where he remained some time, then came back and settled in Howard Township, where he died in 1855.

In 1836 John S. went with a party of surveyors to Wisconsin and was employed in running out the land between the Fox and Rock Rivers, where he remained eight months without seeing the face of a white man, with the exception of their own party. In 1838 he went back again and made a claim, seven miles west of Milwaukee, and remained on it about eighteen months. While out the first time, he assisted in raising the Belview Hotel, which was the second frame house in Milwaukee, and during the first winter he and another man killed one hundred deer. Since his return from Wisconsin he has made Cass County his home, with the exception of four years, when he lived in Berrien County.

The younger brother has always remained in Michigan, and until 1863 in Cass County. In that year he went to Niles and engaged in the grocery trade, where he still resides.

EBENEZER COPLEY.

Ebenezer Copley was born in Hartford, Connecticut, in December, 1786, and came to Michigan in May, 1835, settling near Little Prairie Ronde, where he remained until the time of his death, in March, 1841. His wife, Annis, or aunt Annis, as she was universally called, was born in Granby, Connecticut, and lived until 1848. Their sons, A. G., T. N., D. B., and Ebenezer, all remain in Michigan, and with the exception of T. N., in Cass County.

HON. JAMES O'DELL.

The subject of this sketch was born in Virginia, on the 20th of July, 1779. When twenty-one years of age he moved to Highland County, Ohio, where he remained until coming to Michigan, in 1831. He first settled in St. Joseph County, where he lived but one year, moving into this County in 1832, settling just south of the present site of Vandalia, and at what was known as the Carpenter Mill, and afterward as the O'Dell Mill.

He was a miller and farmer by occupation. He was a member of the first Constitutional Convention, and also represented this County in the State Legislature. He died on the 23d of August, 1845. His two sons, John and Nathan, still live on the old homestead, and another son in Ohio.

JAMES COULTER.

The subject of this sketch was born of Irish parentage, in Hamilton County, Ohio, on the 17th of May, 1808.

Soon after the birth of James, his parents moved to Clinton County, in the same State, where he remained until coming to Michigan, in 1834. He first came in company with his father, and brought a drove of cattle, which were disposed of and five hundred and sixty acres of land purchased in Howard Township. He remained during the winter and worked at making sash, by which he realized the sum of two hundred dollars, and in the spring went back to Ohio on foot.

In June, 1836, he was married to Ann Wilson, and immediately set out for their future home, in the then wilds of Michigan, where they arrived after a tedious journey of seventeen days, with an ox team.

He was a man of strong convictions and decided character, although not demonstrative, yet his will was law. In religious and moral matters he knew no half way ground, but pushed everything with a zeal worthy the cause.

In politics he was a partisan, which for a man of his organization, he could hardly have been otherwise. His religious belief was in accordance with the M. E. Church, which faith he espoused about fifty years before his death, and soon after coming to Michigan his house was thrown open for public worship, and remained so until school houses and houses of worship were built, making it unnecessary.

Coulter's Chapel was built on his land. The site for the Church as well as the Cemetery, was donated by him, beside paying liberally toward the erection of the Church building.

He filled numerous Township offices during his lifetime, and retained the esteem and confidence of all that knew him, until the time of his death, which occurred on the 16th of February, 1874.

THOMAS McKENNEY.

Thomas McKenney was born in Washington County, New York, in the year 1781. When sixteen years old he moved to Cayuga County, where he remained until 1813.

During the war of 1812 he acted as a home guard,

and was at Sodus Bay when the British surrendered that place.

In 1817 he came to Huron County, Ohio, where he lived two years, then moving to Wayne County, Indiana, where he remained until coming to Michigan, in the fall of 1827.

He and his oldest son came out on horse-back, in the fall of the year, on a prospecting tour, and stopped a while with the settlers on Pokagon Prairie. He was so well pleased with the country that on his return he immediately set about preparing to move to the country he had determined to make his home. He came again in March, 1828, built a cabin and put in crops, and moved out his family in October of the same year.

Mr. McKenney's description of the country induced a number of his neighbors to join him in the expedition, among whom were some of the most intelligent and enterprising of Cass County's citizens. His reputation for generosity and hospitality will last scarce longer than the prairie that still bears his name. He was the first Judge of Probate in the County, and filled numerous other positions. He died near Council Bluffs, Iowa, in 1852, at the age of seventy-one. Micajah, his son, now living in California, John A., living in Iowa, and one daughter, Mrs. Dickson, the mother of the well known family of that name, are all that are left.

JAMES DICKSON.

James Dickson was born in Westmoreland County,

Pennsylvania, in the year 1794. In 1811 he moved to Huron County, Ohio, and in 1819 he removed to Wayne County, Indiana, where he was married to Lillis, eldest daughter of Judge McKenney. In 1828 he moved to Michigan, arriving on the 23rd of October, and settling on the farm now owned by William Renniston, in La Grange, buying the first quarter section of land that was bought by one man on McKenney's Prairie, and building the third cabin on the prairie.

Mr. Dickson was a great reader and had a large store of practical information. He was appointed and elected to numerous positions, but never accepted anything, preferring to attend to his own business and leave politics to the more aspiring. He died September 16th, 1866, at the age of seventy-two. His family, of nine children, are all living, except one daughter, Mrs. G. C. Jones.

GEORGE FOSDICK.

George Fosdick was born on the Island of Nantucket, Massachusetts. When nine years old his parents moved to Campbell County, Virginia, and from thence to Union County, Indiana, about the year 1822, where he remained until coming to Michigan in 1830. He first settled at Niles, where he worked at blacksmithing two years, when he moved into this County, settling on the north side of Barron Lake, in Howard Township, where he established a shop and laid out a village named Howard. He cleared up and improved the farm now owned by Henry Pryn, and at the same time carried on the manufactory of agricultural implements. A speciality of his was the making of jail locks, which he did for Southern Michigan and Northern Indiana, and one on the old jail in this County was made by him. In 1838 he moved to Laporte, Indiana, where he died in 1865.

G. W. Fosdick, his son, now living in Dowagiac, was born in Lynchburg, Virginia, and has been identified with Michigan interests nearly all his life. He married Sarah, eldest daughter of Levi Hall, one of the pioneers of Volinia Township. He studied medicine in an early day and has made the practice of it his profession through life.

A. C. MARSH.

A. C. Marsh was born in Litchfield County, Connecticut, in July, 1793, where he lived until sixteen years of age, when he removed to Duchess County, New York, where he remained until coming to Michigan in 1836, settling in Edwardsburg, where he has resided ever since.

While living in New York he learned the trade of scythe making. But, soon after commencing business on his own account, owing to the great influx of scythes from New England, the business had to be abandoned in all country shops, and Mr. Marsh turned his attention to country blacksmithing, and followed that calling for two years after coming to Michigan.

In 1838 a stock company was formed for the purpose of carrying on the foundry business, in which Mr. Marsh took an active part, and in 1839, before it was got in operation, he bought out the other stockholders, which business he carried on until the death of his son, in 1874, when it was discontinued. In an early day their chief business was making plows and sleigh shoes, with an occasional country job, among which may be mentioned was mill castings for some of the early manufactories at South Bend. In 1842 he also manufactured steel plows and continued it for some years.

EZEKIEL C. SMITH.

Ezekiel C. Smith was born in Erie County, New York, in 1812, and came to Michigan in 1835, settling in Howard Township, where he has resided ever since. He held the office of Justice of the Peace from the adoption of the State Constitution, in 1836, until 1872 without intermission, except about six months, a period of thirty-six years. He has held the office of Supervisor twelve years nearly in succession.

Mr. Smith is a good representative of the hardy Western pioneer, a large, powerful built man, whose presence bespeaks the force so necessary in contending with dame nature in opening up a new country, withal a genial, kind-hearted, generous man. He has been very successful as a farmer, now owning one of the finest farms in Howard Township.

When Mr. Smith first commenced to build his cabin, getting thirsty he determined to go across some half mile away to his nearest neighbor's to get a drink of water and to get acquainted. He was met at the yard fence by some ten or twelve dogs, who seemed by their demostrations ready to make a meal of him. In front of the house sat a woman astride of a shaving-horse, at work on a hoe handle, who, hearing the dogs making a fuss, turned around, at the same time yelling to the lead dog, "Lord Almighty, Dragon, be down with you, or I will throw a rock at you," which had the effect of quelling the disturbance, and Mr. Smith was enabled to get his drink of water.

PETER TRUITT.

The subject of this sketch was born in Sussex County, Delaware, February 7th, 1801, where he remained until 1831, when he removed to Michigan, settling in Milton Township. For a time he sold goods in Bertrand, and afterward brought the remainder of his stock to where he now resides, and sold it out. He also kept hotel and postoffice for a number of years, and was known far and near.

He came West for the purpose of bettering his condition, and has never had cause to regret the change. His chief occupation through life has been that of a farmer, in which he has been very successful, accumulating over one thousand four hundred acres of land.

When he came the M. E. Church contained but ten members. He and his wife joined, raising the number to twelve, to which Church he has belonged ever since, with the exception of a period of seventeen years, when from some differences of opinion in the Church, he withdrew.

To Mr. Truitt belongs the credit of naming Milton Township. At the time the petition was circulating for the organization of that Township, it was left with him for the purpose of getting signatures, but not liking the name (Southland) as named in the petition, took the liberty of changing it to that of Milton, the same name that his native town in Delaware bore.

JOSEPH WEBSTER LEE.

Joseph Webster Lee was born in Sandwich, Stafford County, New Hampshire, on the 10th day of January, 1807, about six months after his father's death, being left to buffet the waves of life without the aid or counsel of a father, and only a poor widowed mother to rear and educate him. He inherited a more ungovernable set of passions than are the usual lot of man.

In 1828 he married Maria Hastings, and started boldly on the "sea of life." He soon became tired of a New England farmer's life and determined to try his fortune in the far West Territory of Michigan, where he arrived at the house of his brother-in-law, Abiel Silver, in the village of Edwardsburg, on the 19th day of June, 1836, after a wearisome journey of six week's duration, with a two-horse team and a canvas covered wagon, over roads known only to the trader and pioneer.

With him to will was to do, and he at once invested his limited means in land, buying the north-east quarter of section eight, in Ontwa Township, on which he moved the block house formerly built by Ezra Beardsley, and which had answered the purpose of dwelling, Court House and hotel. This was made to answer the purpose of a habitation until his means permitted him to supplant it with a commodious brick residence.

He was a strong partisan, being politically, a Whig and Republican, and religiously, a Methodist, a stern moralist, a worker in the cause of education, a firm and unflinching supporter of law and order, never fearing the mob nor flattering the powerful; *popularity* was not a factor in any of his calculations. He always had an opinion of his own and was ever ready to express it, and he was loved by his friends and respected by his enemies. He was an intense worker and succeeded in obtaining a competence which was enjoyed through the latter part of his life by himself and family, as well as numerous friends. He died August 24th, 1874, followed by his wife on the 3rd of February, 1875.

JOHN RHINEHART.

John Rhinehart was born in the State of Virginia, in the year 1771. In 1823 he moved to Ohio, where he lived until February, 1829, when he came to Michigan, settling where James E. Bonine now lives, on Young's Prairie, buying the claim of a man named Hinkley. He remained here four or five

—23

years, when he sold out to a man named Collins, and moved to Porter Township, where he resided until the time of his death in 1858.

His family consisted of Jacob, Catherine, (Mrs. George Meacham,) Lewis, Samuel, Susan, (Mrs. Kirk,) John, Abraham, Christiana, (Mrs. Stevens,) and Ann, (Mrs. Hall and afterward Mrs. Sullivan,) all of whom are still living, with the exception of Mrs. Kirk.

Mr. Rhinehart was of German descent, his grand parents on both sides emigrating from that country. In coming to Michigan he was accompanied by John Price and John Donnel, who also settled on Young's Prairie.

ABRAM TOWNSEND.

The subject of this sketch was born in the State of New York, in the year 1771. A portion of his younger days were spent in Upper Canada, and in 1815 he moved to Huron County, Ohio, where he remained but a short time. Moving to Sandusky County, where the town of Townsend was named for him, he remained until 1825, when he came to Michigan, where he moved his family in 1827. He first located in Pokagon and moved on to La Grange Prairie, (then called Townsend's Prairie) in the spring of 1828, and to him belongs the credit of naming the prairie and Township.

His son, Gamaliel, was born in the town of York, Canada West, January 20th, 1802, and came to Michigan with his father in 1826. He has ever since been identified with Cass County interests. For a number of years he has been afflicted with nearly total blindness, which has deprived him of many of the enjoyments of life.

HAIN FAMILY.

John, David, and Jacob Hain were born in Lincoln County, North Carolinia, and with their parents moved to Clark County, Ohio, about the year 1820, where they remained until 1831, when they came to Michigan, settling in La Grange Township, where the two older brothers have lived ever since, Jacob removing West but a few years ago.

John and David participated in the Black Hawk war, making numerous trips to Niles for the purpose of fighting the Indians.

On one of these occasions John relates that he went in company with a man named Boon, who lived about two miles on the way. Their conveyance consisted of a two-wheeled gig, drawn by a blind horse, and returning in the night to Mr. Boon's, where they expected to find their women and children, were surprised to find the house deserted; but continuing on to Mr. Hain's house, they found the two women, one in either corner of the fire place, with their respective children surrounding them, and the big dog lying in the middle.

John at one time, considering that taking care of his family was of more importance than fighting imaginary Indians, did not heed the order to appear at Niles, and the authorities in power gave him the benefit of a court martial, but the penalty was remitted after the war was over.

David commenced blacksmithing in 1832, and has carried on the business ever since. In early times he manufactured the "Bull Plow," in which he was quite successful, customers coming a distance of twenty miles to get his plows and repairs. He assures me that he could make three a day, which he readily sold for seven dollars each. In 1837 or '38 he made for Daniel Wilson a plow out of steel, which worked well on prairie soil, and was probably the first steel plow in the County.

The first winter after coming to Michigan, David lived in a small log cabin with two other families, (seventeen members in all) in which there was neither door, window, chimney, or floor. At one time their breadstuff ran very low, and he and a man named McPherson started for Ford's Mill, distant eight miles in a direct line, but much farther the way they had to travel. The snow was three feet deep, without a beaten path. Their stock of provisions for the trip consisted of a biscuit each and a quantity of boiled venison. After a hard day's travel they arrived at the mill to find a full day's grinding ahead of them; but by taking turns with the miller through the night in attending the mill, they were enabled to start home at three o'clock in the afternoon following. Night coming on soon after leaving the mill, the only way to proceed was for one to go ahead and feel the sled track made the previous day, the other following and driving the team. At one place, where there was a short turn in the road, they missed the track, going some distance out of the way, which had to be retraced, no small task in the night and in thick timber. About daylight they arrived at a widow lady's house, two miles from home, so nearly famished that they could go no farther. Here they stopped and had a cake baked to last them home, where they arrived about noon, to find their families in great distress, fearing that they had become lost in the woods and consequent starvation would be their portion.

DAVID BRADY.

David Brady was born in Sussex County, New York, in May, 1795. When twenty-three years of age he moved to Franklin County, Ohio, where he lived five years, then moving to Sandusky County, where he remained until coming to Michigan in 1828, settling on La Grange Prairie, where he has remained ever since.

Mr. Brady is a good representative of the hardy class of pioneers who made the early settlements of the West, possessed of an iron constitution and a will that knew no obstacle, elements absolutely necessary in subduing natural obstacles and bringing the wilderness under subjection for the use of civilization. He is of rather rough exterior, but kind hearted and generous to a fault.

JARIUS HITCHCOX.

Jarius Hitchcox was born in Oneida County, New

York, in the year 1795, and came to Michigan in 1830. He settled in Porter Township on the land now owned by his son, J. H. Hitchcox, and moved his family out in the following year.

He was a brick and stone mason by trade, which occupation he followed most of the time through life. His death occurred on the 14th of April, 1850, at the age of fifty-five years.

JESSE GREEN.

Jesse Green was born in Welsh County, Georgia, in the year 1790. When fifteen years old his parents moved to Preble County, Ohio, where he lived until coming to Michigan in 1831. He was a Quaker by birth-right, but, from some differences arising in regard to the liquor question, he never acted in concert with them after coming to Michigan.

His first location was on the north side of Young's Prairie, where he remained a year or two, when he moved into Wayne Township on the farm since owned by his son, Eli Green, Esq. While in Ohio he followed merchandising and brought a small stock of goods to Michigan, which, after selling out, was not renewed.

AMOS GREEN.

Amos Green was born on the 10th of December, 1794, in the State of Georgia. While quite young, with his mother, he moved to Randolph County, North Carolinia, and afterward to Preble County,

Ohio, where he remained until coming to Michigan in 1831. He settled on the east side of Young's Prairie, where he lived until the time of his death, which occurred on the 6th of August, 1854, at the age of fifty-nine years, his wife, Sarah, following him on the 13th of December, 1863, at the age of sixty-seven years. They reared a family of fifteen children, all of whom grew to man and womanhood except three.

JOHN TOWNSEND.

John Townsend was born in Wayne County, Indiana, in the year 1804. He came to Michigan in 1829, settling north of Young's Prairie, on the farm now owned by Jay Rudd, where he lived until the time of his death, which occurred on the 20th of November, 1835. While a young man he carried on the manufacture of edge tools in Butler and Preble Counties, Ohio, and also dealt in merchandise, but after coming to Michigan followed the occupation of farmer, with the exception of the time occupied by the Black Hawk war, in which he was a captain. His three sons, William, George and James, all remain citizens of this County.

DAVID HOPKINS.

David Hopkins was born in Washington County, New York, in the year 1794, where he lived until 1816, when he moved to Cayuga County, remaining there until 1834, when he came to Michigan. He first settled on the river below Niles, where he lived two years, then moving to Volinia, where he died on the 7th of April, 1850, at the age of fifty-six, his wife surviving him but two days.

He was a man of many peculiarities, especially in dress, frequently going bare-headed and bare-footed, when others required heavy winter clothing; a great hunter and trapper, at home in the woods wherever night overtook him. His special forte was bee hunting, and it is said that not unfrequently every available vessel about the house would be filled with honey from the woods. He was a man of considerable native ability and shrewdness, and served a number of terms as Supervisor and one term as County Commissioner.

RICHARD V. HICKS.

Richard V. Hicks was born in the County of Cornwall, England, in the year 1818. When seventeen years of age, in company with his father, he came to Cass County. His three brothers had preceded them two years. One of them was killed at a raising in Ohio. The second fell overboard from a boat on the Ohio River, and being struck by one of the paddle wheels was never seen afterward. The third was a lake captain for thirty years and died at the house of R. V. about two years ago, and still another brother died about the same time at the house of his son-in-law, Emmet Dunning, in Howard Township.

The first season after coming to Michigan he

settled in Ontwa Township, on the farm now owned by Mr. Hadden, but in the fall of 1838 he went to Niles and hired out to feed hogs at a distillery at that place. Being of an ingenious turn of mind he soon rose to the position of forman of the distillery, which business he followed six or seven years at different places in the County. In 1843 he abandoned distilling and settled in the Truitt neighborhood, where he remained six or seven years until he removed to the place where he now resides. In 1843 he was married to Catherine Ullrey, with whom he still lives.

DANIEL McINTOSH, Sr.

The subject of this sketch was born in Scotland in the 1765. When about thirty-two years of age he imigrated to this country, settling at Baltimore, Maryland, where he remained a year or two, then moving to Alleghany County, in the same State. He afterward moved to Wayne County, Ohio, and from thence to Michigan in 1829. His occupation was that of wagon and carriage maker, but while in Baltimore he followed the business of sawing veneerning.

It was late in November when they started for Michigan and extreme cold weather overtook them when near Tecumseh, where they were encamped for the night. In the morning they found that their horses had all ran away in the night except one kept hitched to the wheel. Instructing his son Daniel to push on with the family in the ox wagon, he set out to look for the horses, employing a man named Dorrel to pilot him through the woods. This man proved to be a treacherous wretch, and, as soon as out of sight, he abandoned Mr. McIntosh, who soon became bewildered and, overcome by the extreme cold weather, he wandered around for five days and nights, finally crawling to a house on his hands and knees with his feet so badly frozen that he could not use them. In this condition he remained fifteen days after coming in, or until word could be got to his family and he could be removed home. One of his feet paining him very badly, his son was sent to White Pigeon for a surgeon to amputate it, but finding the Doctor had gone to Detroit on business that would detain him some time he came home without him.

On his arrival at home his father, who was in great pain all the time, importuned him to cut off his foot with a knife, the only instrument of a surgical character in their possession, which he did after putting his father off as long as possible in the hope that some one more skilled could be procured, but mortification setting in made it a matter of necessity. The foot was unjointed at the ankle and done up in the best manner with such materials as were at hand, and some time afterward the other foot was amputated by a surgeon. He was a man of great energy—after loosing both his feet he would work at chopping wood, sawing with a cross-cut saw or hoeing corn, using his knees to walk on instead of feet. He seemed to enjoy himself best when busy, and long after his family wished him to quit work he would beg to be carried to the field where others were at work, that he might take part in whatever was going on. His sons, William, Daniel and Duncan, all came with their father, and are, at the present time, citizens of the County.

EZRA MILLER.

Ezra Miller was born in Onondaga County and town, New York, July 6th, 1808. In 1818, with his parents, he moved to Erie County, settling on land belonging to the Holland Land Company. By the rascality of some outside parties, Ezra was swindled out of all the money he had paid on the land and the improvements he had made, which was the cause of his coming to Michigan, in the hope of retrieving his fortune.

He came to Detroit in 1833, where he followed the occupation of driving team for two years, when he came to this County, in May, 1835, settling in Edwardsburg, where he has ever since remained. When he arrived here, he had but forty-eight dollars in money; but with the assistance of friends, he was enabled to raise enough to enter forty acres of land, and in the fall of the same year he added another forty to his possessions, all of which he still retains.

Previous to his coming West, he was married to Maria A. Best, by whom he has had six children, of whom two only are now living. Mr. and Mrs. Miller have been members of the Congregational Church over twenty years.

REV. JACOB PRICE.

The subject of this sketch was born in Breconshire, South Wales, on the 28th of March, 1799. His father was a Deacon in the Baptist Church, and a man highly respected for his integrity and good judgment, but died when Jacob was but five years old, leaving him and a sister, but four years older, to be supported and educated by the mother. This proved a hard task in that country, but she worked with energy and faithfulness, and lived to see her son a steady youth of seventeen, with good mind and morals.

Young Jacob had early formed the intention of making his future home in America, and his mother's death loosened the last tie that bound him to the Old World. He determined to gain an education, if possible, before leaving, and for this purpose entered the Baptist Academy, at Abergavenny, where he completed a regular course of study. Here, of necessity, he learned the English language, in which all the text books were printed. When twenty-two years old he united with the Church, and soon after commenced to preach, and while in the Academy he filled various appointments in the southern Counties of Wales.

After completing his studies, he resided with his sister a year or two in Hay, in which time they settled their affairs, preparatory to embarking for America.

In 1830 he married a Miss Ann Price, an English lady, and, in the following autumn, with his wife and sister, bade their old friends a last good-bye and sailed for the new country, the voyage occupying nearly the entire month of September, 1831. While yet on shipboard, he was waited upon by a number of prominent Baptists, who had heard of the young minister and welcomed by them to his new home. They made their home in New York the remainder of the year, and on the 6th of January, 1832, he was ordained pastor of the Second Baptist Church, of Brooklyn, where he remained a little over eighteen months.

Mr. Price had intended from the start to settle in the West and preach the Gospel to that far off people, and while in Brooklyn made additions to his library for this purpose.

In the summer of 1833, M. C. Whitman, a merchant from Cass County, was in New York on business, and inquired of Dr. Going if he knew of any minister who would be willing to come as a pioneer and preach in the scattered settlements of Western Michigan. Dr. Going introduced him to Mr. P., who soon after made his arrangements to come to this County.

On the 1st of September, 1833, he was in Detroit, and two Sabbaths later, he preached in La Grange, where he had taken up his residence. His next place of preaching was at Geneva. On the 27th of the same month he preached at South Bend, and on their return from this place, his wife was taken with a fever, from which she died on the 19th of the following month, and his own health was so poor at this time that he was hardly able to sit up at the funeral.

While at La Grange he had regular appointments for preaching at Bertrand and Edwardsburg, and besides these three appointments, he preached occasionally in nearly all parts of the County, as well as attending funerals far and wide. In 1836 he removed, with his sister and only child, to Edwardsburg, where he bought eighty acres of land, on which he lived seven years, at the same time preaching in Southwestern Michigan and Northern Indiana.

In 1836 he was married to Miss Sarah Bennett, who still survives him, as does his sister, who came to the County with him.

In 1842 he removed to Cassopolis, where he made his home until the time of his death, a period of twenty-nine years. He was pastor of the Church at Union from about the year 1850 until the time of his death, in 1871. Were there a record of all the funerals preached and the marriages solemnized by Elder Price in this County, it would include a large part of its domestic history.

ALEXANDER COPLEY.

Alexander Copley was born in the Town of Granby, Hartford County, Connecticut, on the 22nd of November, 1790. His grandfather, in company with his brother, emigrated from England to this country when young men, settling in Connecticut, where he was married, and, within two years, was drowned in the Connecticut River while returning from his weekly labor one Saturday evening in a canoe, a belt around his body, containing his accumulated earnings in silver, is supposed to have been partially the cause of his misfortune. He left one son, the father of the subject of this sketch.

Mr. Copley was the youngest of six children. His father dying when he was but six years old, his education and support devolved largely upon his own efforts. He first learned the trade of carpenter, and then that of machinist, in which capacity he arose to the position of superintendent of the Mattawan Manufacturing Company's works, which he held three years.

On the 12th of September, 1829, he left Mattawan for Dayton, Ohio, where he arrived on the 18th of November, and in October of the next year, as superintendent, he started in operation the first Cotton mill at Dayton, the machinery for which he had superintended while at Mattawan.

On the 9th of June, 1833, he left Dayton for Michigan, arriving at Little Prairie Ronde on the 1st day of July—averaging eleven miles a day with ox teams and camping out every night while on the route. He bought the land where Nicholsville now stands, and built a saw mill in 1835, which was the first in the Township, and, in connection, run a cabinet shop until the financial depression of 1837 and '38, which, with ill health, made it necessary to abandon this department.

He brought with him, from Ohio, three sizes of Wood's patent cast iron plows, two head of Durham cattle, bred by John C. Brooks, of Ridgeville, Ohio; and in 1836 manufactured a revolving rake from a description furnished by a man from New York. The first school in the Township was taught by his oldest daughter, in his house. He afterward built a school house, which was used by the first district organized in the Township until it was burned down.

He was a man of very superior native and acquired ability, and far in advance of the necessities of pioneer life. Upon first arriving in this vicinity he examined the water privileges of the Christianna and St. Joseph and prepared a detailed map of the peculiarities and advantages, which is still preserved by his family. He always kept a full and accurate journal of current events which has been of service in the construction of this work. He died January 6th, 1842, aged fifty-one.

His oldest son, A. B. Copley, at present President of the First National Bank of Decatur, was a pioneer and resident of this County until 1874, and has exerted a marked influence upon its progress, both socially and politically. He has satisfactorily served his Township as Supervisor for six years, and has been three times sent to the Legislature—twice by this County and once by Van Buren.

He is a man of strong will and honest impulses, and, although largely self educated, has acquired a fund of general information and culture which secures to him a leading position among his fellows.

JOSEPHUS GARD.

The subject of this sketch, and father of the numerous family bearing the name, who were among the early pioneers of Cass County, was born in Morris County, New Jersey, August 24th, 1774. In 1801 he moved to Ohio, settling near Cincinnati, where he remained six years, then removing to Union County, Indiana, where he remained until coming to Michigan, in the fall of 1830. His business through life was farming, but while in Indiana carried on a tan-yard. His wife, Sarah Goble, was born in New Jersey, December 15th, 1773. He settled on the farm now owned by Loomis H. Warner, where he lived until the time of his death, August 4th, 1840.

JONATHAN GARD.

Jonathan Gard, the second son of Josephus, and one of the first settlers of Volinia Township, was born April 6th, 1799, in New Jersey, and came to Michigan the season of 1828, on a prospecting tour. So much pleased was he with the country, that immediate preparation was made for coming hither, which he did in the spring of 1829, arriving the 30th day of March, settling on the farm now occupied by his sons, at that time consisting of a small prairie of about two hundred acres, entirely surrounded by heavy timber, where he lived until the time of his death, in 1854. He was a man of great force, both mentally and physically, of very generous disposition, his hospitality hardly knowing any bounds, always ready to help the needy. He left a record in the hearts ot the people that will not be obliterated while the present generation lasts. His wife still survives him, living among her children in the immediate vicinity, a quiet, serene old lady, of whom no one would judge from her looks that she had been through the vicissitudes of the settlement of a new country.

JOHN B. GARD.

John B. Gard, or Brookfield, as he was commonly called, was born October 4th, 1808, in Indiana. He came to Michigan in the fall of 1829, settling on the farm now owned by J. Vancuren. He was the first Collector of Volinia Township, when it comprised what is now Marcellus, and all of Van Buren County. He was of a restless disposition, and must be on the move, and not satisfied with the tameness of civilization. On the breaking out of the California fever, he was among the first to take up the Westward march, and is now a resident of one of the Western Territories.

SAMUEL RICH.

The subject of this sketch was born in Rowana County, North Carolina, in August, 1802. While quite young, his parents moved to Adams County, Ohio, where he remained until coming to Michigan, in the spring of 1829. He was married to Charity

Gard, November 23d, 1827. He died February 20th, 1873. John H. Rich, his son, born October 21st, 1829, was the first white child born in the Township.

Mr. Rich was a quiet, unassuming man, much respected by all that knew him, a farmer through life. His wife still lives at the old homestead.

HIRAM ROGERS.

Hiram Rogers was born in Morris County, New Jersey, in the year 1802. When quite young his parents moved to the State of New York, first settling in Steuben County, near Crooked Lake, but afterward moved to Ontario County, and again to Niagara County, where he remained until coming to Michigan in 1831, settling on section one of Milton Township, where he has remained ever since. He came to Michigan in company with Luther Chapin, who remained in this County for many years, but is now a resident of Naperville, Illinois. Mr. R. became a member of the M. E. Church early in life, and has remained an earnest, consistent worker with that body ever since. His occupation throughout his life has been that of a farmer.

ALLEN DUNNING.

Allen Dunning was born near Albany, New York, July 27th, 1796. When he arrived at manhood he removed to Erie County, Pennsylvania, where he lived until coming to Michigan in 1836. He was married to Minerva Reynolds January 12th, 1824. Mr. Dunning settled in Milton Township, where he resided until the time of his death, December 10th, 1869. Mrs. Dunning still lives on the old homestead with her son. In an early day Mr. Dunning learned the trade of cloth dressing, which he followed for some years, or until about the time he was married, after which he followed farming. Mr. and Mrs. Dunning both held to the faith of universal salvation, and belonged to the church of that denomination at Niles. Their house was frequently used for public worship by that denomination. At the time of Mr. Dunning's death there had not been a death in his father's family in forty years.

HON. G. B. TURNER.

George Brunt was born in Franklin County, New York, in 1822. He was of Irish extraction, but, being left an orphan at an early age, was adopted by Sterling A. Turner, a Virginian, whose patronymic he has since borne.

He received a common school education until he was thirteen years of age, when he removed with Mr. Turner to Detroit. Here he found employment in a commission house for about a year, until in 1836, when he came to Cassopolis. After he arrived at his new and, as it proved, permanent home, he engaged in teaching school at from twelve to fifteen dollars per month, and at the same time pursued a settled and rigorous course of study with a view to fitting himself for acquiring the profession of the law.

Upon the advice of Nathaniel (afterwards Judge) Bacon he made a specialty of history, both ancient and modern, as a preparatory and disciplinary study.

After teaching for several terms he served as clerk for the Kingsbury Brothers about two years and then entered the law office of A. H. Redfield, where he remained four years, being admitted to the bar in 1844.

While a student in Mr. Redfield's office he found remunerative and instructive employment in practicing in the Justice Courts.

Soon after being admitted to practice he was married to Harriet Munroe who died in 1858.

His present wife was an English lady, the widow of John Tytherleigh, who immigrated to this country in 1850.

He quitted the practice of law in 1850, on account of ill health, and moved on to a farm. Was succeeded in business by D. Blackman, afterwards elected Judge of this Circuit. In 1848 he was elected to to represent Cass County in the State Legislature, and was re-elected in 1849. In 1856 he was nominated by the Democratic party for State Senator. The Republican party, organized this year, swept the State, and Mr. Turner shared the fate of other nominees of his party, *i. e.* was beaten. In 1866 he was nominated as Secretary of State, and in 1868 as Presidential Elector on the Seymour ticket, with like results. He has been twice nominated for Probate Judge, and once for Prosecuting Attorney by the same party.

Mr. Turner is a man of unbounded energy and

noted for his great earnestness and strict integrity of character. He was the first editor of the Cassopolis *Democrat*, and has always been a liberal contributor to the press.

He has from early manhood been a staunch Jeffersonian Democrat, has defended stoutly, with pen and tongue, what he believed to be true democratic principles, and has made warm friends and bitter enemies thereby.

WILLIAM SHANAFELT.

William Shanafelt came from Sandusky, Ohio, in 1835, and settled where Cassopolis now stands. The first school house was built on his land. A hole was dug under the floor for the purpose of getting mud to daub the cracks with. It was afterward used by the teachers for a dungeon, in which to punish unruly scholars, by putting them in. Another mode of punishment was by taking the unruly urchin over the knees, and applying the ruler with a brisk motion.

At one time Henry Shanafelt was up for some boyish misdemeanor, and when brought into the required position for torture, Mr. Harper, the first teacher in the school house, made the remark that he was well prepared for such occasions. His grandmother, one of those economical, good old ladies, an honor of their time, had placed numerous patches on various parts of his pants, and particularly heavy on that part where the punishment was likely to fall.

CANNON SMITH.

The subject of this sketch was born in the State of Delaware, where he lived until the spring of 1828, when he started for the West, intending to make the Wabash country his stopping place. In Delaware County, Ohio, he stopped to visit a brother, and while there met a man from the St. Joseph Valley, who gave such a favorable report of the fertility of the soil and the general advantages, that Mr. Smith determined to abandon his first destination and come to Michigan. He was accompanied by a man named Case, who came as an assistant, and also to look at the country.

Through the Auglaize country, for the distance of eighty miles, but one team had preceded him. He arrived at Edwardsburg October 12th, 1828. In the season of 1830 he rented Ezra Beardsley's farm, and in the spring of 1831 built a frame house, the first one in Milton Township. The lumber for this house was all split and shaved out—not a sawed board in it.

Mr. Smith and family were members of the M. E. Ghurch, and were among the first to help organize a Society in the south part of the County. His house was used for public worship until the school house was built, and that until the Chapel, which bears the name of the subject of this sketch. His sons, John H., George, Wesley, and Cannon, are still living in the immediate neighborhood of the old homestead, in Milton Township.

DANIEL BLISH.

The subject of this sketch was born in Cheshire County, New Hampshire, in the year 1812. When five years old his parents moved to Essex County, New York, where he remained until coming to Michigan, in July, 1839. He is a millwright by trade, and the first season worked on Pain's Mill, above Niles, until February, 1840, when he settled in Silver Creek Township, on section thirty-two, where, in the heavy timber, he cleared up a large farm wholly by his own effort and industry, and on which he resided until coming to Dowagiac, in the fall of 1874.

He has served as Supervisor of his Township ten years, eight of which were in succession. He was elected Justice of the Peace in 1843, and served in that capacity thirteen years in succession.

ISAAC WILLIAMS.

Isaac Williams was born near Lynchburg, Virginia, in the year 1800. About 1815 he came to Ohio, where he lived twenty years, until coming to Michigan, in 1835, settling in Pokagon Township, on section five. He was the first settler in this part of the Township. His nearest neighbor for a number of years was four miles distant. He lived on the same farm where he first settled until the time of his death, November 22d, 1874, at the advanced age of seventy-four years.

DAVID M. HOWELL.

David M. Howell was born in Champaign County, Ohio, in the year 1817, and came to Michigan with his father in 1834, at first settling in Bertrand; his father having a contract on the Chicago road.

In 1841 he moved into Howard Township, in this County, where he served as Township Clerk and Justice of the Peace until elected to the office of Register of Deeds, in 1844, when he removed to Cassopolis. He held the office of Register twelve years in succession, and was Justice of the Peace until he moved on his farm in 1858.

Mr. Howell's success in life is a good illustration of what may be done by an honest course, perseverance and energy—from infancy a cripple, dependent wholly upon his hands and head, he has accumulated a fine property. He is accredited as being one of the best farmers in the County, although never able to plow a furrow in his life.

FULTON FAMILY.

Alexander and Samuel Fulton came from Franklin County, Ohio, in 1829, settling on the south side of Little Prairie Ronde, David and James coming in July, 1833.

The three oldest brothers, Alexander, Samuel and David, after staying five or six years, removed to Berrien County, selling a part of their interest in the land to Dolphin Morris, now the farm of Samuel Morris, and the remainder to the brother James, who remained where he first settled until the time of his death, last year. David died in Berrien County about the year 1844, and Alexander in 1865. In 1852 Samuel went to California, where he remained until the time of his death, some two years ago.

WILLIAM R. WRIGHT.

The subject of this sketch was born in Sussex County, New Jersey, about the year 1779, and while a young man moved to Butler County, Ohio, where he lived until coming to Michigan, in the season of 1828.

The experience of Mr. Wright and family the first winter after coming in, was of the most severe character. Breadstuffs became very scarce and dear. Potatoes and Johnny-cake were staples, while pork and flour were rarities.

The family have always been noted for keeping fine horses, and these had to be kept mainly on hackberry bark for several weeks at a time. The manner of preparing it was to cut the timber into suitable lengths for rails, draw the cuts up before the cabin door, when they would be split into rails, carried in before the fire and warmed sufficiently to start the bark, which would be peeled off, broken up, and carried to the animals by the bushel basket full.

His son, Stephen D. Wright, still lives on the old homestead, his father having passed away many years ago.

WILSON BLACKMAR.

Wilson Blackmar was born in Connecticut, in 1792, removed with his parents, when fourteen years old, to Buffalo County, New York, where he remained until three years previous to coming to Michigan, when he moved to Huron County, Ohio. Came to Michigan in 1829, arriving at Edwardsburg on the second day of July. On their arrival preparation was in progress for a celebration of the coming 4th of July, and Mrs. Blackmar made a flag from two red silk handkerchiefs for the occasion, sewing on the stars and stripes.

His family consisted of four girls and two boys. Nathaniel B. Blackmar, the oldest son, was born in Erie County, New York. When ten years old he came with his father to Michigan, and, with the exception of two years, has resided here ever since.

ISAAC SEARS.

Isaac Sears was born near Hartford, Connecticut, in the year 1795. While quite young, he, with his parents, moved to Cayuga County, New York, and from thence to Erie County, Pennsylvania, in 1809. He was in the war of 1812, serving under Commodore Perry.

In 1836, with his wife and eleven children, he moved to this County, settling in La Grange Township, where he remained until the time of his death, in 1839.

He was a member of the Baptist Church, and held the office of County Treasurer at the time of his death. His two sons, William and John, are citizens of this County.

JUSTUS GAGE.

Justus Gage was born in De Ruyter, Madison County, New York, on the 13th of March, 1805. In early life he received a common school education, with a short term at an academy, which was sufficient to stimulate his active mind, from which time forward, through life, he was a diligent student.

In 1822 he became a member of the Universalist denomination, and soon after was licensed to preach, in which profession he continued through life, so far as his health would permit.

In the spring of 1837 he emigrated with his family to Michigan, settling in Wayne Township. He always took an active part in everything tending toward the advancement of agriculture, was one of the first Presidents of our County Agricultural Society; in the fall of 1852 delivered the annual address before the State Agricultural Society, at Detroit, and with the organization of the State Agricultural College he was made a member of the Board of Agriculture, in which capacity he acted eight years.

His interest in educational matters was second to none, engaging in whatever tended to the advancement of our common and high schools. In the fall of 1850 he was chosen Director of the village school of Dowagiac, and at once proceeded to the inauguration of the union or graded school system, under the free school law. He also took an active part in the organization of the Universalist Society of that place, and contributed his full share toward the erection of the house of worship, and served as Clerk of the Church from its organization until the time of his death, which occured on the 21st of January, 1875, in the sixty-ninth year of his age.

His many virtues and good qualities will long be remembered by the people of this County, and his pioneer sketches will be treasured with the things of the past.

ZADOK JARVIS.

The subject of this sketch was born in Roan County, North Carolinia, in the year 1785, where he lived until about the year 1825, when he moved to Wayne County, Indiana. In 1834 he moved to this County, settling in La Grange Township, where he lived until the time of his death, in 1851.

In his younger days he learned the trade of distiller, but after coming to Michigan followed the vocation of farmer. His widow, now nearly ninety years old, is a sprightly old lady in the enjoyment of all her faculties. His four sons, Barton, Norman, Benjamin, and Zadok, all remain in this and Berrien Counties.

ABIJAH HUYCK.

Abijah Huyck was born in Delaware County, Ohio, in the year 1818. When eight years old his parents moved to Lenawee County, this State, and in 1836 removed to this County.

Mr. H. was one of the earliest settlers in Marcellus Township, moving in when there were but three other families. In 1850 he erected a saw mill, on the "Little Rocky," and for a number of years manufactured lumber and wagoned it to Decatur, his nearest market. He is known as a thorough business man, and one of the best farmers in the County.

His brother, Richard J., came to Volinia Township in 1838, and for a number of years sold goods there, but for several years past has followed the life of a farmer.

DAVID S. BALDWIN.

David S. Baldwin and his two sons, Josephus and Silas, left Warren County, Ohio, in March, 1828, for what was then known as the St. Joseph Country, and arrived in this County early in April, and camped on the southwest corner of Beardsley's Prairie.

They found food for both man and beast very scarce, and had to resort to felling trees for brouse for the cattle, and to the streams and woods for food for themselves. They brought with them three yoke of cattle, a cart loaded with camp equipage, provisions, breaking plow, log chains, axes, iron wedges, &c. The weather, while on the journey, was wet and cold and the roads bad. Through the St. Mary's Swamp they made but three miles a day. There was but one house between Fort Wayne and

Benton, at which place they found the Elkhart River so badly swollen from long continued rains that a canoe had to be dug out from a white wood tree before they could cross.

The two lads, then fifteen and sixteen years old, after remaining until June, returned to Ohio. Their outfit consisted of one horse, which they rode alternately, a small supply of provisions, and a five dollar bill.

In the fall of 1830 the boys came back, with the rest of the family, the older brother still residing on the prairie. Silas removed to Elkhart, in April, 1842, where he has ever since remained, and is known as one of the most enterprising of that city's citizens. He was a Lieutenant in the Black Hawk war, and his reminiscences of that struggle are well worth publication.

The third son, William, of auctioneering fame, is probably as well known as any man in Cass County. Although of limited education, having never attended school but eighteen days in his life, yet he carries on quite an extensive business, beside furnishing the windwork for many others.

The father was of a migratory character, and was one of the first to start to California, in 1849, since which time he has never been heard from.

RUDD BROTHERS.

Marvrick, Jeremiah, Barker F., and Stephen were born near the Green Mountains, of Vermont, where they all lived until men grown and married, except the youngest. The three, Marvrick, Barker F., and Stephen, came to this County in 1834, and Jeremiah came in 1836.

Stephen and Marvrick settled on Young's Prairie, the other two locating in Newberg Township, where Barker still lives. Marvrick removed to Oregon about the year 1858, and only lived two years after getting there. His two sons, Harry and James L., are residents of Oregan. Jeremiah died in the year 1855. His two sons, Jay and Orson, are residents of this County at the present time. Stephen died on Young's Prairie in 1864. His only son now lives in Vandalia.

WILLIAM GILBERT.

William Gilbert was born on Long Island, in the year 1790. When three years old his parents moved to Otsego County, New York, where he lived until coming to Michigan, in 1839, settling on the bank of Indiana Lake, in Silver Creek Township.

In New York he followed teaming twenty years, between Albany and Buffalo, and while at this business received the nick name of "Tommy," by which he was ever afterward known. He was a man of rather singular organization; was very fond of having a good time, especially on holiday occasions. His three sons, William, Anderson, and Eugene, all live near the old home, their father dying on the 18th of February, 1864.

THE SILVER FAMILY.

No name is more frequently met or more prominently identified with the development of the southern portion of Cass County, during the first twenty years of its history, than that of the Silvers, and, did space allow, a chapter, detailing their virtues and experiences, could be written, which of itself would be a tolerable history of that locality, but the limit which was placed for this volume, in its inception, having been already exceeded, I must confine these sketches to the barest mention.

John Silver was born in New Hampshire in 1763. He was a mason and taught that trade to all of his boys. In 1785 he was married to Mary Buell, of Somers, Connecticut, by whom he had eight children, six boys and two girls. He served with credit during the war of 1812, and at its close retired to a farm in Hopkinton, New Hampshire, where he remained until in 1837 when he followed his children to the then far West.

He came first to Edwardsburg and Cassopolis, but finally purchased a farm in Cleveland Township, Elkhart County, Indiana, one mile from the Michigan line, where he resided until his death, in 1843. His wife survived him five years.

Jacob, the oldest son, was born in Newport, New Hampshire, in 1786. In 1806 he married Abigail Piper, by whom he had five children, only one of whom—Mrs. E. B. Sherman—is now living. In 1837 he married Mrs. Maria Goodrich, who still survives him.

In 1830 he formed a partnership with his two

younger brothers, Abiel and Benjamin F., for trading in the West, either at Chicago or Ottowa. They shipped their goods to Chicago, Jacob accompanying them, Benjamin remaining to close up his affairs East, and Abiel traveling overland. The latter, while journeying through Michigan, fell in love with Beardsley's Prairie, and was so strongly impressed with a belief in the future greatness of Edwardsburg that he wrote to Jacob to reship the goods from Chicago to that point via the St. Joseph. It was late in the fall before the change could be effected, and part of the cargo was in a boat which was frozen in for the winter, necessitating a long and expensive portage; but they were finally got through and opened out in a log store room.

In the spring of 1832 they opened a branch at Cassopolis, then just laid out and designated as the County Seat, and Jacob removed there with his family some months later. He was the pioneer trader of the village, and was identified with its prosperity for many years.

In 1833 they put up a large distillery, the first in the county. It was a very heavy frame building, and required the aid of nearly the whole able bodied population of the County to raise it. The work lasted three days, and each night Mr. S. took two pans, one filled with gold and the other with silver coins, and passed them around through the crowd, requesting each man to help himself to whatever he considered an equivalent for his day's work. In 1834 the partnership terminated, and the Cassopolis branch and distillery fell to his share.

In 1833 he was elected County Treasurer, and in 1836 was a member of the first Constitutional Convention, at Ann Arbor. He died in 1872, leaving the bulk of his property to the Swedenborgian Church, of which he had been a zealous supporter.

John, the second son, was born in Hopkinton, New Hampshire, in 1788. He was an inn keeper and proprietor of a stage route in Newport for many years, but in 1845 followed his brothers and son to Cass County, Michigan, settling in Ontwa Township. He remained here about ten years, but after the death of his second wife, returned to New Hampshire, where he died in 1864.

His son, Orrin, was one of the first hotel keepers in Edwardsburg, where he still resides, and has always been a prominent representative of the business interests of that place.

Jeremiah, the third son, was born in Hopkinton, New Hampshire, in 1790. He served three years in the war of 1812, but never applied for a pension until 1866, when he received twelve dollars per month until his death.

Upon the conclusion of hostilities, he exchanged the sword for the trowel and plowshare, and soon after married Sarah Hastings, by whom he had six children, four of whom survived him. He removed to Cass County in 1836, and in company with Benjamin F. purchased a farm of two hundred acres in Ontwa. During the pioneer days he was noted as a hunter and trapper, and is said to have destroyed more wolves than any man in Southwestern Michigan. He took the contract and built the first Cass

County Poor House. He died April 19th, 1876.

Josiah was born in New Hampshire, in 1794, and came to this County in 1837. In 1818 he was married to Polly Straw, by whom he had three children, two of whom are still living. He died in 1870.

Abiel, better known as Judge Silver, was born in Hopkinton, New Hampshire, in 1797. In 1825 he migrated to St. Lawrence County, New York, where he engaged in teaching, and afterward married Edna Hastings—by whom he had one child—and engaged in mercantile pursuits. In 1830 he removed to Chautauqua County, and in company with Benjamin F. opened a stock of goods. In 1831 he came to Cass County, as before described. He is a man of more than ordinary ability and culture, and played an important part in the history of those days. He was a member of the first Constitutional Convention of Ann Arbor, an Associate Judge of Cass County, and in 1846 was appointed Commissioner of the State Land Office, which position he held two years. Soon after this he entered the Swedenborgian ministry. He has served in this capacity in Wilmington, Delaware, Newport, New Hampshire, Salem, Massachusetts, and now has charge of a Church in Boston, Massachusetts.

Margaret, the sixth child, was born in New Hampshire, in 1799, married Seth Straw in 1817, and came to this County in 1837. She now resides in Elkhart, Indiana.

Joan was born in 1802, was married to Timothy Straw in 1821, came West in 1837, and still lives on the farm originally purchased, south of Edwardsburg.

The history of Benjamin F., the youngest of the family, has been outlined in that of the others. He was born in Hopkinton, New Hampshire, in 1808, and came to Edwardsburg in 1832, in company with Jacob and Abiel. Upon the dissolution of their partnership, in 1834, he remained in company with Abiel. He next followed farming a few years, and in 1838 married Martha Morrison, by whom he had one child, a daughter, who died in 1874. In 1843 he commenced selling goods in Cassopolis, with H C. Lybrook and S. E. Dow, but in 1847 he gave up mercantile pursuits and settled down on the farm in Pokagon, where he now resides.

An annual reunion of the family is held on Thanksgiving day, at which feasting and merrymaking is diversified by an exchange of mutual confidences and a rehearsal of the traditions of the elders. No display of differences in wealth or social position is allowed. The women wear calico dresses and the men plain business suits, and all meet upon a footing of perfect equality. At the last gathering, at "Uncle Ben's," one hundred and thirty-seven sat down to dinner.

JACOB A. SUITS.

The subject of this sketch was born in Johnstown, Montgomery County, New York, in the year 1798, where he lived until 1836, when he came to Michigan and settled in Silver Creek Township. At that time there was but three cabins in the Township, Mr. Suit's being the fourth.

Mr. Suits died in 1844, but his widow is still living among her friends, and his two sons, Adam and Jacob, are still citizens of the County, the former on the old homestead and the latter in Dowagiac.

The family came from Buffalo to Chicago and then to St. Joseph, on a lake schooner. The voyage, owing to rough weather, was very tedious, occupying seven weeks, during which time, while on the west side of Lake Michigan, their mast was blown away and they had to lie still until another could be brought from shore and put in place.

On their arrival at their new home, Mr. Suits made inquiry where he could purchase some butter, and was informed that their nearest neighbors to the south had, if for sale, which he found to his surprise to be ten miles away.

PLEASANT NORTON.

The subject of this sketch, and father of the numerous family in this County, was born in Grayson County, Virginia, in the year 1806. When two years old his parents moved to Champaign County, Ohio, and afterward to Logan County, in the same State, where he lived until coming to Michigan, in the fall of 1832, settling in Jefferson Township, where he still resides.

In 1826 he was married to Rachel Fukey, who also is still living. Mr. Norton cast his first vote for General Jackson, and has adhered to the Democratic party ever since. He has served two terms in the State Legislature from this County, was Supervisor of his Township eight years, and was Township Treasurer a number of terms, besides holding numerous other offices by election and appointment.

THE BURK FAMILY.

William, Thomas, and Andrew L. were born in Giles County, Virginia, in the years 1788, 1796, and 1810, respectively. In 1824 they, in company with their father's family, moved to Preble County, Ohio, where they remained four years, or until 1828, when the three brothers came to Michigan and settled in Pokagon Township.

William, better known as Judge Burk, who acted as Associate Judge for a number of years, remained a bachelor and a resident of the Township until the time of his death, in 1868.

Andrew lived in the Township but a few years, or until he was married, when he removed into what is known as the bend of the river, in Berrien County, where he still remains.

Thomas is still living in the vicinity of where he first settled. He was married in 1829 to Catherine Lybrook, who was also from Virginia, and by whom he had quite a large family. She died in May, 1863.

The Burk family are of Irish descent. The grandfather on one side and the great grandfather on the other came from Ireland. They have always been known as honest, upright men, and good types of Virginia gentlemen.

The family removed from Virginia to Ohio and then from Ohio to Michigan, with wagons. While on the way from Ohio, Thomas met with a misfortune, by cutting his ankle while falling a small sapling a few miles out of Fort Wayne, where he was carried to have his wound dressed, and was then put on board of one of the wagons and hauled the remainder of the way. He was not able to place his weight on the crippled foot for eight weeks.

THE REAMS FAMILY.

Moses Reams was born in North Carolina, in 1798. While still a lad he removed, with his father's family, to Ohio, where he spent his youth and early manhood.

In 1819 he married Mahala Norton, a sister of Pleasant Norton, who is mentioned elsewhere in these pages, and whom he had six children. He was passionately fond of hunting and fishing, and when the increasing settlement of Ohio rendered game scarce, he moved to Cass County, Michigan, in 1828, squating on Government land in the extreme northern part of Jefferson Township. He changed his location several times within two years before settling upon the farm which he now occupies.

William Dixon, his oldest child, was born in Ohio, in 1820. In 1843 he married Rhoda Collyer, by whom he had seven children, only two of whom are now living.

Mary Jane was born in Ohio, in 1822, and married Christopher Richardson, in 1841, by whom she had five children, three of whom are still living.

Levi was born in 1824, married Irene Collins, in 1847, by whom he had four children, all of whom are still living.

Margaret Ann was born in Ohio, in 1826, married Ichabod Pearson, in 1844, by whom she had four children, three of whom are living.

Lovinia was born in 1834, and in 1851 married Joseph N. Marshall, by whom she had three children, two of whom are living.

Nathan was born in 1842, and in 1872 married Sarah Rumer. All of the children live in Jefferson or Cassopolis.

THE JONES FAMILY.

This family, so well and prominently known in the central portion of the County, are of English descent, the grandfather of the present generation's father emigrating from England about the middle of the last century and settled in North Carolina, and afterward removed to Georgia, where George, the subject of this sketch, was born, on the 28th day of August, 1770.

They were of the Quaker persuasion and in common with their sect early imbibed a distate to human slavery, and finding life irksome and unremunerative to nonparticipants in the National crime, removed to Ohio, where he remained until 1829, when he removed to Michigan and settled on Young's Prairie, where he died on the 4th of April, 1834.

While in Georgia he married Lydia Hobson, by whom he had ten children, five sons and five daughters. Henry, the oldest son, was born in Georgia, in the year 1790, and came to Michigan, with his father, and entered a large tract of land on the prairie, where he died in 1850. His surviving sons are Amos, George W., Henry, Phineas, and Jesse, who all remain in the County with the exception of Henry, who has migrated to Oregon, where he still resides.

Charles, the second son, was born on the 20th of January, 1792, and came to this County in 1829, where he remained until the time of his death. Of his sons, William and Charles remain near the old homestead, and Joseph lives in Iowa.

William, the third son, remained in Ohio.

George, the fourth son, was born on the 30th of April, 1801, accompanied the family to Michigan, but the change of climate proved unfavorable to him, and he died three years afterward. All his sons, Stephen, Nathan, and George D., are residents of Cass County. His widow, familiarly known as "Aunt Polly," is deserving of more than a passing notice, and I regret that my limited space will not allow a detailed account of her ability and virtues. Left alone with a large family, her superior management, thrift, and practicability stood in full stead for their lost father. She built the first frame house on the prairie, superintended the farm and its marketings, and always made time for kind and helpful offices to sick and unfortunate neighbors. She was widely known and universally respected, and though long gone to her reward, her memory is still green in the hearts of her beneficaries.

Nathan, the youngest son, was born on the 16th of October, 1810. He came to Cass County with the family, where he remained until 1850, when he took the gold fever and migrated to California, where still resides.

Of the daughters, but two came to Michigan, and were mothers of the well known Green and Townsend families, which are detailed in another part of this work.

The family hold an annual reunion each year, which is attended by about one hundred and fifty descendents.

THE BARNEYS.

Judge John Barney was born in Connecticut, and while yet a young man moved to Wilksbarre, Pennsylvania, from thence he moved to Mount Vernon, Ohio, and again to Huron County, in the same State. He was a Captain of volunteers during the war of 1812, and was taken prisoner on the Detroit River a day or two previous to Hull's surrender, and kept a prisoner on board an old vessel under a strict guard. After a time their captors relaxed their vigilance in a measure, and while a part of them were below playing cards, Captain Barney and his comrades overpowered them and took possession of the vessel, which they run to the mouth of the Maumee River, from whence they proceeded home.

In 1836 Mr. Barney came to Michigan, settling at

first in Wayne Township, where he lived one year, when he moved to Silver Creek Township, where he died in 1852. He served a number of years as Associate Judge in this County. After he was sixty-five years of age he went to California, making the entire journey on foot.

Henry Barney, Sr., was born in Connecticut, in 1763, and early emigrated to Pennsylvania, where he was married, and then moved to Western New York. He afterward removed to Huron County, Ohio, where he remained twenty years, clearing up a large farm in the time. He came to Michigan in 1838, settling in Silver Creek Township, where he lived until a few years before his death, which occurred in 1850. He had been a pioneer in four States. He was married three times and had ten children, six girls and four boys, three of whom are now living.

His oldest son, Henry, Jr., was born in 1804, and came to this County in 1835, with his brothers, and entered six hundred acres of land, in Wayne Township, upon which they moved in 1837 and remained until the time of his death, in 1851.

He left a wife and four sons, the youngest of whom, and mother, died within three years of the husband and father. Of the others, Henry L., our present Register of Deeds, is still a resident of this County. The other two lie in graves in Southern soil, devotees to their country.

Julius A. Barney was born near Wilksbarre, Pennsylvania, where he lived until coming to Michigan, in 1837, settling in Wayne Township, having been here two years previous to see the country and make a location. He brought with him hogs, cows, and sheep to make a commencement with, and came with a determination to succeed by hard work. He never experienced the privations that many complained of, but suffered considerably from the sickness of 1837–8. He was Supervisor of his Township one year, Township Clerk two years, and was elected Justice of the Peace twice, but never qualified for that office. Mr. Barney remained on the farm where he first settled until the spring of 1874, when he moved to Dowagiac.

John G. A. Barney was born in Cayuga County, New York. While quite young his father moved to Huron County, Ohio, where he remained until coming to Michigan in February, 1838, stopping nearly a year in Wayne township. At this time there was no road across the swamp between Paw Paw and Sumnerville, a distance of over thirty miles. He, having purchased land in the township of Silver Creek, had to wait until it would freeze up to make it passable. Mr. Barney believes himself to be the first man to drive a team across the swamp, which he did the winter of 1838–9. He built the first saw mill in the Township the season of 1840, since known as the Foster mill. For a number of years he carried on quite a trade with the Indians, buying their furs and skins, and furnishing them provisions &c. In the earlier days of Dowagiac he engaged in the drug business with Asa Huntington, where they were burned out in the first fire, after which he removed to Porter Station, Indiana, where he remained six years, since which he has lived in Dowagiac. He was Supervisor of Silver Creek a number of years; he has also held the office of Justice of the Peace. Mr. B. relates many anecdotes of his early career in Michigan, some of which will be found under their appropriate head.

THE TIETSORT FAMILY.

Abram Tietsort, Sr., was of Holland Dutch descent. The family early settled in New Jersey, where Abram was born in 1777. He served in the war of 1812, soon after which he settled in Butler County, Ohio, where he followed the occupation of farmer.

In the year 1828 he and his family came to Michigan, settling on the present site ot Niles, where he raised grain, and in company with his oldest son ran a flat boat on the St. Joseph River.

In 1830 he removed to this County, and settled on the farm now owned by Hiram Jewell, which he afterward exchanged with Mr. Jewell for land on which the Air Line depot now stands, where he lived until the time of his death, in 1847, his widow surviving him seven years.

Abram, Jr., his oldest son, was born in Butler County, Ohio, in the year 1805, and came to Michigan at the same time of his father. In 1830 he settled on the east side of Stone Lake, and was one of the original owners of the villagc plat of Cassopolis, where he lived until the time of his death, in

1842. In pioneer times he carried on the business of cabinet making, undertaking, etc.

His oldest son, John Tietsort, is a resident of the village. Two others are in Detroit, and one in Illinois. His widow and only living daughter reside in Orleans County, New York.

Levi, the second son, settled in La Grange Township, where he lived until the time of his death, about twelve years ago.

Henry, the third son, is a mason by trade, which he has followed many years, in connection with farming. He lives just north of the village of Cassopolis.

The fourth son, Cornelius B., settled just east of the village, on the farm now occupied by his widow and sons, where he died about six years ago.

Squire V., the youngest son, remained on the old homestead until the time of his death, in 1852.

SYLVADOR T. READ.

The subject of this sketch was born in Tompkins County, New York, on the 12th day of January, 1822. When six years old his parents moved to Erie County, Pennsylvania, where they remained four years, when they came to Michigan, in 1832. He first settled in Monroe County, where he remained nine years, then removing to this County, at first settling in Calvin Township, where he served for a time as Supervisor.

Mr. Read's life has been diversified with many callings, and contrary to the general rule, of "too many irons in the fire," has succeeded in accumulating property far beyond the average of mankind. He served as a soldier in the memorable "Toledo War," under Governor Mason, has followed the occupations of itinerant thresher, following the breaking plow, steam saw milling, merchandising, and railroading.

In 1854 he went overland to California with a drove of cattle, the trip out occupying six months. In 1855 he removed to Cassopolis, and has been identified with her interests ever since. He is a thorough, enterprising, business man, taking hold with a will in whatever is for his own benefit or the public good, a genial, social man.

CAPTAIN JOSEPH HARPER.

The subject of this sketch was born in Washington County, Pennsylvania, in the year 1805, where he lived until 1834, when he came west and settled in Cassopolis, which has been his home ever since. In 1836 he was married to Caroline Guilford, with whom he still lives.

Early in life Mr. H. followed the business of carpenter and joiner, and was one of the contractors for the building of the present County Court House. He has been elected and served in the several offices of Register of Deeds, County Treasurer, Sheriff, and is at present Postmaster of Cassopolis. In early California times he made a trip to that golden clime and remained four years, and afterwards went to Pike's Peak and Montana in search of the precious metal. He served as Captain of Company A in the Twelfth Michigan Infantry.

He is known as a stern, unflinching moralist, a man with an opinion and ready to maintain it, a zealous supporter of law and order, and an upright, honest man.

ARMSTRONG DAVIDSON.

The subject of this sketch was born on the James River, Virginia, about the year 1784, where he lived until a man grown, and learned the trade of blacksmith, serving an apprenticeship of seven years. Soon after learning his trade he was married to Rebecca Spears, after which he moved to Wooster, Wayne County, Ohio, where he remained until coming to Michigan, in 1829.

He settled in North Porter Township, where he lived until the time ot his death, over twenty years ago. His oldest son, Samuel, lives at the present time in Cassopolis. Henry and Noah are residents of Oregon, and William lives in California. Catherine (Mrs. Hebron) died last fall (1875), Mary (Mrs. John Hartman) and Elizabeth (the widow Robins) are both residents of Porter Township.

MOSES McILVAIN.

The subject of this sketch is of Scotch-Irish descent. His antecedents left Scotland and went over to Ireland during one of the many turmoils that existed there in early times. The grandfather of the subject of the present sketch settled in Pennsylvania, and in an early day went to Kentucky on a prospecting tour, and while there was taken prisoner by the Indians and kept in bondage two and one-half years. He afterward made a permanent settlement near Lexington, where Moses was born, in 1802.

When three years old his parents moved to Champaign County, Ohio, where he remained thirty-one years, or until coming to Michigan, in 1836. He settled in Jefferson Township, where he lived until a few years ago, when he moved to Cassopolis to live with his son, William W., of the firm of McIlvain & Phelps.

Mr. McIlvain is a quiet, unassuming man, and has never put himself forward, yet has served in numerous Township offices and other positions.

JOHN RITTER.

The subject of this sketch was of German descent and was born in Virginia, on the 31st of March, 1793. About the year 1810 his parents moved to Preble County, Ohio, where he was married to Sarah Lybrook, in September, 1816, after which he removed to Union County, Indiana, where he lived until coming to Michigan, in October, 1828.

He first settled near Niles, where he remained until the following August, when he removed to La Grange Prairie, in this County, where he was killed by lightning on the 31st of the same month, his wife surviving him until the 24th of January, 1834.

Hannah, his oldest daughter, resides with her brother, J. K., in Cassopolis. Henry L., his oldest son, died about four years ago, on La Grange Prairie, where his family still reside.

David M. died about ten years ago. His two sons reside on McKinney's Prairie.

Eve died while on the road to Michigan.

Joseph K., the youngest of the family, is a resident of Cassopolis, and is well known throughout the County, having served in numerous public positions.

INDEX.

Ancient Earth Works, 49
Agricultural Society, 279
Alexander J., 326
Aldrich James, 333
Bogue Stephen, 338
Byrns John, 340
Beeson J. G., 341
Brady David, 357
Blish Daniel, 376
Backmar Wilson, 379
Baldwin D. S., 382
Burk Family, 391
Barney Family, 395
Carey Mission, 66
Cabin Building, 85
Cooking Utensils, 101
Cass County, 110
Calvin, 208
Cassopolis, 236
Cass Co. in the War, 281
Copley E., 344
Coulter J., 345
Copley A., 365
Dowagiac, 262
Dickson James, 347
Dunning A., 371
Davidson A., 401
Edwards Lewis, 313
Fosdick George, 348
Fulton Family, 377
Goodspeed J., 337
Goble Elijah, 342
Gallup Family, 343
Green Jesse, 358
Green Amos, 358
Gard Josephus, 369
Gard Jonathan, 369
Gard John B., 370
Gage Justus, 380
Gilbert William, 384
Howard, 218
Humphrey L., 332

Huntley E., 339
Hain Family, 355
Hitchcox Jarius, 357
Hopkins David 359
Hicks R. V., 360
Howell D. M., 377
Huyck A. 381
Harper Joseph, 400
Jefferson, 213
Jenkins B., 293
Jacks J. L., 316
Jarvis Z., 381
Jones Family, 393
Kentucky Raid, 131
Kingsbury A., 328
La Grange, 188
Lybrook John, 299
Lybrook H. C., 331
Leach J., 342
Lee J. W., 352
Michigan, 5
Michigan Indians, 52
Marcellus, 150
Mason, 222
Milton, 233
Morelan J., 317
McKenney T., 346
Marsh A. C., 349
McIntosh D., 361
Miller E., 363
Meacham George, 302
McIlvain Moses, 401
Newberg, 172
Nash Ira, 311
Newton James, 314
Nixon John, 338
Norton Pleasant, 390
Ontwa, 226
Olmstead S. C., 334
O'Dell James, 344
Pioneer Furniture, 96
Penn, 179
Pokagon, 195
Porter, 202
Putnam U., Sr., 289
Putnam O., 307
Price Jacob, 364
Redfield George, 322
Renniston William 326
Rogers Alexander, 334
Rinehart J., 353
Rich Samuel, 370
Rogers Hiram, 371
Rudd Brothers, 383
Reams Family, 392
Read S. T., 399
Ritter John, 402
Silver Creek, 166
Shurte Isaac, 305
Shanahan E., 318
Shellhammer D., 319
Sherman E. B., 321

Shintaffer P., 333
Smith E. C., 350
Shanafelt William, 374
Smith C., 375
Sears Isaac, 379
Silver Family, 385
Suits J. A., 389
Smith Joseph, 330
Toledo War, 46
Thompson S., 298
Truitt P., 351
Townsend A., 354
Townsend J., 359
Turner G. B., 372
Tietsort Family, 398
Volinia, 155
Wayne, 161
Williams S., 335
Williams I., 376
Wright W. R., 378

www.ingramcontent.com/pod-product-compliance
Lightning Source LLC
LaVergne TN
LVHW020108110826
845151LV00001B/101

9781425544096